# BEGINNING WRITER'S
# ANSWER BOOK

## 30TH ANNIVERSARY EDITION
### COMPLETELY REVISED AND UPDATED

*edited by* Jane Friedman

**WRITER'S DIGEST BOOKS**
Cincinnati, Ohio
www.writersdigest.com

Distributed in Canada by Fraser Direct, 100 Armstrong Avenue, Georgetown, ON, Canada L7G 5S4, Tel: (905) 877-4411. Distributed in the U.K. and Europe by David & Charles, Brunel House, Newton Abbot, Devon, TQ12 4PU, England, Tel: (+44) 1626 323200, Fax: (+44) 1626 323319, E-mail: postmaster@davidandcharles.co.uk. Distributed in Australia by Capricorn Link, P.O. Box 704, Windsor, NSW 2756 Australia, Tel: (02) 4577-3555.

Visit our Web site at www.writersdigest.com for information on more resources for writers.

To receive a free weekly e-mail newsletter delivering tips and updates about writing and about Writer's Digest products, register directly at our Web site at http://newsletters.fwpublications.com.

10 09 08 07 06          5 4 3 2 1

Library of Congress Cataloging-in-Publication Data

Beginning writer's answer book / edited by Jane Friedman. -- 30th anniversary ed., completely rev. and updated.
    p. cm.
"First edition"--T.p. verso.
Includes bibliographical references and index.
ISBN-13: 978-1-58297-365-4 (pbk. : alk. paper)
ISBN-10: 1-58297-365-2
    1. Authorship--Miscellanea. 2. Authorship--Handbooks, manuals, etc. I. Friedman, Jane.
PN147.B42 2006
808.02--dc22                                                    2006022008

Edited by Jane Friedman
Designed by Grace Ring
Production coordinated by Robin Richie

This book is dedicated to unpublished writers everywhere.

# Table of Contents

# INTRODUCTION

"Sit down and put down everything that comes into your head and then you're a writer. But an author is one who can judge his own stuff's worth, without pity, and destroy most of it."

—Colette (1873–1954)

This book is for beginning writers, as clearly indicated by the title, *Beginning Writer's Answer Book*. But not all beginning writers are created equal. Beginners may be young or old, have some writing education or none, and be published or unpublished. So it would be helpful to describe what type of beginning writer this book hopes to assist.

First and foremost, this book is for the thousands of aspiring writers who feel they have a book inside them but don't know what to do with it. While more than a few accomplished editors and authors will say that your book should remain exactly where it is (inside yourself), I believe it's more helpful for you to see what's ahead if you should attempt to write and publish your work. You need to have the right expectations going into this business so that when you're inevitably rejected, it doesn't come as a surprise, and you know what steps to take afterward.

This book is also for writers who have found some success—either as freelance writers or creative writers—but have never been brave enough to call themselves *writers*. Perhaps you don't consider yourself a writer because writing is more like a hobby, or because you haven't published anything "worthy" enough. Whatever your situation, you probably have questions about what it takes to be a "real" writer, and you're serious about getting published and dedicating yourself to the craft.

This book can also help writers who have mastery in one area, such as magazine article writing, but have beginner questions about other areas, such as book publishing. While this book can't cover every topic in-depth, it can ground you in the fundamentals and show you reliable sources to find out more.

## HOW TO USE THIS BOOK

This book is divided into twenty-nine chapters, with useful appendices in the back. It's not meant to be read from cover to cover, though you could try that if you simply want to learn all the basics about all writing topics.

While the book is not divided into parts, it can be thought of as having four distinct sections:

- Core Knowledge for All Writers: Chapters 1–7
- Book, Magazine, and Freelancing Basics: Chapters 8–15
- Additional Complications: Chapters 16–22
- Specialized Areas: Chapters 23–29

If you're completely new to writing and publishing, read chapters one through seven first, then move on to whatever area or genre interests you. The information within Additional Complications is also vital to all writers since it covers rights issues—your own rights as well as the rights of others. Since most beginners have lots of questions about copyright, permissions, and whether they might get themselves in legal trouble, these chapters discuss specific scenarios, plus outline copyright law and fair use.

What *won't* you find in this book? This isn't a how-to-write book, even though you'll find bits and pieces of writing instruction throughout. This book doesn't recommend specific agents, editors, or publishing companies, though it does tell you how to find, research, and query them.

The main benefits of this book are:

- learning the basics of how to get published in any genre
- understanding what it means to be a professional writer and conduct business in an ethical way

- developing the right expectations of editors, agents, and other publishing professionals whom you'll deal with
- avoiding the typical (and sometimes disastrous) beginner mistakes that can sabotage your efforts to get published

The good news is that many things in the publishing world are a matter of common sense, and politeness and professionalism go a long way toward covering up any amateur mistakes you might make.

Finally, you'll find that the answers to many questions in this book begin with *It depends*. That's because everyone's situation is different, and some questions don't have a black-and-white answer. After you become more adept at navigating the ups and downs of the publishing world, you'll instinctively know the right course of action without consulting someone else; you will have internalized the basics and will be able to make your own judgment calls, because so often in publishing, that's what it all comes down to—one person's opinion.

## ACKNOWLEDGMENTS

The wealth of information inside this book could not have been possible without the contribution of many Writer's Digest Books editors, including Ian Bessler, editor of *Songwriter's Market*; Nancy Breen, editor of *Poet's Market*; Robert Brewer, editor of *Writer's Market*; Joanna Masterson, editor of *Guide to Literary Agents*; Lauren Mosko, editor of *Novel & Short Story Writer's Market*; Kelly Nickell, managing editor of Writer's Digest Books; and Alice Pope, editor of *Children's Writer's & Illustrator's Market*.

Additionally, the Tunkhannock writers' group in Pennsylvania gave vaulable feedback and suggestions that make this a stronger resource for all writers.

Finally, this book is indebted to its meticulous copyeditor and indexer, Nicole Klungle, and the patience of its designer, Grace Ring.

Thank you all.

## FINAL NOTE

This book pays tribute to earlier editions of the *Beginning Writer's Answer Book* by featuring flashback questions. Keep in mind such questions do not necessarily pertain to *today's* writer, but provide nostalgic amusement.

# 1

## DO I HAVE WHAT IT TAKES?

One of the biggest problems that plague beginning writers is self-doubt. Whether that doubt results from age, gender, profession, lack of experience, or limited education, it creeps into the minds of beginning writers and often dampens hope and hinders progress. Unfortunately, self-doubt doesn't go away with experience, age, or even success. Writers will always wonder if they have what it takes; even after a long career of publishing, you may wonder if you've been faking it all along.

The answers in this chapter provide a starting point for thinking about some of these existential problems, but many of the final answers will be unique to you and will change over time. Writers tend to have opposing views on the role self-doubt plays in the creative life. Sylvia Plath said, "The worst enemy to creativity is self-doubt," while Sidonie-Gabrielle Colette said, "The writer who loses his self-doubt, who gives way as he grows old to a sudden euphoria, to prolixity, should stop writing immediately."

This chapter also addresses questions that relate to setting up life as writer—the tools, space, and time that you will need. Again, the answers to these questions often depend on knowing the best way to remove distractions and allow for productive writing time. All writers work a little differently, and no one way is best.

### What does it take to become a writer?

Mostly passion and persistence—the passion to write and the persistence to keep writing in the face of failure. Curiosity and an awareness of human behavior are also signature qualities of successful writers. Knowledge about the publishing industry can be vital and helps you avoid frustration and wasted time.

### I'm interested in writing, but not sure I have the aptitude for it. Are all good writers born with writing talent?

Certain writers may be born with more talent than others, but writing is mostly learned through practice; talent often boils down to having the discipline to write regularly and frequently. Anyone with the energy and willingness to develop as a writer can learn the craft and become successful at it. It's also possible for a talented and gifted writer to lack the energy and persistence necessary to publish with any degree of success.

### How can I be sure I really have creative writing ability?

You'll never be sure. It's best to believe in yourself and keep moving forward. Most writers cycle between periods of self-doubt and periods of confidence.

### How can I decide whether to write fiction or nonfiction?

Look at what you most enjoy reading, and see if that leads you to an answer. Many talented writers have made names for themselves in both fiction and nonfiction, so it's not necessary to limit yourself to one or the other.

### What causes writer's block, and how can I combat it?

Ask twenty writers what causes writer's block, and you'll probably get twenty different answers. The causes of writer's block usually don't have anything to do with writing, but rather are connected to factors that distract writers, keeping them from concentrating on the craft.

Frequently asked question

Look at your work and see if you're actually ready to begin writing; it may be that you haven't done all your preliminary work yet. Step away from the work and try to look at it objectively. You may not have a clear understanding of how you want it to turn out. You may be writing it one way, when you know subconsciously that it would be better if it were treated some other way.

Some say a writer should make sure he *wants* to write about his current subject; if you're trying to make yourself write about something you just don't like, your mind could be rebelling.

Anxiety about the quality of one's writing is frequently cited as a cause of writer's block. Novelist Dean Koontz claims this is easily solved: "Read a novel by a really bad writer whose work you despise, and tell yourself, 'If this junk can get into print, publishers will fight one another for the rights to *my* book.'"

### What's the best book I could write to make sure I'd be published?

The best book you can write is *your* best book. In other words, your best shot at selling a book to a publisher is to write about what you want to write about, and write it as well as you can. It doesn't necessarily matter what's currently selling; the book business is full of unknowns and the unexpected. Choose whatever interests *you*, and hopefully others will be informed, inspired, or entertained by what you've written.

### What is the best market for writers? What sells most easily?

There is no such thing as one best market, since so much depends on the type of writing each individual writer does. A market is good for a particular writer if he writes the kind of material that market needs.

### I'm only interested in writing nonfiction. Is there any reason why I should read fiction?

Nonfiction writers should be familiar with fiction techniques, as they're often used in nonfiction. The most successful nonfiction writers use dialogue, suspense, characterization, description, and emotion—all part of the fiction writer's craft—in their work. In fact, a writer should be able to learn from the study of any good writing—be it fiction, nonfiction, poetry, or script.

### I sometimes wonder if I write fast enough. Are there any standards I can measure my writing speed against?

It's said Marcel Proust would spend three or four days working on a single paragraph. In contrast, Jack Kerouac is said to have written *On the Road* in a single protracted session at the typewriter. It's best for each writer to set his own goal, since writing speed seems to vary with the individual. When setting your daily quota of pages or words, you should make it a little higher than you think you might be able to reach, so you can have something to shoot for. Or, consider that if you wrote one page per day, you'd have a book-length work in a year.

**Some days I just don't feel like writing. Are there any secrets or formulas for disciplining oneself to write regularly?**

Discipline can separate the would-be writer from the published writer. You should think of yourself as a professional and regard your writing as any other job. Techniques that make the writing task seem easier include (1) finding the time of day when you think best and writing during those hours, (2) dividing a project into easily accomplished parts, so the entire job doesn't loom above you, and (3) choosing a writing time when distractions are few.

**I work at home and sometimes have trouble starting work at the beginning of the day. How can I overcome this problem?**

One good way to begin is to edit or revise work that's already been written. Some writers deliberately stop a writing session in the middle of a thought, section, or sentence, so they will know exactly where to resume the next day and will be less likely to procrastinate. Browsing through writing magazines or reading a chapter from a how-to book on writing can also put you in the mood. (Reading about writing is an important part of your workday, but know when to stop reading and start writing.)

**A few months after one of my article ideas was rejected by an editor, a similar article appeared in that magazine. This has also happened when an entire manuscript was rejected. How can I protect myself from editors who steal my ideas?**

Frequently
asked question

Beginning writers (and sometimes established ones) are quick to suspect their ideas have been stolen by editors. Such assumptions are almost always false. Since a magazine often has three months or even one year of lead time between an issue's creation and its publication, the published piece was probably written or assigned before you even wrote your query letter. Unless the published article uses, word-for-word, the same paragraphs and sentences as the rejected work, there is no proof of editorial piracy. The truth is that the better your understanding of the market, the greater the chance of similarities between your ideas and published articles or manuscripts.

Writers also frequently ask how they can protect their ideas from other writers. When fellow writers gather and talk shop, a writer will casually mention a piece he's working on. Months or years go by, and another writer ends up doing an article or book on the same idea. This other writer hasn't intentionally stolen from you, and may not even remember that you were working on the same idea, since most writers get ideas from many different sources—newspapers, magazines, books, television, films, neighbors and co-workers. Once you've discussed your idea with others, you've put it out where others can get at it—consciously or unconsciously. (Ideas can't be copyrighted.) A good rule is: Don't discuss a work in progress with other writers if you fear it being stolen.

### I'm fourteen years old. Am I too young to get my stories published?

You're never too young to submit your work for publication. Editors everywhere are looking for good writing. If a fiction editor is sent a short story that is compelling and entertaining, or a magazine editor is sent a feature story that is direct and informative, he wouldn't pass just because the writer is young. (And how would he know unless you told him?)

That said, a young writer is likely to face a tougher challenge breaking in to an adult publication market than an older writer would. This has nothing to do with age, and everything to do with experience. Writers who are twenty to thirty years older than you are going to have ten to twenty more years of trying-to-get-published experience under their belts. They're likely to have a more developed sense of what a query letter should look and sound like, what markets accept what kinds of pieces, etc. Although this information can be researched and learned by anyone, it is something that is only fully understood with practice.

So, get started now. The earlier you dive in and try, the sooner your chances of success will manifest themselves. Do not be discouraged if your writing is not accepted at first. Rejection is a fact of the writer's life, and every writer of every age must face it.

### I recently retired, and I've found the time to write. Am I too old to begin?

You're never too old to start writing.

Writers always want to know the secret, the shortcut, the key phrase or practice that will bring easy publication or success. But there is no magic bullet.

**I've been submitting my work for months without any luck. How can I increase my chances of getting published?**

The first step is understanding why your work is not being published. Analyze (and objectively evaluate) your work in light of what's being published in the places you've targeted. The publishing industry is very competitive and very subjective—editors change and so do editorial preferences. Your work may not appeal to editorial tastes, or it may not measure up to other work submitted. But don't give up. Several months (or even several years) is not an adequate test of your writing skills. Remember: Persistence is essential.

**How do I get an editor to say yes?**

Research what that editor is publishing—what he *has* accepted. Know that editor's target audience and market, and make sure your work fits. When you're sure that's taken care of, make sure you're querying and submitting not only in a professional manner, but in the manner preferred by the publication or editor. (See chapters four and five for more.)

**Are there shortcuts to writing success that most beginners don't know?**

No. Knowing someone on the editorial staff can sometimes help your work get a closer read, but if the publication is reputable and respected (and who'd want to be published in a publication that isn't?) only excellent work will pass the test.

**Do writers who live in New York or Los Angeles have an advantage over those who live in other parts of the country?**

No matter where you live and write, you must be able to turn out quality work, and external environment is only part of what enables you to do so. Top-quality writing attracts the attention of editors everywhere, no matter where it originates.

**I'm intrigued by the idea of being a writer, but, having no experience, I'm afraid to get my feet wet. Can you give me ideas for basic, challenging writing projects I could do to get some practice?**

One often overlooked but excellent way to get practice is by writing letters to the editor. Everyone has ideas and opinions, but the ability to get them down on paper in an organized and concise manner is the mark of a good writer. Although you won't receive a response from the editor, you can compare what you wrote to what was printed to see how your copy was edited to exclude repetition, awkward sentences, and wordiness.

Many clubs and local organizations use volunteer writers to create newsletters and to handle publicity. Any such writing is excellent training and bolsters your confidence; it also gives you published work for your portfolio.

Frequently
asked question

**Some editors won't consider my work unless I can show them clips of my previously published work. But how can I get clips if I can't get published without them?**

This seeming catch-22 situation is not new to writers. But you *can* get published without clips. You have several options.

First, if you have a strong idea for a publication that accepts first-time writers, then clips become a nonissue. So seek out those publications, brainstorm a stellar idea, and send it their way.

Another way to obtain publishing experience is by writing for free. Some writers will argue that you should not write for free—that your work deserves pay—but writing for local school, community, or group newsletters without pay is charitable, as well as smart. The main reason editors want to see your clips is to confirm that you can actually write. A nonpaying published clip confirms this as well as a paying one does.

Finally, if you have a spectacular idea for a magazine, but the magazine only deals with previously published writers, send a complete manuscript to break in. Some publications state that they do not accept complete manuscripts, but if you have an idea that interests them and no clips to show them that you know your writing stuff, sending the complete article may be the only option. The editors will forgive you for breaking their rules if you send a killer complete manuscript their way.

**Friends love hearing me tell stories and say I should write a book. Should I?**

Unless you have a passion for writing, you should probably ignore your friends' advice. As Heather Sellers says in *Page After Page*, "Writing is a ton of work. It's exhausting. You can hardly do it when you are tired—it's that hard to do well. It's a way of life, and you have to really look inside yourself. It's like cleaning house—fun to have finished, less fun to do. Writing is not always the answer. It's not always right to say to people, 'Yes, you have a great story. You should write it.' Maybe you should write. Maybe not."

**What does it mean to be professional?**

A writer who is professional has a firm grasp of the skills of his craft, understands the techniques required for writing successful fiction or nonfiction, and constantly strives to improve. Professionals study markets before submitting their work, so they know their audiences and the needs of specific editors, making their acceptance rate higher. When a professional receives a rejection slip, he realizes that his manuscript is a product for sale, and that there was not a need for the product in that particular market at that time. Therefore, he proceeds by looking for another suitable market, or by analyzing the strengths and weaknesses of the work itself.

Most importantly, professionalism is an attitude. For the beginning writer, it means professional presentation of queries and manuscripts, a thorough study of the markets, and the ability to deliver assigned work on time.

**It seems every topic I want to write about has already been covered. How can I use my idea without duplicating another writer's work?**

You're unlikely to duplicate another writer's work simply by using the same idea. Even if you use the exact same idea, you're sure to execute it differently. Writers have different styles, attitudes, voices, and approaches, and it's nearly impossible for two writers to execute the same idea in the same way or with the same slant.

### Where do writers get their ideas?

Frequently asked question

From the world around them. Look at your experiences, your family, your workplace, your home, your reading, the newspaper, the television, and the places you've been. Things you're familiar with can provide a gold mine of ideas and make more viable stories than things you know little about. For instance, suppose a responsible woman in your office just didn't show up for work for an entire week. Would you wonder during that week what had happened to her? Where she went? Whether she would come back? Constantly ask yourself questions. If an idea comes to you, write it down immediately. It may never pass through your mind again. Keep in mind that most ideas need to gestate for a while before you develop them.

## MATTERS OF PERSONAL PREFERENCE

### Is it a good idea to keep a journal?

A journal can be invaluable to a writer, since it records ideas, impressions, and anecdotes for future use. Even if your journal entries never get into print, journal writing can help your career by instilling in you the habit of writing regularly.

Julia Cameron popularized journaling in her best-selling book *The Artist's Way*, in which she advocates doing "morning pages" (writing a few pages, no matter what the quality, first thing in the morning). Some writers have found this advice to be life-changing, while others, such as Pulitzer Prize winner Richard Russo, have scoffed at journal keeping. It's a matter of what works for you.

### Where's the best place to write?

Wherever you can get the work done. You can write at a desk in a home office, in a rented office away from home, on the kitchen table, or even in the garage. The most important thing about where you write is that you write there consistently, and that others respect your writing place. Using the same place every time you write helps you establish a routine so that you'll write regularly.

**If I want to work on my writing in my spare time, would it be better to hold a job completely unrelated to writing?**

Unfortunately, there's no simple answer to that question. Some writers find that doing any sort of writing, even if it's not related to their personal work, sharpens their skills and is infinitely preferable to any other sort of work. Other writers find that holding down a writing-related job makes it more difficult to devote energy to writing at home. There's no way to know unless you try it.

**How much time should I put into developing my skills? Should I write every day?**

You should devote as much time as possible to writing if you expect to accomplish very much. Most serious writers put in time every day; other writers, especially novelists, have intense work cycles when they write all day every day for several months to finish a project, then take a period of time off.

**I find it difficult to find enough time to write. What should I do?**

Never say you don't have enough time to write. You make time for the things you care about; if you care about writing, you will make time.

**Is it in my best interest to write only about a specific topic and build a reputation in that field, or should I write about what interests me at any given time?**

It's probably best, at least early in your career, to play the field. By doing so, you'll have the opportunity to sample different types of writing to determine which brings you the most satisfaction and success. Many writers who specialize continue to write on other topics in which they're interested, even after they've established a name for themselves in one field. If a specialist limits his writing to one field, he runs the risk of being without an outlet for his work should that market go sour, or of being so closely associated with it that his credibility in other fields is weakened.

## TOOLS AND EQUIPMENT

No avocation in the world has as little start-up expense as writing. Ideas, energy, a scrap of paper, and a pencil are all a beginner requires. As your skill develops, only a few more tools are necessary to create work that is properly formatted and looks professional.

**I'm trying to keep expenses to a minimum. What equipment and supplies do I need to get started?**

All you need to begin is paper, pens, and access to a computer and printer, though your equipment needs will expand with your success. If you plan to become a freelance writer, a telephone and daily access to e-mail and the Internet will become essential—both are your connection to clients and research resources.

If you become a career writer, a good, sturdy office file will become necessary. Many writers have tried to do without a file cabinet, but sooner or later have realized the need for organizing correspondence, old manuscripts, financial records, etc. Once you begin getting paid for your work, you may need an accounting software program like QuickBooks to keep track of your finances.

Important
information

**I don't use computers. Will an editor accept work typed on a typewriter?**

Probably not. If you produce a manuscript with a typewriter, you won't be able to submit it as an electronic file, and very few (if any) editors will be willing to rekey your work—it's costly and time consuming. Editors will also be turned off by your inability (or refusal) to use computers.

**Should I buy a desktop computer or a notebook?**

What type of writer are you? Are you frequently traveling, on the go? Do you prefer to work outside of the home, in coffee bars or parks? Or do you want to frequently move your computer between many rooms of your house? Would you like to use it on research trips to the library or bookstore? If the answer to any of these questions is yes, you may prefer a notebook. If you write only at home or in an office setup, or if you can only get work done without distractions, then consider a desktop model.

A desktop model is likely to be more expandable (upgradeable) and less expensive than a notebook.

**I keep reading about PCs and Macs—what are the differences between the two and which should I buy?**

It's totally up to you. Macs tend to be more expensive, but they are more resistant to viruses (and infected less often) than PCs. You'll find that many editorial offices, especially those concerned with graphic design, use and prefer Macs. PCs are more common in offices and homes, and more software is available for PCs than for Macs. Not surprisingly then, software for PCs is often cheaper. (For a discussion of file compatibility across platforms, see the next question.)

**What word-processing software should I use?**

Ask yourself how fancy you'd like it to be. For basic writing that requires minimal or no professional layout, you can get away with bare-bones text editors. Text editors are very simple programs that come with your computer, such as TextEdit (for Mac) and WordPad (for Microsoft Windows). This software will allow you to edit, save, and print your work, but it's not recommended for formatting and submitting professional queries and manuscripts. Professional work requires that you have additional capabilities, such as margin settings, paragraph formatting, running heads, and page numbering. For this, you need a program like Microsoft Word.

Most writers and businesses—whether using Macs or PCs—use Microsoft Word. Word files are highly compatible between platforms and versions, meaning that a manuscript created using an older version of Word on a Mac, for instance, will still be readable by a newer Word program on a PC. Microsoft Word won't set you back more than a couple hundred dollars, and it might even come packaged with your computer.

If you prefer not to use Microsoft products, or if you just want free, downloadable word-processing software that's more powerful than a basic text editor, look for OpenOffice.org (www.openoffice.org). Also, see the Appendix for information on how to set up your word-processing program to format your manuscript properly.

**Please set me straight once and for all. Half the time I read that manuscripts should be prepared on non-Corrasable paper because it smudges less, and the other half of the time they say that liquid erase should be avoided, and that a good eraser is best. This leads me to believe that neither is a steadfast rule. I would, however, appreciate knowing what the general consensus is.**

It's general knowledge that erasable bond is an "editing nuisance." Most editors prefer good quality bond paper, and the use of either liquid erase, or strike-over erase. If you have more than three corrections on a manuscript page, though, it's best to retype that page—and avoid the first-draft look that editors are impatient with.

[Editor's note: Today's writers should not worry about these issues. Simply use the standard white copy paper available from any office supply store. If you spot a mistake on your print-out, correct it and print a new version—don't use correction fluid.]

### What extras should I look for when purchasing a computer?

Today's computers have several times the capacity that most writers require. Any new, off-the-shelf computer is guaranteed to have the essentials you need to start writing, e-mailing, surfing the Internet, and sharing photos. Unless you (or your children) have a video-game hobby—or you plan to use or store lots of photos, music, or movies—don't worry about speed, hard-drive size, or memory when buying a new machine.

If you have a writing archive on older disks—such as the 3.5″ disks that are becoming obsolete—be aware that many new computers don't come with any disk drive except a CD/DVD drive. However, even if you do buy a computer that doesn't have the right disk drive, you can typically buy an external disk drive to plug in to your computer.

For writers with archived material on older disks, consider transferring your files (which will likely become damaged and inaccessible over time) to writeable CDs or DVDs, or other available media—such as flash memory sticks, external hard drives, and even iPods. Most flash memory sticks are small enough to fit in your pocket, and they plug right in to your computer. External hard drives are a good choice if you have an enormous amount of information to store or archive. (iPods are external hard drives that are designed and sold as music players.) Do realize that transferring material from very old floppy disks might require professional help.

If all this sounds confusing, consult with a young person or computer geek in your social circle. She'll help you find the best option for your situation. In general, you should keep at least two or three copies of your important work on separate media. Think about how much would you miss if your current working copy suddenly disappeared.

**Is it necessary to have a portable audio recording device? What kind should I get?**

Many writers find audio recorders useful in a variety of situations. Recording an interview allows you to concentrate on your subject, the surroundings, and the questions you want to ask. Using a recorder is a good way to verify quotes and can help establish credibility with editors. You can also use it to record your impressions and ideas when driving home from an interview.

The model you choose should have a built-in microphone, a tape counter (so you can note points in the tape where the interviewee makes important comments), and a telephone adapter (to record interviews conducted via the telephone).

**Are stationery and business cards necessary for a writer? How elaborate should they be, and how can I obtain them?**

Printed stationery is not necessary for a beginner, but as you develop—and especially as you publish—you may want to accompany your professional manuscripts with professional letterhead. It doesn't need to be elaborate or expensively designed. Most office-supply stores and quick-print shops offer standard imprinted letterheads in a variety of type styles, colors, and paper quality.

Business cards can enhance your image as a professional writer and help you network; you generally give them to potential clients, editors, agents, people you interview, people you meet at writers conferences, etc. When you're just starting out, you don't need to invest very much to have a business card made. A chain print shop can create, print, and cut a hundred black-and-white, one-sided business cards for about fifty dollars.

## WHERE TO FIND OUT MORE

### BOOKS

*Page After Page: Discover the Confidence and Passion You Need to Start Writing and Keep Writing—No Matter What!* by Heather Sellers, is the perfect inspiration book if you're a non-writing writer.

*The Artist's Way: A Spiritual Path to Higher Creativity,* by Julia Cameron, helps you find the discipline to write every day.

*Writing Down the Bones,* by Natalie Goldberg, brings a touch of Zen to the writing life.

*Bird by Bird: Some Instructions on Writing and Life,* by Anne Lamott, tackles the toughest psychological questions of the writing life, with wit and verve.

### WEB SITES

Author Holly Lisle (www.hollylisle.com) maintains a great collection of articles and information for writers, particularly those just starting out.

# 2

# Do I need further education?

Education—any kind of education—is often valuable and sometimes necessary for writers, but formal education, however valuable, is not absolutely necessary. It can be fairly said that all writers are largely self-educated, and that their training continues throughout their productive lives. This chapter tackles questions related to formal education as well as informal education such as writing courses, writing conferences, and writing groups.

## FORMAL EDUCATION

**Which is better for a writer: a college education, or a variety of experiences?**

If your goal is to obtain a staff job at a publication or with a publisher, a college degree is a near must. Creative writing programs, too, can be extremely valuable; they force you to write and they include regular criticism by professors and peers. On the other hand, the habits (and even rules) learned while writing for an academic degree may have to be broken before you can produce a salable book or magazine article.

Most creative writers—those with MFA degrees and without—claim that experience trumps education, as nothing can be a substitute for experience. As Virgil said, "Trust one who has gone through it." But even if you live a rather humdrum existence, you can usually find material for your writing simply by exercising your imagination. Emily Dickinson, for example, created perceptive poetry though her lifestyle was, by most modern standards, frightfully dull.

**I'm interested in a career in journalism. What college courses should I take to prepare for work in this field?**

Most media organizations look for a college degree in job applicants, though they don't insist it be in journalism or English. Some alternative fields of study recommended by professionals are history, political science, psychology, and economics; knowing a foreign language also can give job applicants an advantage. Of course, whatever subject you choose to study, you must have a broad knowledge of literature and a command of composition skills and English grammar and usage. If possible, work on your college newspaper or literary magazine for hands-on experience, or participate in an internship program.

**Where can I find a list of the best creative writing schools?**

What is the best creative writing school for you depends on what you expect from it, how much you can afford to pay, your own talents, the school faculty, and many other factors. The Association of Writers & Writing Programs (AWP) publishes *The AWP Official Guide to Writing Programs*, which lists hundreds of creative writing programs in the U.S., Canada, and the United Kingdom. It can be ordered online at www.awpwriter.org. You can also refer to *U.S. News & World Report* magazine, which publishes an annual ranking of graduate schools, including creative writing programs.

## INFORMAL EDUCATION

**I read a lot both for pleasure and for improving my writing. Some writing instructors have told me to concentrate on the classics, while others have suggested reading different magazines, especially those for which I want to write. Which is better?**

You need to do both: Read the classics and read your market. Reading literary classics is basic to all good writing. If you're a fiction writer, your market reading should consist of popular novels and stories, or literary fiction—whichever you hope to publish. If you hope to write magazine articles, you should be reading magazines, especially those you consider future markets for your work. By reading magazines, you grasp their style and editorial needs.

**I have a college degree and have sold some articles, but I want to learn more about the craft and business of writing. How can I do this?**

The most obvious way to learn more is to go online. See appendix one for dozens of Web sites that have proven helpful to writers, and use these sites as a jumping off point to find other sites that cater to your specific needs. Every year, *Writer's Digest* magazine publishes a list of the top one hundred sites for writers; this list can help you stay up-to-date on the newest and best online resources.

Make sure you're reading the trade journals related to your area of interest. *Editor & Publisher* can keep you abreast of news in the newspaper field, as can *Folio* for the magazine business and *Publishers Weekly* for the book publishing industry. If you're looking for magazines that focus on the craft and business of writing, you'll want to look at *Writer's Digest* and *The Writer*. These publications provide excellent education over the long haul for very little investment.

Look around your area for one-time writing workshops and courses, which are usually sponsored by adult education programs, nonprofit organizations, or community centers. Not only will you learn more about the craft, you'll likely be able to network with other writers and develop connections that will serve you well over time.

If your local area has little to offer in the way of writing education, consider attending one of the thousands of writers conferences held every year. Writers conferences feature dozens of workshops and seminars to help you write better and get published, no matter what your genre, and usually have editors and agents available for appointments. (See the next section, Writing Conferences and Workshops, for more information on the benefits of writers conferences.)

Finally, no matter how much formal education you've had, it's best to read as many literary classics as possible and keep abreast of today's popular reading, especially in the area to which you hope to contribute.

I write in times of extreme despair, sorrow, or distress. Might this be some indication of writing ability, or is this merely a form of comfort or therapy instead of alcohol, ungovernable temper, over-eating, or other?

A need to write does not necessarily denote an indication of ability or talent. It is not the motivation but the end result that counts. The channeling of tortured emotions into acts of creativity has some-times been responsible for great works, such as the paintings of Van Gogh and the poetry of Keats.

### What about online courses for writing?

An online writing course or workshop is a good choice if you lack easy access to local programs, or if your schedule prevents you from attending regular classes. Online courses usually last four to twelve weeks and offer one-on-one instruction with the same teacher for the length of the course. But choose your course wisely. You cannot always adapt the course to your needs if you require specialized instruction, so pick one that suits your specific goals.

The most important factor in your choice should be the instructors: Who are the instructors and what are their qualifications? Any reputable institution will share information about the caliber of its instructors. Look for instructors who not only know the subject, but have recent sales in their chosen genre. Feedback from the instructor can make or break your experience, so it's important to get a good match. Inquire about the level of feedback that you can expect from your instructor. Ideally, you will want frequent detailed critiques of your work—not just overall evaluations.

Also, seek answers to some or all of the following questions:

- Are references from former students available?
- Does the site offer assistance (via phone, e-mail, or regular mail) to answer questions beyond the scope of lessons?

- How long has the site or organization been in operation?
- How much writing will have been critiqued at the end of each course?
- Are the deadlines rigid or flexible? Will you be able to stay on schedule?

The cost of online courses can vary widely, so compare different courses against each other; the most costly do not always offer what is best for you. Look for a course that allows you to get a full or partial refund if you are not initially satisfied.

Some of the most popular places to find online workshops are Writers Online Workshops at www.writersonlineworkshops.com (owned by *Writer's Digest*), MediaBistro at mediabistro.com (which has a heavy journalism focus), and the Gotham Writers' Workshop at www.writingclasses.com.

## WRITING CONFERENCES AND WORKSHOPS

**What will I gain by going to a writing conference or workshop?**

Writers workshops and conferences are considered a great source of information and inspiration for all writers, beginning or experienced. They allow you to establish friendships with other writers and editors and escape the loneliness of writing. They offer not only encouragement but practical advice and information on current trends and needs, writing craft and technique, and marketing and promotion. At a conference, you may hear lectures from published authors, get to talk with an editor or publisher, or even acquire an agent—it all depends on the type of conference you attend.

ShawGuides (www.shawguides.com) maintains a free searchable listing of writing events all over the globe and is a good starting place to find an event that fits your style and budget. If you prefer to stay close to home, look for regional or state writers organizations; many host an annual conference for both members and the public.

You don't have to be published to attend a conference; in fact, beginners have the most to gain by meeting other writers and establishing contacts with editors. Conferences can also fuel your enthusiasm for writing.

**I'm about to attend my first writers conference. What should I do to ensure I get my money's worth?**

The most important thing you can bring with you to a writers conference is an open and alert mind, ready and willing to listen and learn. Aside from that, take advantage of everything the conference has to offer—attend all the informal events as well as the structured ones. You may learn as much at lunch as you do in a lecture room, because the best shop talk always occurs at luncheons or banquets. Even if you don't get to talk to a faculty member or speaker, you'll learn a lot just by staying in the circle and listening. Always ask good questions, but don't overstep your bounds by monopolizing speakers' time.

### How do I select the right conference or workshop?

Make sure the focus of the conference or session matches your writing interests and goals. Then study the conference program for quality speakers and instructors. Research them carefully to see what they've written or what experience they have—that way you'll know what they are qualified to speak about, and you'll be able to ask pertinent questions. Also seek out past attendees of the conference and get feedback from them—did they learn something new from the sessions? Did they meet people who proved important to their writing life? If you take the time to do this basic research, you should feel confident that the conference you select will give you your money's worth.

Some additional tips:

1. Your chances of up-close contact with speakers or instructors can be greater at a small conference, but large conferences often feature well-known or famous authors, agents, and editors. Determine what's important to you: intimate interactions with a small group, or a wide cast of speakers (and choices) with less personal treatment. It can be more helpful to know how many people are in an average session than the total conference attendance number; you'll have a greater chance to ask questions or discuss your work with the instructor if the session sizes are small. (Some of the larger conferences have intensive workshops led by well-known writers or publishing professionals, with limited enrollment—and sometimes the participants are screened or specially selected by the instructor. These can be excellent experiences.)

2. A one- or two-day workshop can cost up to two hundred dollars or more; conferences that last up to a week can cost eight hundred dollars or more, which might include the cost of lodging and some meals. One way to work a conference into your budget is to combine it with a vacation.

3. Some conferences offer individual consultations with instructors, editors, or agents, either as part of the registration fee or for an additional fee. Such personal feedback must usually be scheduled ahead of time, especially if it includes a manuscript critique. If you are paying for an appointment, you have every right to know what to expect from the meeting, so ask the organizers, if you're unsure. However, never expect to instantly find an editor who will want to publish your work or an agent who will want to represent you. Such overnight success stories are few and far between. Instead, learn from the professionals (take questions with you!) and simply make a good impression. Agents' and editors' memories are long.

4. Some conferences attract writers of a variety of skill levels and are structured accordingly. Check the program for clues as to which sessions are geared toward your skill level; sometimes the conference program will split sessions into different tracks for beginners and professionals.

5. A conference's format can make a big difference in your overall experience. The best conferences are set up to provide interaction between attendees and the instructors/speakers, rather than just lectures. Also look for panel discussions where agents, editors, and authors offer their opinions on subjects that most interest you.

**Is it worth going to the same writer's conference you attended a year or two before?**

Since the people who are recruited to act as workshop leaders, panelists, and luncheon speakers usually vary from year to year, most writers find it worthwhile to attend a particular conference more than once. But first ask yourself why you attend conferences: Are you attending because the conference is a good way to rejuvenate your writing life and find inspiration? If so, then it may not matter that you're going to the same conference, and it may even be beneficial if you're returning to a group you know and like.

If, however, you're attending conferences for the networking and consultations, it's better to attend different events to open yourself up the widest possible range of writers, editors, agents, and experiences.

## YOUR HOME REFERENCE SHELF

### What books should I buy first for my home reference shelf?

Fiction and nonfiction writers will each have their own basic references, depending on their interests and specialties, but the following general references are appropriate for nearly every writer.

- *The Elements of Style*, by William Strunk Jr. and E.B. White, is a helpful aid to writing clearly and concisely. The book covers grammatical points and principles of writing style in such a way that even the novice writer can learn to communicate well.
- *Formatting & Submitting Your Manuscript*, second edition (from Writer's Digest Books), is a visual guide to formatting and submitting your work correctly in all genres.
- *Merriam-Webster's Collegiate Dictionary* is a standard dictionary favored by many writers and editors.
- *Garner's Modern American Usage* covers the proper usage of words and is frequently referenced by editors, copyeditors, and proofreaders.
- *The World Almanac and Book of Facts* details facts and events of every description and is a useful brainstorming tool.
- *The Chicago Manual of Style* is an essential reference for anyone involved in book publishing, as it covers everything from publishing formats to editorial style and proper documentation.

### What books would you recommend for improving my grammar and punctuation?

The right grammar guide for you depends on how fearful you are of grammar. If you're looking for something to teach you the basics in a fun and approachable manner, look for a mainstream, popular guide such as *Woe Is I* or *Write Right!* For people who already have a solid understanding of grammar, but need a detailed and technical reference, *The Writer's Digest Grammar Desk Reference*, by Gary Lutz and Diane Stevenson, is an excellent choice.

**What are some other useful and enjoyable writing books?**

You might want to invest in a good book of quotations. *Bartlett's Familiar Quotations* has been the favorite for many years because it contains the memorable words of history's greatest public and literary figures. A thesaurus is also helpful; you might complement your word processor's thesaurus (or online thesauri) with J.I. Rodale's *Synonym Finder*.

Best-selling how-to books on writing include the following:

- *On Writing Well: The Classic Guide to Writing Nonfiction*, by William Zinsser, will help you write more clearly.
- *The First Five Pages*, by literary agent Noah Lukeman, can help your novel avoid an editor's rejection pile.
- *Bird by Bird*, by Anne Lamott, is an inspirational guide to the writing life.
- *On Writing*, by Stephen King, was a classic from the moment it was released.
- *Writing Down the Bones*, by Natalie Goldberg, is a more New Age approach to the writing life.
- *Self-Editing for Fiction Writers*, by Dave King and Renni Browne, delivers just what the title promises: a guide to editing yourself before you submit your work to be judged and edited by others.
- *On Moral Fiction*, by John Gardner, is more of a literary argument than a how-to book, but even if you disagree with its message, there's much to be learned here.
- *Story*, by Robert McKee, is technically for screenwriters, but any storyteller will find useful advice in this book.

# WRITING GROUPS AND ORGANIZATIONS

### Should I join a local writing group?

There are many different opinions on the value of writing groups, mainly because there are many different types of writing groups. A good group can provide the opportunity for you to establish friendships and contacts while gaining valuable tips from professionals who are currently writing and selling. Clubs that criticize manuscripts honestly, discuss only writing-related topics, and invite prominent local writers to speak can motivate you and help you learn what's going on in the publishing world today.

Writers dislike some groups because they have a nonprofessional atmosphere in which the emphasis is more on socializing than writing and critiquing. These groups also serve a purpose, though it may not be the purpose you want. The key is to find a group that shares the same goals as you—whether it's getting published, getting critiqued, getting support, or getting away from the house. Avoid those that seem to do nothing other than sit around and gripe.

When seeking out a group to join (check your local newspaper or entertainment news source), ask about the experience level or publication record of the members. A group of beginners may be fun, but you won't necessarily learn very much (though if you're looking for a new social circle, such a group may work for you). If you're serious about reaching your writing goals, then find a group with at least one member who has recently achieved your goal.

### How do I start a new writing group?

If you're looking to start a new writing group and need to find like-minded writers, then the best way to recruit members is to post a flyer at your local bookstore, café, or community gathering place—wherever writers are likely to gather. Here are a few tips:

Frequently
asked question

- *Determine your goals.* Your members must agree on the key purpose, whether that's getting published, improving writing, critiquing each other's work, or cheerleading. Groups will naturally do many of these, but what's your focus?

- *Limit the size.* It's best if you keep the group to somewhere between six and a dozen members. Much smaller, and you run the risk of quickly losing freshness; much bigger, and there won't be an opportunity for good interaction.

- *Set a meeting place and time.* You can rotate among each other's homes, meet at a workplace, or get together at a local establishment. The starting time should work for everyone, and the meeting schedule should be regular and dependable (usually once or twice per month).

- *Set ground rules and follow them.* An effective writing group must have some order. What will the standard agenda be? Will all members share work? Will manuscript copies be distributed prior to each meeting? Who will distribute and how? Does the work being shared have to be new? How will critiques be run, and what's expected of a critiquer? What happens when a member doesn't show or has nothing new to contribute for many meetings?

## What about online writing groups?

Online groups—usually focused on critiquing—give you the opportunity to have your work critiqued without having to accommodate the schedules of every member. They also allow for a more diverse group, which means more diverse opinions. Online groups can offer support and assistance in all aspects of your writing, from grammar to overall structure, and they can provide you with links and newsletters about writing. It may seem that online groups would be impersonal, but you're likely to become just as close to your online critiquers as you would with people in the same room.

## Should I join a national writers organization? Are there specific organizations for different types of writers?

Membership in a national professional writing group can help you establish a professional image (as it increases your visibility), and may help you land assignments. Some of these organizations can also help you by acting as your representative in certain legal cases or disputes, as well as by giving you access to specialized information and publications. Most national organizations require that you qualify for membership as a "professional," which may mean you must have sold your work to various reputable publications or publishers.

There are organizations for just about every type of writer, from International Thriller Writers to the Poetry Society of America. You should join the organization that is aimed at your field of writing. Membership fees are usually modest. The three major (and most general) organizations for writers are the National Writers Union (www.nwu.org), the Authors Guild (www.authorsguild.com), and the Writers Guild of America (www.wga.org and www.wgaeast.org). Other popular writing organizations include Romance Writers of America, Mystery Writers of America, and the Society of Professional Journalists.

**What's the difference between the Authors Guild, the National Writers Union, and the Writers Guild of America?**

The Authors Guild is a national professional organization of book and magazine writers. The Writers Guild consists of movie, TV, and radio scriptwriters. The National Writers Union is the only labor union that represents freelance writers in all genres, formats, and media, and has the support of the UAW.

The Authors Guild is probably of most interest to beginners. Its members are required to have published a book at an established American publishing house within seven years prior to application for membership, or three fiction or nonfiction pieces in a general circulation magazine within the previous eighteen months. The Guild is involved in such issues as free speech, copyright, and taxes, and has represented the interests of writers both in Congress and in the courts. The organization also provides writers with information on contract provisions.

The Writers Guild of America (WGA) has two branches, East and West (divided by the Mississippi River for administrative purposes), each of which publishes its own monthly newsletter and operates a manuscript registration service for the purposes of verifying the date of script authorship. You must have sold or been employed to write a TV, radio, or movie script within two years prior to your application.

You are eligible for membership in the National Writers Union if you have published a book, a play, three articles, five poems, a short story, or an equal amount of newsletter, publicity, technical, commercial, government, or institutional copy. You are also eligible for membership if you have written an equal amount of unpublished material and are actively writing and attempting to publish your work.

### Are there organizations that provide services for writers in prison?

PEN American Center, a writer's organization, operates a prison writing program. See details at their site, www.pen.org.

### What can you expect at a writer's colony?

If you are looking for a peaceful place away from the hustle and bustle of the everyday world, a place where you can write, uninterrupted, for hours each day, a writer's colony is the place for you. Though each colony is slightly different from the others (for example, some accept beginners, and others do not), all provide a comfortable and private atmosphere meant to encourage writing, and the opportunity for interaction and discussion with other writers, if you desire it. The cost of a stay at a writer's colony varies greatly—some are free, while others offer scholarships or charge a weekly or seasonal rate. The cost may or may not include meals (again, depending upon the colony). Some require you to submit an application, which may ask for writing samples and recommendations from former residents or other notable people. Information about writers colonies is available from *Poets & Writers* (www.pw.org) and *The Writer's Chronicle*, published by the AWP (www. awpwriter.org).

## WHERE TO FIND OUT MORE

## BOOKS

*Writing Alone, Writing Together: A Guide for Writers and Writing Groups*, by Judy Reeves, is an excellent reference if you're interested in starting a writing group or want to improve the one you're in.

*The AWP Official Guide to Writing Programs* is indispensable if you're trying to find the right creative writing program.

*An Insider's Guide to Creative Writing Programs: Choosing the Right MFA or MA Program, Colony, Residency, Grant, or Fellowship*, by Amy Holman, is a solid guide to all types of writing communities and opportunities.

## WEB SITES

ShawGuides (www.shawguides.com) keeps a listing of writing workshops and conferences around the world.

Alliance of Artists Communities (www.artistcommunities.org) is an excellent resource if you're looking for a retreat, colony, or community.

# WHAT DO THEY MEAN
# WHEN THEY SAY ...?

To beginning writers, it can seem as though editors and established writers speak in a foreign language. Publishing jargon can be a stumbling block for the beginner struggling to enter the inner circle. Here are some down-to-earth explanations for terms you read in editorial listings, writing magazines, and on Web sites.

### What's a market, and what does the phrase *marketing your material* mean?

A market is a magazine, publishing firm, or company to which you sell what you write. *Marketing your material* means selling what you write. *Study the market* means just that—read back issues of the magazine or, in the case of a book publisher, study the company's catalog, and visit bookstores to view the books in person. Also study the magazine or publisher's editorial requirements in the market listings found in publications like *Writer's Market*, so you can understand what type of material the market is purchasing.

### What are writers guidelines?

Writers guidelines (also called submission guidelines), are instructions from editors on the sorts of submissions they'd like to see from writers. Guidelines often briefly describe the publication's or publisher's audience, the types of articles or books published, and the types of material that are *not* accepted. Magazine departments open to freelancers may be listed and described, and the editors may offer some tips on the article

Important
information

structures and writing styles they favor. Reviewing writers guidelines is an important element of researching a magazine market, and should be combined with studying several recent issues of the magazine. Most magazines and book publishers post their writers guidelines on their Web site, and many are happy to mail the guidelines if the writer provides a SASE.

### What's a SASE?

Do not break
this rule!

*SASE* is the acronym for *self-addressed, stamped envelope*. A SASE should be enclosed with snail mail queries or submissions to editors or agents. When requesting information from an editor or from a magazine's subscription or service department, it's always best to enclose a SASE for the reply. Make sure the envelope is a no. 10 (business-size) envelope—not the tiny personal-size stationery envelopes, which are useless when sending reprints, fliers, publications, or other literature that's requested. And, when submitting a manuscript, always enclose the proper size envelope (usually the same size as the one the manuscript was mailed in), with adequate postage for return. Always apply the stamps to the return envelope, rather than using a paper clip to attach them. (If you only clip them, there's a chance that they might get separated from the manuscript.) Remember: Most editors won't reply to a query or return material submitted without a SASE.

### What's a query?

See chapter
four to learn
how to query.

A query is a letter to an editor or agent attempting to sell him on the idea of your article or book. It can be as short as a few sentences or as long as several pages, depending on the particular market and the complexity of the subject. You should generally limit your query letter to one page, especially if you're querying a magazine or if you're querying an editor or agent with a novel idea. Longer queries are more acceptable when querying nonfiction book projects.

If your query appeals to the editor's interest, he'll contact you for further information. For magazine article queries, a positive response results in an assignment; for novel or book queries, a positive response results in a request for a complete proposal or the complete manuscript.

Not all publications (or editors and agents) accept queries directly from writers; their guidelines or Web site may state, "No unsolicited queries" or "No unsolicited submissions." But many publications do accept queries; they just don't want unsolicited *manuscripts*.

### What's an unsolicited manuscript?

Important information

When you submit a book, article, story, or poem without the publisher requesting it, your manuscript is unsolicited. In such a case, the editor or publisher has not given any indication he will read the work; he and the writer have not previously communicated. Many book publishers and magazines won't read unsolicited manuscripts; they expect a query first. Since publishers have no legal responsibility for unsolicited manuscripts, the author should always consult *Writer's Market* to make sure a specific publisher accepts them. Always include a SASE when submitting unsolicited manuscripts or queries.

### What's meant by the term *slush pile?*

*Slush pile* is a collective term for all the unsolicited material received by magazine editors and book publishers. It refers to any queries or manuscripts not specifically assigned by an editor or submitted by an agent.

### What's meant by *over the transom?*

*Over the transom* is another collective term for unsolicited material received by a publisher; for example, "It arrived over the transom." It's an old phrase that implies works were slipped into the publisher's office illicitly, as in through the small windows (transoms) above office doors.

### What can a writer do when a magazine or book publisher will not look at unsolicited queries or manuscripts?

Not much. If the magazine or publisher will accept agented materials, then you should seek an agent to represent you. Otherwise, you're out of luck unless you network your way in or find someone the publication trusts—like a current freelancer or contributing editor—to recommend you.

See chapter six to learn more about agents.

### What is an agent and what does an agent charge?

An agent acts as a liaison between writer and publisher (editor). An agent shops a manuscript around to editors, receiving a commission only when the manuscript is accepted for publication. Agents usually take a 15 percent cut from the advance and royalties after a sale is made.

### What is a simultaneous submission?

A simultaneous submission is a manuscript submitted for consideration to more than one publishing company at the same time. Some editors and agents don't like (and don't accept) simultaneous submissions because they want to be sure their competitors aren't considering the same material at the same time they are.

Once taboo, simultaneous submissions have become a common practice, particularly when submitting to book publishers and literary agents, mainly because today's lengthy response times place too great a burden on a writer, who would have to wait years to receive a meaningful number of responses on their work.

Should you inform the editor in the cover letter that others are considering the manuscript? Opinions vary. Most editors and agents will assume that the submission is simultaneous unless you indicate otherwise, but it's considered polite to let them know anyway.

As for submitting your work to people who don't consider simultaneous submissions, you may want to break the rules—life's too short to wait for any one person, especially for more than a month or so, unless he's someone you prize highly. (Furthermore, few editors or agents would refuse to look at a submission just because it's simultaneous—even if they claim not to accept simultaneous submissions.)

Finally, it's acceptable for a writer to make simultaneous queries or submissions to magazines, especially if the article idea is timely.

### Is a multiple submission the same as a simultaneous submission?

The term *multiple submission* refers to sending more than one story, article, poem, or manuscript at the same time to the same editor or agent. However, it's often incorrectly used to mean simultaneous submission. Most editors do not like receiving more than one submission at a time—it's overwhelming. Limit yourself to submitting one idea.

## What's a proposal?

Proposals are used to sell nonfiction book ideas; instead of writing an entire nonfiction book and then trying to find a publisher or agent, you generally write the proposal first, which should convince the editor or agent to contract you (and pay you up front) to write the book. Book proposals aren't something you dash off in a day or two. They can take weeks or months to write if properly developed and researched, and can run to a hundred pages in length (or more).

See chapter ten for more about proposal writing.

Some beginners might find it easier to simply write the book first, then use it to prepare a proposal—which isn't such a bad idea, since many editors and agents want assurance that an unknown writer can produce an entire book before they commit to the manuscript. However, drafting a proposal first can give you a better idea of what your book needs to include to make it stand apart from competing titles. There is no one right way to write a nonfiction book proposal, just as there is no one right way to write a book.

You may occasionally hear someone refer to a novel proposal, which would include a query or cover letter, a synopsis or outline, and a partial or complete manuscript, along with any other information the editor or agent requests.

## What's a synopsis? Is it the same as an outline?

*Synopsis* can be a very confusing term, since its meaning depends on the context. *Synopsis* most frequently refers to a brief summary of a novel, but *synopsis* can also refer to a section of a nonfiction book proposal. Michael Larsen's book *How to Write a Book Proposal* is an excellent resource for learning how to write a synopsis for a nonfiction book.

See chapter nine for more about synopses.

Editors and agents often require a synopsis for novels, but synopsis requirements can widely vary. Some ask for a one- or two-page novel synopsis; others look for ten- and twenty-page synopses (or one page of synopsis for every twenty to twenty-five pages of manuscript). A helpful resource on writing a synopsis for your novel is Evan Marshall's *The Marshall Plan for Getting Your Novel Published. Give 'Em What They Want*, by Blythe Camenson and Marshall J. Cook, is another excellent resource on this topic.

Some editors and agents use the word *outline* interchangeably with *synopsis*. For nonfiction writers, *outline* refers to a chapter or organizational outline, but people working with novel-length fiction often use the word *outline* as well, in which case they simply mean *synopsis*.

### What's an advance?

An advance is a sum of money a publisher pays a writer prior to the publication of a book. It is usually paid in installments: for instance, one-half on signing the contract; one-half on delivery of a complete and satisfactory manuscript. The advance is paid against the royalty money that will be earned by the book, which means that royalties will not be paid to the author until the publisher has recouped the total sum of the advance from the author's royalties.

## FLASHBACK QUESTION

### What is a pot-boiler?

This term refers to something done only for the money, that is, to keep the pot boiling. The writer who turns out work of little or no artistic merit just so he can earn a living may be said to be producing "pot-boilers."

### What is a galley?

In book publishing, *galley* refers to a collection of typeset, unbound pages. A *bound galley* has been bound into book form, and sometimes you'll hear about the *advance reading copy* (or ARCs), which can considered a galley, though ARCs sometimes have full-color covers and closely approximate the final product. You might also hear the term *galley proofs* or *page proofs*, which can refer to first or second proofs that are used for proofreading and indexing. You'll find the term *galley* often used in reference to early copies of a book sent to reviewers or other publicity outlets.

### What are clips?

A clip (or clipping) is a sample of a writer's published work, usually taken from a newspaper or magazine. Editors often indicate that clips should be included with a query letter. Clips show an editor how a writer handles a variety of topics, and they serve as proof of a writer's published credits. When sending clips, a writer should make sure they are neat and readable; a high-quality photocopy is preferable to the original, especially in the case of newspaper articles, since newspapers tend to deteriorate quickly. Be sure you have sufficient postage on the return envelope if you want your clips returned, but never send the only copy of your clips. For information on how to send clips electronically, see chapter eleven.

Writers also use the term *clips* to refer to newspaper or magazine articles written by other writers. They file the clips for research purposes, for reference, and for future article ideas.

### What's a tearsheet?

*Tearsheet* is another term for a clipping, a sample of writing that has been cut (or torn) from the newspaper or magazine in which it appeared.

### What's meant by the term *freelancer*, and how much work and pay is involved in freelancing?

The term *freelancer* is used to describe an editor, writer, or other full- or part-time self-employed person who works for a variety of clients on a temporary or per-assignment basis. The term originated in medieval times, when a knight or soldier who offered his services—his lance—to any available employer was called a free lance.

How much work you do as a freelancer depends on how much time you wish to devote to the job. Most freelancers begin their careers part-time, writing in the evenings and on weekends while holding down a full-time job. Some writers remain part-time freelancers, moving in and out of the field as their lives and careers change, but many choose to leave their day job to pursue a full-time freelance career. Full-time freelancers are writers who have achieved the track record and reputation to make freelance writing a permanent career. These writers include authors of new books, as well as those whose articles appear in issue after issue of national magazines.

Freelance writing, as a full-time occupation, is not easy. While it's possible to earn a living wage as a freelancer, it requires a great deal of time, skill, discipline and dedication. For more information on how much a freelance writer can expect to earn, see appendix one.

### What's the difference between a trade magazine and a consumer magazine?

A consumer magazine is intended for the general public (e.g., *Esquire, Newsweek, Cosmopolitan*), while a trade magazine is published for workers in a specialized industry (e.g., *Airport Operator, Clear Day Limousine Digest, Medical Imagery*). Trade magazines usually contain articles written by members of the profession that make up their readership, but many also welcome submissions from freelancers. Publications that refer to themselves as journals are usually published by and for a professional or trade group, such as orthopedic surgeons, microbiologists, or history professors. Consumer magazines, on the other hand, appeal to a general-interest audience or to consumers and businesspeople with special interests. Examples of special-interest consumer magazines include *Writer's Digest, Fast Company,* and *Backpacker*. (For a long list of trade journals and consumer magazines, see *Writer's Market*.)

### What is meant by rights? What rights are you supposed to sell?

Important information

A writer owns all rights to his literary creation. He is entitled to decide who shall own the right to print his story for the first time, or reprint it, or make it into a movie, or adapt it to any other print or electronic format. Such rights are his protection against those who would come along and freely use his work for their own purposes. The rights most commonly offered for sale to magazines are first North American serial rights, which are the rights to be the first to print a particular work, for the first time, in a magazine or newspaper. All other rights still belong to the writer. When selling your rights to a book publisher, the contract you sign will indicate what rights you keep and what rights you give to the publisher. See chapter eight for more information.

### What is the difference between first North American serial rights and first serial rights when submitting to a major magazine?

Both phrases mean almost the same thing—the right to publish the material once for the first time. The word *serial* refers to newspapers, magazines, and publications that are published on a continuing basis. First North American serial rights cover first publication rights in both the United States and Canada (American magazines that distribute in Canada usually want this extra protection); first serial rights cover first publication rights anywhere in the world.

**What does** *buys all rights* **mean? Does it mean a publisher buys first and subsequent rights? Or that it buys any rights offered?**

*Buys all rights* means a publisher buys the rights to *all* possible avenues of sale on that manuscript—such as book, movie, TV, syndication, reprint, and other rights. Some publications that buy all rights will reassign rights to the author after publication. Check this point with the editor.

**Are second and reprint rights the same? Can they be sold more than once?**

The answer is yes to both questions. Most magazine editors use the term *reprint rights* (or *second serial rights*) to refer to the right to reprint an article, poem, or story after it has already appeared in another publication. These reprint rights may be sold as many times as the author or copyright owner wishes, to any number of publications.

**What's a work-for-hire agreement?**

A work-for-hire project is one that permanently gives all rights of a work to the person or business that assigns or purchases it. A freelance writer who signs a work-for-hire clause gives up his copyright and also his right to any further income from that material. Work-for-hire agreements and transfers of exclusive rights must appear in writing to be legal.

## WHERE TO FIND OUT MORE

### BOOKS

*Writer's Encyclopedia*, forthcoming from Writer's Digest Books in fall 2007, is an alphabetical reference to writing and publishing terms throughout all genres.

# 4

# HOW DO I GET PUBLISHED?

Getting published is a step-by-step process of (1) researching the appropriate publications or publishers for your work, (2) reading their submission or writers guidelines, and (3) sending a query letter. The query letter is the primary tool for writers seeking magazine or book publication. A nonfiction writer with an article or book idea can elicit, through a query letter, the interest of an editor and sometimes even the particular slant an editor prefers. For fiction writers, a query letter attempts to persuade an editor or agent to request a full or partial manuscript for review. The questions and answers in this chapter will fully explain the query letter and its advantages.

## RESEARCHING THE MARKET

**Do all magazines and book publishers read unsolicited manuscripts or accept unsolicited queries?**

No. Publications that accept unsolicited manuscripts or queries usually indicate that in their listings in *Writer's Market*, on their Web site, or in their guidelines. Some places only accept material submitted by agents. With few exceptions, no agent or editor will accept a complete manuscript on first contact; you have to query first.

**Are there any rules concerning which editor or department should receive requests for submission guidelines or writers guidelines?**

Always look online first or in *Writer's Market* for guidelines. If you absolutely can't find them, then resort to mail. Write on the outside envelope, in the lower left corner, "Request for Submission Guidelines," and address the envelope and the letter to the editor of the publication. (If you don't know the editor's name, just address the request to "The Editor.") Your request will be routed quicker and get a faster response with the corner notation.

**I am interested in having my book published. However, I've had no experience with these things. Where do I start?**

Use a market guide (such as *Writer's Market* or *Novel & Short Story Writer's Market*) to find places likely to be interested in your particular book, or check the library or bookstores to find books similar to your own, and note who the publishers are. The listings in the market guides will tell you what to submit, where to submit it, and how to submit it. Send a SASE with every submission.

Frequently asked question

**How can I find out which publishers are most likely to be interested in a new novelist?**

There are several ways. You can research publisher listings through a market guide and look at the percentage of new writers they publish; you can read magazines like *Booklist*, *Writer's Digest*, and *Publishers Weekly*, which periodically give profiles of first novelists and information about their books; or you can browse through the fiction shelves at the bookstore or library and look at author bios, then note the publishers of first-time novelists. One company particularly known for its support of new novelists is MacAdam/Cage, an independent book publisher based in San Francisco. They still read unagented manuscripts.

## MAGAZINE QUERIES

**Do editors usually choose pieces from the slush pile to publish in their magazines and, if so, how frequently do they choose from the pile?**

If an editor works at a publication that accepts unsolicited submissions, then the answer to the first question is yes, they do use pieces from the slush pile—but only if the queries fit the bill. This means that the queries should first and foremost exhibit that the person querying the publication is familiar with the content of the publication. The query should also reflect that the person has read the publication's guidelines. Guidelines are important because they let the freelancer know what sections of the magazine are open to freelance submissions and what sections are not.

In addition to being on target, the query needs to be fresh and creative. Editors see lots of queries by lots of writers who all present the same article ideas. Make your idea stand out in that slush pile by finding a new slant on a topic of interest to the publication.

How frequently are queries from the slush pile actually assigned? That depends on how often editors see queries like those described above, and it depends on the publication's inventory of articles. If a publication has its editorial lineup for the upcoming year well in hand, as well as a significant number of unused articles, that particular publication may not be purchasing many articles. It is "overstocked." If this is the case, then no matter how on target your query is, the publication may be unwilling to purchase it for fear it will sit in its yet-to-be-published files for an unreasonable length of time.

**What information should a query letter contain for a magazine article?**

Important information

The information in a query letter serves two purposes. It should convince the editor that your idea is a good one for her publication's readership, and it should sell you as the best writer to turn out a good article on the subject. The query letter should contain an alluring (but concise) summary of the article's central idea and the angle or point of view from which you intend to approach it. Outline the structure of the article, giving facts, observations, and anecdotes that support the premise of the article. Don't give *too* many facts; the idea is to leave the editor wanting more. The letter should tell the editor why the article would be important and timely, and it should present a convincing argument for why the article would fit into this particular magazine.

You should also give the editor some indication of why you think *you* could write a good article on this particular subject. Share some sources of information and describe any special qualifications you may have for developing the idea. For example, if you are proposing an article on a topic in which you have some professional expertise, you should mention that. Samples of your published work will also help the editor see what you can do. The close of the query can be a straightforward request to write the article. You might also specify an estimated length and delivery date. If photographs are available, mention that, too. Don't discuss fees or request advice.

These are guidelines, of course, not a hard-and-fast pattern for a query letter. Good query letters are as individual as the writers who send them and as unique as the ideas that are proposed.

### How long should a query letter be?

Most successful query letters run only one page. Two or three pages of single-spaced typewritten copy is more than a busy editor wants to read. If that much copy is needed to give an editor the gist of the article, you probably have failed to focus on a specific angle.

### I have no previous publications, but I don't want to hurt my chances of having my article accepted by admitting that to an editor. How much must my query letter tell about my background?

If you've never been published before, it's best to ignore the subject of past credits and discuss instead your qualifications to write the article at hand. Discuss only those aspects of your background that relate to your subject. If you're proposing an article about how small businesses use computers, for example, mentioning your computer knowledge through education or employment would be a plus. What's important to an editor is not how many articles you've had published, but how much promise is shown by your query letter. Even if you've never published anything, a thorough and professional approach to the query letter will allow you the same chance to sell an article as someone who has a few articles in print.

### Should I include two or three samples of my work when sending a query letter?

It's always a good idea to include a few clips of your previously published articles. If an editor is not familiar with your work, looking at other pieces you've written is one way she can familiarize herself with your abilities and the quality of your work. The articles you send with your query ideally should be of the same category as the article you are proposing; a suggestion for an article on easy house painting could be bolstered by your published article on how to reupholster furniture. Even if the clips you send differ from the type of article you're proposing, send only your best published articles. Showing insignificant clips to the editor of a major publication could defeat your purpose. If you are dissatisfied with something you wrote, chances are the editor will not be too impressed with it either.

### How do I obtain clips or tearsheets of my work?

Publishers frequently furnish free contributor copies, tearsheets, or clips to freelance writers. If none of these are offered or provided, you may offer to buy copies of the issue your work appeared in from the publisher.

### Do I always have to query before sending a manuscript, or are there times when querying isn't necessary?

For certain types of articles, editors prefer to see the finished manuscript rather than a query. For example, personal experience articles, humor, nostalgia, and editorial opinion pieces rely so much on the writer's personal style that reading the finished product is the best way an editor can assess their acceptability for her publication. Articles requiring extensive research, however, are best attempted after an editor has responded favorably to a query. That saves the writer time, since the editor may prefer a different approach to the subject than the one the writer originally had. If you have any doubts, check *Writer's Market* for the specific magazine's policy on various types of articles.

### It seems so presumptuous for a beginning and unpublished writer to query first. How much attention would be paid to a beginner?

A busy editor would much rather read a query to decide whether she's interested in a certain idea than plow through a lengthy manuscript for the same purpose. From the writer's standpoint, think of the savings in postage and wear and tear on the manuscript. What *is* presumptuous is the writer who disregards an editor's stated request to query first and deluges the editor with completed manuscripts. Editors pay as much attention to beginners as they do to professionals, as long as the query letters are professionally written and the ideas are suitable to the magazine's readership and the editor's needs.

**A magazine recently published an article strikingly similar to one I have been trying to sell to the same magazine for some time. What can I do about this?**

First, don't assume that the idea was stolen by the editor and given to someone else to write. One frustrating fact of a writer's life is that you're often beaten to publication by someone with the same idea—sometimes even using the same words. But you're not forced to forget about selling your idea elsewhere, because many articles are published on the same subject in a variety of publications within a two- or three-year period. If your article is well written, and hits the right magazine at the right time, publication of the other article will not be a deterrent to publication of yours.

**I submitted a query to a magazine's top editor. The assistant to the editor replied: "Although we can't use this idea, we'd like to see more of your work." Now I have another idea for that magazine. Do I now correspond with the assistant, or with the top editor?**

Direct all future ideas or manuscripts to the person from whom you received the last correspondence. Top editors rarely are the first to review incoming manuscripts. It's best to submit to an articles editor or associate editor.

**It's not unusual for a single publishing company to produce several magazines with similar editorial content. Will my manuscript automatically be considered for use in all the magazines, or should I submit to each one separately?**

Unless otherwise noted in *Writer's Market* or in a magazine's guidelines, you should query each magazine separately. This allows you to personalize your submission—addressing it to the proper editor, mentioning a previously published article you admired, etc.

**I submitted a seasonal article idea too late and received a rejection slip. Should I resubmit to that same market in about four months?**

Seasonal queries should be submitted at least six months ahead of schedule. Some editors prefer queries at least one year ahead of season. If you receive a rejection for seasonal material with a note stating "received too late," resubmit it again in plenty of time for the editor to consider it for next season. See *Writer's Market* for publications' policies. "Received too late" may also mean that it is not good enough to keep on file for the following season.

**After I have received a favorable reply to a query, how soon will the editor expect the manuscript?**

If an editor gives you a favorable response on an article idea and doesn't specify a deadline, ask for one.

## GENERAL ETIQUETTE

Do not break
this rule!

**I'm going to New York with my husband to a convention at just about the time I'll have my book finished. Would it be to my advantage to visit agents there with it?**

No, it is not to your advantage and would likely kill your chances with that agent. Never go knocking on doors—it is considered rude, obnoxious, and unprofessional. Neither agents nor editors want personal visits from potential authors (and sometimes they don't even want visits from their established authors, especially unannounced visits).

**Is there any situation in which I can query by telephone?**

Very few, especially for beginning writers, but check the submission guidelines to see if phone queries are accepted. In almost all cases, you should query by mail or e-mail. A written query allows the editor to examine the proposal at her convenience, and to show it to her associates for their opinions. An editor is better able to judge the merits of an idea if it's in tangible, written form than if it's related to her over the telephone.

To the writer, the time and energy required to develop a carefully written query or proposal seems a large investment, especially when a telephone call might sell the editor on an idea with far less effort. However, a phone call interrupts the editor's work day and forces her to answer without proper time to think the matter through. Except in rare instances, an unexpected phone query usually receives either a no (whether deserved or not), or a response which puts you back at square one: "We're willing to look at it if you send a detailed query by mail." If you receive a negative response by phone, you have closed the door to a query that might have been considered more carefully had it come by mail. Once you have sold an editor several articles, or otherwise have an established relationship, she may be more receptive to phoned queries.

## What about fax queries?

The fax is falling out of favor, especially with the proliferation of e-mail. It's best not to use a fax to communicate with an editor unless the submission guidelines clearly state that fax queries are accepted.

## What about e-mail queries?

The number of publications that accept e-mail queries is growing as more publications find that it saves them time and money. The benefit to writers is that it can improve overall response time and make it easier for you to track submissions. The key is to first ascertain how a particular editor or publication prefers to receive electronic submissions, if it accepts them. Just as you would for a paper query, you must do your homework to determine the best way to reach a particular editor. Check the publication Web site or submission guidelines and see if they have a policy on e-mail queries. Sometimes you will be asked to complete and submit a form from their Web site or to use a specified format for your e-mail query. Follow such instructions to the letter. If no such instructions are given, then follow the rules for any good query letter.

## I have an e-mail address for an editor who works for a publisher that states it doesn't accept e-mail queries. May I e-mail this editor anyway with a query?

You can give it a try, though most industry professionals frown on the practice. There is some merit to e-mailing an agent or editor a *very succinct* description of your project and an offer to send more information. Such an e-mail should be only a few sentences long so it will not look like a time investment to read or consider. The worst that can happen is that you'll receive no response, which almost always means the editor or agent was not interested—and then you have your answer. Do *not* try to follow-up or badger the editor via e-mail.

**If I e-mail a query to a magazine publisher that requires clips, what's the best way to provide them?**

You can approach this in a few ways. You could post your clips on your personal Web site, if you have one, and give the editor the site URL. If you don't have a site, you could attach your clips as a PDF file, but only if the editor accepts attachments. If neither of those options are feasible, you could fax the clips or send them through the mail. Try to find out if the editor has a preference for any of these options.

**How soon can I follow up a query letter if I don't get a response? Should I phone?**

If you've not heard from the editor or agent after a month (or after the response time indicated in the market listing in *Writer's Market*), don't hesitate to send a *brief* follow-up note. The note should describe the query (or include a copy) so the editor or agent can readily identify it, and should simply ask whether she's had time to consider it. Be sure to include the date of the original query, since some offices file unsolicited queries and manuscripts by date of arrival. If your follow-up note does not elicit a reply, then assume the editor or agent is not interested, and move on. You should not phone.

**Is it permissible to submit a query to two different editors (at two different publications) at the same time?**

Yes, but do keep in mind that if you make simultaneous submissions to editors, you'll face the possibility of having more than one editor ask to see or purchase the material. This might be flattering to your ego, but it can also be incredibly awkward and can irritate editors (and agents as well).

In the case of a book, it can be preferable to have many editors vying for the same material so that you get the best possible advance and contract, but it's much better to have an agent handle that situation than to attempt to negotiate it yourself.

**I've noticed that many publishers in New York will not accept unsolicited submissions, even if you query first. What's that all about?**

Many of the largest publishing houses have stopped reading manuscripts that come in directly from authors—it's just too much work and hassle to go through the hundreds they would receive each week. Instead, editors have come to rely on agents to bring them quality work that fits their needs. So if you dream of being published by a big house, you'll have to get an agent to represent you. See chapter six for more about agents.

**Should I send with my query photocopies of one or two friendly rejections I've received from previous editors?**

Absolutely not—near misses do not work in your favor! However, if an editor who rejected you provided a referral to someone else, you might mention it—but avoid stating the fact you were rejected. Simply say, "Joe Editor said you might be a good fit for my project."

**I have several questions for various departments of a magazine, dealing with a query, my subscription, and other facets of their business. Is it OK to write just one letter?**

Such a practice can save you postage, but can also try an editor's patience. Honoring all those requests takes a lot of time (making photocopies, routing to various departments). It's best to send separate letters. Not only will doing so ensure that your requests get to the right people, it will make the editor look more kindly on you in the future.

**Is it OK to send editors to my Web site?**

If you are sending an e-mail query and wish to provide clips of your work via your personal Web page, you may do so if the editor accepts clips this way. Otherwise, you should provide everything the editor needs to make a decision in your query letter. Do not force editors to view or print your manuscript or proposal from your site, unless it involves something very unusual (like a portfolio of art, or demonstration of your Web design work). If you do provide your Web site address in your query, make it part of your letterhead or business card, or otherwise ensure it is peripheral to the main point of your query. Keep in mind that many editors and agents will search for you on the Web anyway to see what turns up.

**While most how-to books about freelancing advocate specifying rights for sale on manuscripts, others claim this is a mark of amateurs. What is the accepted practice?**

Most magazine or journal editors will assume you're offering first North American rights unless you specify otherwise, so it's not necessary to spell it out in the query. Once you're given an assignment, you'll want to get a contract or letter that spells out rights, payment, deadlines, and so on; more details are in chapter eleven. If you're querying a publication that's known for buying reprints or buying all rights (according to its writer's guidelines or market listing), and that's not what you're offering, then you should make that clear up front.

## BOOK QUERIES

Do not break this rule!

**What does a novel query look like?**

A novel query gives a brief overview of your novel's protagonist, plot, and setting, while also giving a little bit of information about yourself; a good novel query does not exceed a page. *Do not query until you have a completed manuscript!* An editor will not accept your work based on a partial manuscript if you're an unpublished or unknown writer.

A novel query usually includes five elements: (1) why you're querying this particular editor or agent, (2) your novel's title, genre, and word count, (3) a concise 100- to 200-word description of your novel's characters and plot, (4) a brief bio, and (5) a closing.

This may not sound like enough information for an editor to know whether or not she's interested in your novel, but it is. Your concise description of your novel, or its hook, should spark sufficient interest for the editor to request the first three chapters or complete manuscript. Most beginning writers make the mistake of giving too much detail (and boring detail at that) and attempting to mention every plot device and minor character. Focus on your main character (the protagonist), that character's conflict, the setting, and whatever sets your story apart from the rest. That's it.

Don't forget to establish why this particular editor or agent would be interested in your work—perhaps she's published work similar to your own, or you read an interview that described her interests, and she seemed like a good match. Whatever the case, let her know you've done your research and haven't blindly sent the exact same query to dozens of others.

It doesn't matter in which order you tackle the five elements of a novel query, though you should put your best foot forward. If your connection to the editor or agent is strong (you've met at a conference, for instance), that should go first. Perhaps your hook is so riveting that it should serve as the opening. If you have impressive credentials, a strong record of publication, or a prestigious writing degree, you might start with that. See chapter nine for more about novel submissions.

**Can I include the first few chapters of my novel manuscript with my query?**

No, unless the submission guidelines indicate that's what you should do. However, if you want to tuck in the first five pages, that's almost always acceptable—especially when you're confident about the quality of those pages.

**Should I send a synopsis with the query?**

If editors or agents request a synopsis with your query, they're probably looking for a quick summary of your entire novel. Synopsis lengths vary, but a few pages is typical; see chapter nine for synopsis tips. Sometimes agents or editors ask for an outline when what they really want is a synopsis. Or, when asking for an outline, an agent or editor may want a chapter-by-chapter outline (a synopsis of each chapter). When in doubt, ask.

**Is it acceptable to submit copies of my book manuscript simultaneously to different editors?**

Yes, but it's a good idea to advise the editors that you've done so. Don't worry about offending editors with a simultaneous submission; most of them assume that's the case anyway, and wouldn't expect you to give them an exclusive submission unless requested.

**I have sent several query letters to different publishers to see if they're interested in my book, and I received a letter from a publisher who said she would like to see the material immediately, so I sent it to her. In the meantime, I've received answers to all my letters, all saying they are interested and would like to see the material. What's the best way to answer these letters?**

You should write the other publishers that your book is under consideration by another editor, and enclose a copy of the manuscript. This might either heighten their interest or turn them off completely, depending on the editor.

**Is it proper to indicate in a query letter that my novel is the first of a series?**

Yes, but your query should focus only on the first book in that series—don't attempt to give a rundown of every title you have planned.

## I'M ANXIOUS ABOUT MY FIRST TIME

**How can I get up enough courage to send out a manuscript?**

You must put distance between yourself and your work after you've finished writing it, and realize that most writers have to send out a lengthy succession of queries before having one accepted. In fact, you should lower your expectations to rock bottom when you first start submitting your work—expect rejection.

**How does a beginner accumulate writing credits?**

Novice writers accumulate credits the same way that experienced writers accumulate them—by researching the markets to which they want to submit. The biggest mistake a writer can make is not taking the time to fully understand the publications she queries. By taking the time to read the writers guidelines, study a publication's demographics, and read a few sample issues of the publication, any writer can begin to accumulate writing credits.

That said, it can be much easier to start publishing with local and regional magazines or other small publications. One of the biggest mistakes beginners make is to target national magazines without any credentials or experience to back them up. If you must target the big glossies right out of the starting gate, then look at the shorts and fillers used in the front of the magazine; an editor is more likely to take a chance on you if you propose a 100-word factoid instead of a 2,000-word feature.

**If an editor keeps my manuscript a long time, does that mean she likes it? Or am I setting myself up for disappointment by thinking that?**

You'll probably be disappointed. It takes most editors anywhere from two days to six months (or longer!) to comment on a manuscript. Check *Writer's Market* for a publication's stated response time. If that time passes without any report, it's possible that your manuscript passed one editor's approval and is now being read by the other editors. However, it could also mean that your manuscript is buried under a pile of submissions, or that the editor is out of the office, or even that your manuscript was lost in the mail. So it's best not to get your hopes up. If you still haven't received word two to four weeks beyond the stated response time, write the publication (include a SASE) and ask for an update. If that letter receives no response, move on.

**I've been submitting my work for months, and I haven't made a sale. How can I increase my chances of getting published?**

Keep in mind that the publishing industry is very competitive and very subjective—editors change frequently and so do editorial preferences. The first step to understanding why your work is not being published is to thoroughly analyze (and objectively evaluate) your work in light of the material being published in the places you've targeted. Second, don't give up. A few months of trying (even a few years of trying) is not an adequate test of your writing skills.

**I have an idea for a nonfiction book that I want to write. What should I do first?**

You don't have to write the manuscript for a nonfiction book before you query publishers. You can write a book proposal first. The book proposal is a very in-depth analysis of your book project, sometimes as long as a hundred pages, that details the book's contents, the book's market or audience, and your qualifications to write the book and sell it. You also must explain how your book is different from or better than others that have been published on the same topic. The most comprehensive guide to writing a nonfiction book proposal is *How to Write a Book Proposal*, by Michael Larsen.

As you're preparing your book proposal, you will likely become familiar with publishers known for publishing books on your topic. To further research publishers (or agents), use a book like *Writer's Market* or *Guide to Literary Agents* to compile a list of who would be best suited to be your publisher or agent. Or check libraries and bookstores to see who has published books that are similar to what you want to write. You might only find a few suitable publishers if you're writing on a very specialized topic, or you might find dozens if your topic has general appeal. Once your proposal is fully complete, send out queries (or your complete proposal—check submission guidelines) that detail why there's a need for your book. After that, it's up to the editor or agent to decide whether she is interested in your book. See chapter ten for more detailed information on nonfiction book publishing and proposals.

**Is it OK to send my book proposal to editors on first contact, without querying first?**

Generally you'll be OK if you send the proposal first without querying—many editors need to see the entire proposal anyway to make a decision. However, it's always wisest to consult the submission guidelines first and make sure you won't be breaking an editor's or agent's cardinal rule.

**I'd like to query publishers with an idea that is extremely timely. If they take several months to reply, the material I have researched and collected will become outdated. Do you have any suggestions to speed up the process?**

For starters, make sure you query many publishers at once, and make sure you're querying the right people. Nothing wastes more time than sending your material to inappropriate publishers. If your topic is *extremely* timely, then you may want to look for writer's conferences where you can set up an appointment with an appropriate agent or editor to discuss your idea. Keep in mind, though, that most traditional publishers take one or two years to get a book to market.

## WHERE TO FIND OUT MORE

### BOOKS

*Writer's Market*, published annually by Writer's Digest Books, contains information on more than four thousand places to publish your work, plus query letter and submission tips.

*Novel & Short Story Writer's Market*, which is also published annually by Writer's Digest Books, is the most comprehensive resource on where to publish your fiction; it includes many nonpaying markets that *Writer's Market* does not list.

In *The American Directory of Writer's Guidelines*, about 1,600 magazine editors and book publishers explain what they're looking for. This resource differs from *Writer's Market* in that it offers unedited self-descriptions of what publications are looking for.

*Give 'Em What They Want*, by Blythe Camenson and Marshall J. Cook, is a complete guide to writing novel queries, synopses, and outlines, as well as to how the publishing process works.

*The Writer's Guide to Queries, Pitches & Proposals*, by Moira Allen, is a solid query-writing guide, and includes some valuable extras on securing an agent, syndicating your work, and other topics of interest to aspiring writers.

### WEB SITES

Miss Snark (misssnark.blogspot.com), a blog by a literary agent, features excellent commentary and Q&A on the querying process, and also occasional query letter critiques.

Evil Editor (evileditor.blogspot.com), a blog by a book editor, offers novel query critiques.

MediaBistro (www.mediabistro.com), offers excellent articles and online workshops about querying, particularly for magazines.

# 5

## HOW DO I FORMAT AND SUBMIT MY WORK?

The first impression an editor has of your manuscript is how it *looks*. The quality of your writing can change that impression for better or worse, of course, but why make your good writing work to overcome an unprofessional presentation of your manuscript? Here are some guidelines to help properly format and submit manuscripts to ensure you look like a professional.

All of these questions concern situations that normally take place *after* you've queried and *after* you're been given the go-ahead to submit an article or a manuscript, but you should also follow these guidelines, when applicable, when formatting and submitting query letters.

### What does it mean to format a manuscript?

Manuscript formatting refers to the process of making a manuscript as attractive as possible while making it conform to industry standards of presentation.

### So, what are the standards?

The most important goal is to produce a manuscript page that is readable. All manuscripts must be typed on 8.5″ x 11″ white paper. Type on one side of each sheet only, and don't use typing paper—it's too thin. Your printer should produce crisp, dark, black letters. The text should be double-spaced, with margins of one inch. (Query letters should be single-spaced.) You can use your word processor's settings to double-space your document and to set appropriate margins. Choose a standard font like Times or Arial in twelve-point size. See appendix one for visual examples.

**Does my manuscript have to be typed?**

Absolutely. No exceptions.

**I've heard that editors don't like dot-matrix printers. Why?**

The prejudice against dot-matrix printers is a legacy from early dot-matrix technology, which delivered nearly illegible manuscripts to editors' desks. But if your dot matrix printer produces manuscripts that are indistinguishable from those printed with inkjet printers, your work will be welcomed. (Just make sure the printer ribbon is fresh.)

**Photocopiers—and even some printers—can make two-sided copies; is it acceptable to print on both sides of paper when submitting my book manuscript to a publisher? Such a practice could certainly save tons of paper and postage.**

Manuscripts copied on both sides of a page are not acceptable because they are not *workable* in that format. Editors often rearrange material, send sections of the manuscript to another editor for input, and otherwise manipulate the content. The standard manuscript format developed to what it is today because it is efficient and extremely workable for editors.

**Is it acceptable to use italics, boldface, headlines, and a variety of typefaces in my manuscript?**

Your extra formatting, with the exception of necessary italics and boldface type, will be removed by the editor, so don't use any special formatting unless directed.

**What kind of paper should I print on?**

Editors are firm on two points: The manuscript must be on white paper, and it must measure 8.5″ x 11″. Whatever printer papers are available at your local office store will work. Don't bother spending more money on heavier stock, such as résumé paper; it doesn't work to your advantage.

**Is it acceptable to submit a photocopy of my manuscript, or must I submit the original?**

Since it's generally impossible to distinguish between a photocopy and the original manuscript, yes, a photocopy is fine. But it should be a *good-quality* photocopy that doesn't appear to have been reviewed many times. It may make more sense to print off a second copy than to make a photocopy of the original, unless you're sending off multiple copies of a lengthy manuscript.

**I've been asked by my editor for my social security number. Is this necessary?**

Book publishers and major magazine publishers require social security numbers for all accepted manuscripts, since publishers who pay six hundred dollars or more to a nonemployee must report such payments to the Internal Revenue Service. You don't need to give your social security number to the editor until your piece has been accepted.

**Should I include the word count on a manuscript when I submit it?**

For book projects, definitely—let the editor know your total word count. (Your word-processing program can do a word count for you.) Most magazine editors prefer to have the approximate word count noted when you submit an article. If the magazine pays by the word, they'll pay for the number of words in the final accepted version of your manuscript, or whatever you agreed to in a written contract.

**How do I treat the first page of a manuscript?**

See appendix one for a visual guide.

**Do the rest of a manuscript's pages differ from the first in format and appearance?**

Yes. Again, look in appendix one for a visual guide.

**Are there different manuscript formats for short stories, magazine articles, and book-length projects?**

No. There is only one standard manuscript submission format: double-spaced on 8.5″ x 11″ white paper.

### How should I indicate on my manuscript that I am writing under a pseudonym?

On the first page of your manuscript, in the upper left corner, type your real name, then your pen name in parentheses, then your address. Type your pen name as the byline under the title of your manuscript. On subsequent pages, in the upper right corner, type your real name, followed by your pen name in parentheses, then the page number: "Jones (Smith) 2." Of course, if you don't want even your editor or publisher to know your real name, then you'll have to use the pseudonym everywhere. If this is your wish, you'll have to notify your local post office and bank that you are using a pen name in your work.

See chapter nineteen for more about pen names.

### How do I prepare a manuscript for a how-to book? About half of the book will consist of pictures and diagrams.

The manuscript should be typed in the same way as other book manuscripts, with appropriate illustration references, such as "(See Figure 1)" or "(See photo, page 12)." All diagrams and photographs should be numbered so that they correlate with both the text and a separate sheet listing captions. Check with the editor for any specific guidelines he may have.

### Is it okay to include photographs when submitting my manuscript for consideration?

You shouldn't submit original photos unless they are an integral part of the manuscript. Find out from the editor the best way to submit them. He'll probably accept them via e-mail attachment or on a CD or DVD.

### When submitting a book manuscript for consideration, what information concerning rights should be attached?

It's not necessary to discuss the matter of rights when submitting a book manuscript to a publisher. If the publisher decides to purchase the book, you will negotiate a contract that spells out the rights.

### How do I type a sidebar in manuscript form?

Sidebars should be typed in the standard manuscript format. Begin the sidebar on a separate sheet of paper and clearly mark it "Sidebar." Type an identifying caption after the word *sidebar* to indicate what article or chapter it accompanies. Place the sidebar at the end of the article or applicable chapter.

## FLASHBACK QUESTION

**Is it essential that a manuscript be typed perfectly? I have a 480-page manuscript that I've retyped three times, and it's still a mess. Every time I retype it, I reread it, which is disastrous because my pen flies with revisions (usually of words, not sentences). If I retype it again, I'll be wasting weeks that could be used in creating. Or should I send it out with the word substitutes neatly penned?**

Since you can't resist revising every time you retype, you would probably find a professional manuscript typist the answer to your problem. The cost of this service would be worth the considerable savings in time and effort. Under no circumstances should you send out a manuscript that has more than three corrections per page marked on it. Also, to save wear and tear on the finished product, send the publisher a query letter first instead of submitting the complete manuscript. A clean photocopy can cover a multitude of sins. Certain pages or the entire manuscript can be corrected and photocopied to appear professionally typed.

## SUBMISSIONS

**Should I submit my manuscripts via e-mail? And if I do, should I still send a paper copy?**

Most editors, especially magazine editors, expect you to submit short assignments via e-mail attachment (as a Word document). Book publishers and agents vary in their preferences; if you're sending in a manuscript or book proposal for consideration, they may accept hard copy or e-mail attachment—usually, they prefer hard copy. (If you've been contracted for a book project, and you're wondering how to submit your manuscript, ask your editor for guidelines.) Agents often send hard copies of proposals and manuscripts to editors because doing so ensures quality of presentation and prevents widespread distribution via e-mail. You may wish to submit hard copies at first for the same reasons.

### Is there any scenario in which I should submit my work on disk?

E-mail is usually the best way to submit electronic files; a disk is rarely necessary. However, if you're asked to submit your work on disk, the most popular way is to use a CD or DVD. Check with your editor to find out requirements.

Unless otherwise noted in *Writer's Market* or in submission guidelines, you should not include a disk with an unsolicited submission. Use hard copies exclusively.

### Is it necessary to include a cover letter with a requested manuscript?

A cover letter should accompany a manuscript that an editor or agent has asked to see. When you are submitting finished material at an editor's request, cover letters can serve to remind the editor that he asked you to send the material. A cover letter should be short and to the point, and should not mention rates or fees. Do provide full contact information, and mention any times when you might *not* be available.

Cover letters should be used when submitting short stories, poems, and other short creative works to literary journals and magazines. Preceding a submission with a query is not required in these situations because the editor must read the actual work to know whether it works for the publication.

### I have a requested manuscript ready to send. Now what?

If you must send it as a hard copy, use a no. 10 (business-size) envelope for short pieces; longer works should be sent in a 9″ x 12″ envelope. Book-length manuscripts can be shipped in a padded envelope or a copy-paper box. Always include a self-addressed stamped envelope with your submission, and affix enough postage to get your work home. If you don't need the manuscript returned, attach a note to that effect on the manuscript and send just a self-addressed, stamped, no. 10 envelope for the editor's reply.

I have twenty-four manuscripts, including novels and books of short stories. All are complete; not all are typed. I have written/edited/re-edited these over forty years. I have a spreadsheet with all the titles, word counts, etc. Should I include this with submissions? Isn't it a good overview for the planning and business end of publishing?

Choose your strongest work and market that first. There's no need to mention other manuscripts you've completed until you find an editor or agent who likes your style. Once you have someone interested in your work, he will ask what else you have written, and then you can share your list.

**When submitting a manuscript, should I include a copyright notation?**

No, it's considered a mark of an amateur to prominently declare your copyright on the material. Your work is copyrighted and protected under law whether you type it on the manuscript or not. Editors and agents know this and don't need to be reminded by you.

**Can I mail my manuscript folded instead of flat?**

Yes. Short stories, articles, and poems of five pages or fewer may be folded in thirds and mailed in a no. 10 business envelope. However, any manuscripts *longer* than five pages should be mailed flat. Be sure to include a SASE of the proper size with any submission.

**If I use a special express delivery service, will my work get more immediate attention or have an advantage?**

Many express services require that the recipient sign a receipt, so you'll know for sure (and have evidence) that a publisher received your work. But using such services will not impress the editor or get your work read more quickly.

**Can you explain the difference between certified mail and registered mail? And when is it necessary to use special types of mail when submitting manuscripts?**

Certified mail is used when you just want a record of receipt of mail at a certain address. It's handled like regular mail, but a signed receipt is mailed to you. Registered mail is used to send valuables, such as stock certificates and jewelry, because the post office signs a receipt when it receives the package and it knows where the package is at all times. Certified mail is the best way to withdraw a manuscript or to follow up on a manuscript that's been held too long by an editor. A receipt is mailed to you, so you have a record that the editor received your correspondence. That record should be kept in your files. (You may also want to send your manuscripts via certified mail, so you can be sure the material was received to begin with.)

## FOLLOWING UP ON YOUR SUBMISSION

**Is it permissible to follow up regarding the status of my submission?**

Yes, but make sure you're not bothering the editor or agent before the stated response time. Don't ever phone to follow up; instead, send a very brief letter inquiring about the status of your submission, and use a return-receipt service (such as certified mail) to be certain the editor received your letter. If you still don't hear anything, move on.

**After querying a publisher with my novel, I was asked to mail a synopsis and four chapters. The publisher acknowledged receipt, but I did not hear from the publisher again. After three months, I wrote a letter inquiring as to its decision. The editorial department replied that my manuscript had been misfiled; they did not know it had arrived until receipt of my letter. Within a few weeks, the senior editor wrote a vague letter saying the chapters had not lived up to the outline and that the manuscript was being returned. Nearly three months have passed, and the manuscript has not arrived. The publisher says it has asked the post office to trace it. If the post office is unable to locate it, as now seems possible, do I have recourse against the publisher? There's something illogical about the publisher's explanation.**

Major publishing houses deal with thousands of manuscripts annually, and while yours is an unfortunate incident, you are probably unduly suspicious of the publisher. In this situation, it's best to cut your losses and make a new copy of your materials to send out again.

**After sending my submission, I waited three months for a reply, then sent a letter asking about the status of my manuscript. The publication had no record of it. Is there a way I can trace the manuscript?**

No, you're out of luck unless you sent it by certified or registered mail.

**I have two minor changes I'd like to make in a manuscript I mailed to a publisher last week. Would it be all right to send the editor a note specifying the changes I'd like made in my manuscript?**

No. For better or worse, the manuscript you mailed is the one the editor now has. Any changes will have to be made after the work is accepted. Sending in the corrections now would only exasperate the editor. If your manuscript is accepted, you will probably have an opportunity later to suggest the changes.

**I submitted a manuscript to a publisher a few weeks ago, and have heard nothing since. Is it okay to phone the editor to ask about the status of my manuscript?**

No. Most publishers and magazines receive so many manuscripts that it is impossible for the average staff member to know the status of a particular piece at any given time. Write a note requesting a report on your manuscript. Editors don't like phone calls from writers requesting immediate reports.

**How long does it usually take an editor or agent to read a manuscript or sample chapters?**

It take anywhere from a few days to a few months—or more. If your work gets read in a few weeks or less, consider yourself lucky.

> **How long should I wait for an editor's decision on my manuscript?**
>
> Wait until the stated response time has passed, follow up (if you wish) with a written note, then move on to the next potential publisher.
>
> **I've submitted manuscripts to small publications that never returned them or notified me if the pieces were published. How can I find out if they were ever printed so I can sell them to larger markets without infringing on other publications' rights?**
>
> You can proceed with confidence that the publications never used your work and that you are free to pursue publication elsewhere. It's incredibly unlikely they did use your material, and even if they did, they clearly didn't pay you for it, which means you retain the right to sell it elsewhere.

**What are the mechanics of submitting manuscripts to foreign markets?**

The submission techniques are the same as those for submitting to American publishers. The main difference is that the manuscript must be accompanied by International Reply Coupons (IRCs) in sufficient number to cover the cost of return postage. The number of coupons required for a manuscript is determined by the weight of the manuscript at the post office, which is where the coupons are purchased.

**Do Canadian writers stand the same chance as Americans in the American market? How can a Canadian writer manage return postage?**

Yes, Canadians stand an equal chance in the American market. The easiest way to purchase U.S. stamps is to use the U.S. Postal Service's Web site, www.usps.com.

## WHERE TO FIND OUT MORE

### BOOKS

*Formatting & Submitting Your Manuscript*, by the editors of Writer's Digest Books, is a visual guide to formatting and submitting any type of work, with extra information on queries and valuable do's and don'ts of writing and publishing.

## MULTIMEDIA

*Submit! The Unofficial All-Genre Multimedia Guide to Submitting Short Prose,* by Elephant Rock Productions (www.erpmedia.net), is an excellent DVD guide to the submission process for short fiction and nonfiction in all genres.

# 6

# How do I find an agent?

While many writers believe their key to fame and fortune is finding a literary agent, many more writers don't understand what a literary agent does. A literary agent markets (or sells) your work to publishers. If an agent believes in you and your work, she will take you on as a client and advise you about your work's quality and marketability, and the strategy for securing its publication. This chapter tells you how to search for an agent and what to expect from one.

## GETTING AN AGENT

### How can I find an agent?

The better question is: How can I find the *right* agent? Not any agent will do. Just like editors, agents have personal tastes, preferences, and attitudes, and you need to find one who understands and believes in your work enough to go through the submission and rejection process on your behalf. It's certainly easy to find names of agents through directories like *Guide to Literary Agents* or any of a dozen Web sites, but it's not so easy to find the perfect match.

Therefore, just as you would research a market, research an agent. What types of work does she represent? Who does she sell to? Does she have other clients who are like you? How many new writers does she work with? Once you have a list of potential agents who would be interested in your project, query them just as you would an editor.

Alternatively, writers conferences sometimes have agents as guest speakers, and these agents often take appointments. When you meet with a prospective agent and pitch your project, you often know right away whether she is interested, which saves you the time of researching, querying, and waiting for a response. Sometimes agents are kind or knowledgeable enough to recommend you to another agent if your project simply doesn't fit their area of expertise.

No organization regulates literary agencies, although hundreds of agencies belong to the Association of Authors' Representatives. To be a member of AAR, agencies must agree to adhere to a written code of professional practices. This Canon of Ethics is listed at www.aar-online.org. Do note, however, that even if an agent isn't a member of AAR, the agent may be perfectly reputable and professional in her practices.

Frequently asked question

**How will I know whether an agent is reputable? Is there a list I can obtain of recommended agents?**

In addition to checking agents out through AAR or the Better Business Bureau (www.bbb.org), look for Web sites where writers post information about agents they believe are dishonest or disreputable. (See the end of this chapter for some listings.) If the agent charges an upfront reading fee, that's the first red flag—it's against the AAR Canon of Ethics and is not considered standard practice. Generally, you shouldn't have to pay an agent any fee unless she sells your work, although some agents will charge you up front for expenses related to submitting your work (photocopying, postage, etc).

**Are there different types of literary agents?**

It's possible to categorize agents in terms of the material they handle. Sometimes agents deal only in certain genres, or in nonfiction (or fiction), or in scripts. Dramatic agents who handle plays are usually located in New York, whereas those agents handling scripts for films and television are on the West Coast.

**What agents are most open to new writers?**

Junior agents and newly established agencies are often hungry for new clients and can be more open to new writers. Even some of the better-known and established agents might be willing to look at your material. Whether they will represent it depends, of course, on the material. It's usually not worth your time to submit to the superagents—those who represent the biggest names and sell projects for top dollar—unless you have a referral. (You usually know if an agent is a superagent if she only takes referrals or has other restrictions on submissions.)

**Does having an agent increase the chances my material will be read by a publisher?**

In today's market, almost 80 percent of books that major publishing houses buy are sold to them through agents. Agents are experts in the publishing industry. They have networking contacts with individual editors and know better than writers what editor would be most likely to buy their work. If an editor receives a manuscript or query from an agent, that book has a better chance of getting considered first—the editor knows the agent has already weeded it out of her slush pile and that the agent wouldn't send something along that wasn't at least the genre or type of book the editor was seeking.

**When an agent asks for my complete manuscript, does she expect that she now has an exclusive right of refusal for an unspecified period of time, or is it okay to continue sending the manuscript to other agents who might request it? And should I tell these other agents that someone else is considering the whole manuscript?**

Agents have different policies regarding simultaneous submissions. Unless an agent specifically requests an exclusive look at your manuscript, you're free to continue marketing your work to other agents simultaneously. Do mention in your cover letter if it's a simultaneous submission. This lets the agents know that if they're interested in your manuscript, they'll need to get back to you quickly. If an agent does request an exclusive look at your manuscript, you have the right to decide whether to grant that request. You can also decide the length of time you'll give her exclusive consideration.

If you don't hear back from the agent within a reasonable amount of time—a month or two—it's fine to follow up with a polite phone call to check with the agent and ask if she's had a chance to review your manuscript. If she has not yet gotten to your submission and you decide to submit your work elsewhere, let the agent know you've had other requests for your manuscript and that you'd like to go ahead and send your work out for other agents' simultaneous consideration. Remember, it's within your control to decide whether to give the first agent more time to consider your manuscript on an exclusive basis or to notify her that you'll resume marketing your work to other agents.

## STANDARD PRACTICES

**What is the standard percentage an agent receives as her commission?**

Generally, agents receive 15 percent of your advance and royalties. Anything else is outside of standard practice.

Important information

**Is it routine for agents to charge a fee for reading a manuscript? What does this fee entail?**

It is not routine nor a standard practice, but a handful of reputable agents do charge a reading fee. When dealing with an agent who charges such a fee, you should always check her background—what books she has sold recently, who she represents, and if her clients are satisfied. Find out if the agent offers criticism on manuscripts, and if the agent will refund the fee if she agrees to represent you and sells your book. Make sure you know what you're getting for the fee you pay. And try to determine if reading fees or sales commissions make up the agent's *primary* source of income. Obviously, you'd prefer to be represented by an agent who is most successful at selling—not reading.

**Do agents sign contracts with clients?**

Some agents require a contract before they'll do business with a writer. They feel that written agreements offer the agent protection, since the author doesn't pay her any money until a contract is drawn up containing a clause that provides for payment to the agent. There are, however, agents who prefer not to have a written agreement with authors; it doesn't mean an agent isn't reputable—that's just her working style.

Your signed agreement with the agent should cover several areas to benefit you both and spell out the scope of representation. Will the agent be handling all your work, or just this particular book? Is the agent obligated to inform you of every offer she receives? How may the agreement be terminated?

## How do I dissolve my relationship with one agent and go with another?

Sometimes a writer believes that her agent is not spending enough time on her projects and is no longer the person she wants representing her interests. But the agent will remain tied to the author by any works the agent sold for her, so the relationship should be kept as friendly as possible, even if discontinued. If the time comes to sever ties with an agent, send a simple letter suggesting that parting company would be better for both of you—or follow the guidelines laid out in your contract with the agent.

## If I discontinue my relationship with an agent, do I continue to pay her a percentage of royalties on works she sold?

Yes. Your former agent remains the agent of record for all works she sold before you left her representation. Therefore, the publisher will continue to send your royalties in care of that agent whether or not she continues to represent you. She sold the book, so she gets the royalty checks, from which she deducts her commission. If the book goes out of print and your new agent negotiates a reprint edition (or you do so yourself), whether your former agent would receive any royalties would depend on the terms of the initial sale.

## I have many manuscripts that need work. Is there an agent who will revise and sell, take her share of the money, and send me the rest?

No agent is willing or financially able to do revisions in the hope that she will be paid eventually out of the sale of the work. It would be better to learn to revise your own manuscripts by reading books like *The First Five Pages* or *Self-Editing for Fiction Writers*, and then resubmit your manuscripts for sale. Or, you could look into joining a writers group that provides manuscript critiques or gives advice on how to revise.

**If I authorize an agent to sell one or more of my works, am I committed to pay a fee to the agent for other work I subsequently sell myself?**

Normally, if you acquire an agent, you are committed to pay the agent a fee for any of your work sold after that date, unless there is an agreement between you specifically exempting from commission certain work sold by you yourself.

**My agent has represented my novel for a month and I've heard nothing. What's going on?**

Just because you've heard nothing doesn't mean the agent isn't trying to sell your book. Remember, if she doesn't sell the book, she won't get her commission; a book sale would be to her benefit as well as yours. It takes time for the agent to find the right publisher for your book, and the agent represents other authors, so there isn't always time to report every move of a manuscript.

Nevertheless, it is your manuscript, and you want to know how it's doing. If you haven't heard anything for a month, e-mail a short letter of inquiry or call, and the agent should get back to you. A writer can avoid this problem by establishing at the outset when she can expect to hear from the agent.

**If an agent decides she isn't going to handle a particular manuscript of mine, is it okay for me to start submitting it to publishers on my own?**

Yes. The agent has decided she no longer has any prospects for your work, or cannot sell it for some other reason. Therefore, it would be perfectly acceptable for you to submit it yourself to any publisher you think might buy it, or to contact another agent who might handle it.

**Is it ethical to have two agents? I have two agents and each handles the same type of material, but each in his own locale (New York vs. Los Angeles). Do agents frown on this procedure, even though the material submitted to each is not the same?**

One agent will expect to handle all of your work. If that one agent rejects a project, then you're free to go elsewhere with it. Literary agents often use co-agents to sell film rights, foreign rights, and other rights they don't sell themselves, so you shouldn't need multiple agents for multiple rights sales. However, sometimes one agent will give her blessing for you to use another agent for a genre she has no interest in handling. But it's more likely she'll take it on anyway or find a co-agent.

**If a book or story is being represented by an agent, is it possible to submit it to another agent or to a publisher?**

Once a manuscript has been turned over to one agent, it is not ethical to submit copies either to another agent or to a publisher. If you feel the agent is not handling your work to your satisfaction, terminate your arrangement with her. You will then be free to try marketing the material yourself or to place it with another agent.

**I found an agent to represent my novel. She notified me of the opinions of various publishers (who rejected the work), but when I asked to whom she showed these stories, she wouldn't say. Do I have a right to ask the names of the publishers?**

You do indeed. Any reputable agency would not hesitate to reveal the publishers to whom it submitted material.

## DO YOU NEED AN AGENT?

**Is it a good idea for a beginning writer to get an agent?**

It depends on what you're selling, but it is possible for a first-timer to sell a book herself. Dean Koontz sold his first three books without the benefit of an agent, and claims to have gained valuable marketing experience as a result.

However, Koontz was selling his work at a time when most publishers would consider unagented or unsolicited submissions. It can be downright impossible these days to sell a book to any major publisher without an agent, simply because publishers won't accept material directly from authors. Evaluate whether your project is suited for one of these big houses to help determine whether you need an agent.

It's probably not worth your while to get an agent if any of these apply to you:

- Your book has a niche audience that would work best with a small publisher who accepts unsolicited submissions and is likely to offer a small advance. (Projects like these are rarely worth an agent's time.)
- Your book is best suited to an academic or university press. (You can sell these types of projects very well on your own.)
- You know the market for your book better than any agent and know specifically which publishing houses would be likely to buy it—and maybe even know the editors in question.

An agent will benefit you the most when you need her connections and insider savvy to find the right editor and publisher for your book, when you need to reach the big houses, and when you lack the business sense to negotiate your contract or manage your business relationship with the publisher. An agent can also be vital to writers who seek a lifetime career of writing books for the big houses, and need an advisor who can help them build that successful career.

### Can I get an agent to sell my short stories or magazine articles?

No. Unless the agent is also making a lot of money on an author's book sales, she won't handle magazine pieces or short stories because such sales aren't economically feasible for the agent. Editors of magazines and journals buy shorter pieces directly from writers on a regular basis, so an agent isn't needed on these sales. However, if you've done a series of articles on a specific topic and are considering incorporating them into a book proposal, an agent might be interested in that.

### I am a poet who needs a literary agent. Who do you suggest?

There is such a small market for poetry that almost no agent will handle an author whose sole output is poetry. Most poets attempt to sell their poems individually to magazines, hoping to gain enough published credits to interest a publisher in a collection.

**I write religious material—what about agents in the religious publishing field?**

Not all agents are familiar with or understand the religious market, so your search for an appropriate agent will need to be more restrictive than the typical agent search. The exceptions are those agents who regularly deal with major publishers with a special department or imprint for religious books. Try starting your search with *Christian Writers' Market Guide*, an annual market directory for Christian writers.

**Do agents offer manuscripts to publishers for review, and receive money only after they make a sale?**

Yes. The only way agents should earn their money is by selling your manuscript and deducting commissions from the sales.

**I've read in *Publishers Weekly* about agents auctioning off a book, and getting escalation clauses if the book hits the New York Times best-seller list. Can I get my agent to make such deals for me and my book?**

It depends on the sales potential of your book. Auctions take place when an agent has what she thinks is a really hot property. She might establish a floor price—the minimum for which she will sell the book—and then make multiple submissions to prospective publishers, giving a deadline for responses. If one publisher's bid is topped by another, the first publisher is given the opportunity to top the competitor's offer. Escalation clauses increase an author's royalty percentage if the book sells particularly well; this provision is determined by various sales reports, including the number of weeks the book is on the *New York Times* (or other) best-seller list.

Obviously, these contract provisions all hinge on one factor: The book must be one that everyone believes is going to be a big seller. So these deals are often obtained by established authors whose books the publishers *know* will be promotable and salable. Nothing is more embarrassing for an agent than holding an auction that no one wants to participate in.

**Can you tell me the requirements for becoming a literary agent, or where I can obtain such information?**

The main requirement for becoming a literary agent is knowing the publishing market incredibly well and having insider information on what editors are looking for. This usually requires that you have prior experience at a publishing house or in the publishing industry. There is limited information on how to become an agent, but sometimes you can find courses on the topic in the New York or Los Angeles area.

**My friend, who has published some poetry and short stories, is writing a novel that I think is excellent. I've been editing and critiquing her work on this project and would like to be her agent. My question is: How does one become an official agent? Everyone must start somewhere with that first client, correct? What steps should I be taking to become my friend's agent and see her book all the way to print by a major publishing house?**

It's a mistake to think that being an agent or a sales representative begins with one client. It begins with knowledge of the industry and with connections to both the seller of the product and the potential buyers. Deciding to become an agent because your friend is writing a book is like deciding to become a realtor because your friend is selling her house. To become a literary agent, you'll need to study publishing much more extensively than you can by reading this book. Anyone can call herself an agent and mail her friend's work out to publishers, but this won't compel an editor to give your friend's book more consideration than she'd give an unagented writer. Calling yourself an agent before you're ready won't impress an editor who's never heard of you, since agenting is a profession built on reputation and relationships.

To be an effective agent, you'll have to read the trade magazines to keep up with the industry: who's buying and selling what. You'll need to establish a reputation by working with a larger agency that can introduce you to the editors at the major publishing houses, or else find another way, like meeting the editors at conferences or moving to New York and knocking on doors. You'll need to study book contracts and learn about rights negotiations. And you'll need to build a client list with more than one name on it to make it worth an editor's time to meet with you.

In short, agenting is a profession, not a part-time hobby. If this sounds like too much of a commitment, there are other things you can do to help your friend. Encourage her to keep writing by doing exactly what you're doing—objectively editing and critiquing her novel. An agent may not have the time to give her that one-on-one editing help, and your service to her is invaluable as it is. You may help her find an agent by assisting her in writing a strong query letter, attending writers conferences with her, and helping her submit her work.

## SCRIPT AGENTS

### Do I really need an agent for a script?

Once you have a completed script that's the best it can be, you must find someone in the business to read it, and an agent is sometimes the only way to do that. Anybody who receives a script direct from an author wonders why it wasn't submitted by an agent. If you want to be a professional, then find yourself an agent. Unfortunately, it's often said that getting an agent to represent you is tougher than getting your first film produced.

### How do I find a script agent?

One of the best methods is to have a friend who is already represented recommend you; some of the biggest agencies (Creative Artists Agency, William Morris Agency) won't read your unsolicited script unless you have such a referral.

With any agency, it's best to query first, just as you would query for a novel. Stick with one page that contains a concise description of your idea, a brief summation of your accomplishments, and a request for the agent to read the script. Don't go into detail about your script in the query—doing so gives the agent more reason to reject you. You can find a list of script agents in *Guide to Literary Agents* or through the Writers Guild of America.

In Hollywood, knowing somebody—or knowing somebody who knows somebody—is a big help in breaking in to the industry. Try to find a connection and save yourself the frustration of querying cold. One of the best ways to get someone to look at your script is to have someone who already works in the business recommend it to a friend.

**I have no connections in Hollywood and no possible way of finding an agent. Now what?**

See chapter twenty-six for more about scriptwriting.

First, it's a good idea to register your script with the Writers Guild of America. Registration provides a dated record of the writer's claim to authorship and can be used as evidence in legal disputes about authorship.

Next, you need to match your script with the appropriate market. The best bet for a beginning writer is an independent movie, not a big-budget, special-effects-laden extravaganza. This means you should focus on original story line and compelling characters. Study films and film credits; note what types of movies a producer, director, or actor typically makes, because you can pitch your script to any of them. (Sending scripts to actors' agents is the worst thing to do, because these agents are trained to turn people away. See if you can find a creative way to reach the actor.) Also, try to identify production companies that might be interested in a script similar to yours, then find the telephone number for its story department and get the name of the story editor. Write that person a one-page query letter and hope it grabs her attention.

Competition today is so fierce that scriptwriters must be innovative in finding ways to get people to read their material. If you can get a studio head to look at a script by funneling it through her dentist, don't hesitate.

Former UCLA film chairman Richard Walter has said that beginners might try writing flattering letters to other writers or producers. The letters may help you make a friend of someone who knows how hard it is to break in, and who, eventually, might agree to help you.

## WHERE TO FIND OUT MORE

### BOOKS

*Guide to Literary Agents* is an annual directory by Writer's Digest Books that lists hundreds of agents and what types of work they sell.

*How to Be Your Own Literary Agent*, by Richard Curtis, is a must-have guide if you're attempting to negotiate your own contract or if you need answers about the publishing process in the absence of an agent.

## WEB SITES

The Association of Authors' Representatives (AAR) (www.aar-online. org) can help you find reputable agents; be sure to read up on the Canon of Ethics for agents while you're visiting this site.

Preditors & Editors (www.anotherealm.com/prededitors/) lists complaints against agencies and publishers.

Writer Beware (www.sfwa.org/beware/), a site from the Science Fiction and Fantasy Writers of America, is another site to double-check when you're in doubt about the legitimacy of an agent or publisher.

Agent Query (www.agentquery.com) is a free directory of agents.

Miss Snark (misssnark.blogspot.com), a blog by a literary agent, gives you a firsthand look at what makes agents tick.

Agent 007 on Publishing (agent007.blogspot.com), a blog by an editor turned literary agent, gives excellent insight into the agenting and publishing world.

# 7

# WHY AM I GETTING REJECTED?

There is no easy way to face rejection, and editors give little information about why they rejected your work. These are the tests of the writing life. When you encounter them—and, at some point, all writers do (beginners more so than others)—face them with renewed determination. Success begins where most people quit.

Rejections tend to happen for two reasons: (1) your work isn't ready to be submitted, or (2) you queried incorrectly, either by choosing the wrong market or by querying unprofessionally. The first reason can only be remedied by making your work the best it can be, through constant analysis and revision. The second reason for rejection can be completely eliminated by following the advice in this book and getting information from other expert sources.

**Why are editors rejecting my work when family and friends love it so much?**

Your family and friends love you and see you in your work. An editor doesn't know you and can be much more objective. *(Thanks to Jennie Pitkus for providing this important question and answer.)*

**I get lots of form rejections that have little or no feedback on my individual work. What might be wrong?**

Reasons for rejection can be incredibly subjective (indefinable issues of taste), but you might consider the following possibilities:

• Something similar is on file or was recently published: You're not the only person with your idea. Often your work will be rejected simply because someone else beat you to it.

- The timing is wrong. Editors change. Publishers cut back on their lists. The market changes. Sometimes it's hard to hit things just right.

- You don't have adequate credentials (particularly if you're writing a non-fiction article or book), or you don't have an attractive marketing platform—a way to reach readers and promote yourself and your work.

If you're attempting to get your book published, keep in mind that most New York agents and editors take on a new project or new author only when they feel there's solid potential for a significant or guaranteed return. Your book may be too "small" for some publishers to consider; if you believe that's the case, start querying small or regional presses.

### What should I do after an article is returned with a rejection slip?

Send a rejected query or manuscript to another appropriate publication the day it is returned to you—or decide it's time to revise or recast it. Always keep your work in circulation.

### How many rejection slips do you consider the cutoff point—where I should give up completely?

If you put a lot of time and effort into a project, don't abandon it too quickly. Look at the rejection slips as bits of advice for improvement, or as patterns of criticism. Rejections, if used properly, can be lessons to improve your writing.

If you've been sending the same magazine query around for many months, your idea may have grown too stale for you to keep circulating it. If you've been attempting to sell a book manuscript, and have had some near misses, then your timing or your luck may be off; some books circulate for many years before finding the right agent or editor. As long as you feel passionate about the work, you shouldn't give up on it—even if it means returning to the manuscript a few years down the road. Some ideas and manuscripts have to be set aside because the market isn't ready for them.

### If I'm aiming at a specific type of market, should I continue to submit to (or query) publications that have rejected my past work? Do editors begin

**to recognize certain authors as "losers" and push their work aside because of past rejections?**

Just because a market has rejected your manuscripts in the past doesn't mean it will in the future. Editors reject manuscripts for many reasons that have nothing to do with your manuscript's value. For example, the editor could have recently bought a manuscript on a topic similar to yours. Don't assume that the sight of your name on a manuscript will cause an editor to automatically reach for a rejection slip. Assuming your manuscripts are neat, appealing, and suited to the publication, the next manuscript you send may be the happy combination of the right idea in the right place at the right time, while your earlier pieces weren't. On the other hand, tread carefully. If you've submitted six stories in the past six months, and they've all been rejected, you might want to back off from that market for a while. Watch the publication closely and try to make your articles as good as the ones the magazine is publishing.

**Frequently asked question**

**May I submit the same manuscript more than once to an editor (or agent) who has rejected it?**

In the case of magazine articles, if the editor tells you he's rejecting it because he's overbought at the time, or he's recently bought something similar, you might have a chance at a later date. Also, watch the magazine's masthead. If an editor leaves, the new one might have different tastes, and you might be able to sell him your manuscript. But use your best judgment before resubmitting. Try to ascertain if the editor was simply being polite, or if your manuscript may really stand a chance at a later date.

In the case of book editors and literary agents, once you've been rejected, you've killed your chances with that person on that particular project—unless the editor or agent instructs you to revise and resubmit. If there's no invitation to resubmit, then you shouldn't try again, even if you do revise the work later on. While your revised work may indeed merit another look, editors and agents don't want to see it again.

Beginning writers often look for ways around this hard truth, especially if they realize later the rejection was due to an unprofessional query letter or unpolished manuscript. They wonder if they could change their book title, use a pen name, or alter the characters' names or otherwise disguise the fact they're resubmitting the same material. You can always give it a try, but it's not recommended; editors and agents often see through the ruse.

That's why it's so important you query and send your manuscript only when you're really ready. In book publishing, it's tough if not impossible to get a second chance on a manuscript. Make it the very best it can be before sending it out.

**I am puzzled by writers who claim that after mailing a piece nineteen times and having it rejected, they mail it once more and sell it. Are they telling the truth?**

These writers are telling the truth, because they have carefully explored all possible markets and recognized that, even though their work wasn't right for one editor, it still might appeal to another.

**I've got an article that I've submitted to several different magazines, all without success. *Vogue, Cosmopolitan, Woman's Day*—it's made the rounds of all the women's magazines. I've researched and written my article carefully, and I think I ended up with a good manuscript. Why isn't it selling?**

Although it's true that all the magazines you've mentioned come under the general category of women's publications, each one has a different audience; each magazine's readers have interests and characteristics that attract them to that particular publication instead of others. The fact that you have submitted the same article to four very different publications might reveal that you have not slanted the article to one specific publication. Each magazine has different needs to satisfy its readership. *Cosmopolitan*, for example, caters to the sophisticated single woman; *Woman's Day* concentrates on family-oriented topics. An article written for the needs of one would clearly not meet the needs of the other. *Woman's Day* would be the place to market an article on problems of child-rearing; *Cosmopolitan* would not be interested.

**After four years of freelance writing and not selling a word, I would like a personal remark from an editor about why my manuscript didn't qualify, instead of the usual cold-blooded rejection slip. What you can recommend?**

An editor's job is to find publishable material, not explain rejections. Most editors have too much work and too little time, so personal analysis of the thousands of manuscripts that cross their desks is impossible. For constructive criticism, take a writing course, join a writers group, or attend a writing conference to find out how to improve your chances.

**Since magazines depend on advertising for revenue, would they reject articles because of controversial subject matter that might offend some advertisers?**

Magazines are businesses, so they are sometimes forced to think long and hard about running controversial material. Any article likely to offend a regular advertiser probably won't be accepted. Some editors have been courageous enough to run controversial material, but most magazines choose carefully the controversies they start.

**I submitted a book proposal about a year ago that was rejected. I've now come up with a better title that I think is a natural for one of the houses that rejected the initial proposal. Should I resubmit it?**

As long as the same editor is at that publishing house, changing the title isn't likely to make the book idea any more appealing than it was the first time. Think up new ideas, not just new strategies to sell your old ones.

**I have a cousin who is in sales with a leading book publisher, and I sent him my manuscript, asking him to pass it along to the right editor. Shortly after that, I got a form rejection letter. Am I wrong to have expected a more personal response?**

If the manuscript had interested the editorial department for possible publication, you would have gotten the personal response. Some beginning writers think that knowing someone at the publishing company will be an advantage. It isn't. Your manuscript has to sell itself.

## WHAT DOES IT MEAN?

**I receive letters from editors saying my manuscripts are interesting, but "not quite right for us." What does this mean? If it's so interesting, why isn't it right?**

These letters expressing interest are meant to encourage you and show that your work does have a degree of promise. The material's style or content, however, was probably not in keeping with what the editor usually publishes. Get to know the markets better by studying what they are buying. Current magazine issues and book catalogs give writers valuable clues as to what kinds of work editors are looking for.

**If an editor writes "Sorry. Try us again" on a rejection slip, what does that mean?**

When an editor indicates interest in future submissions, it means he thinks enough of your work to offer the encouragement of a personal note. It means your writing style and approach are suitable for his readers, and he wants to see more ideas from you.

**On recent rejection slips from greeting card companies were handwritten messages, "Terrific possibilities but more punch" and "Ideas good but lack sales appeal." I don't know what composes "punch" and "sales appeal." Should I take these handwritten remarks to be encouraging?**

These handwritten criticisms certainly should be regarded as encouraging. By referring to "punch" and "sales appeal," these editors probably meant that your work lacked the impact necessary to make the prospective card buyer immediately react favorably to the cards. It would seem, then, that your underlying ideas are good, but you need to present them in a more colorful, entertaining, or dramatic way that will catch the customer's attention and make him buy. If, after studying published cards and revising your own work, you feel your ideas capture the right sales appeal, don't hesitate to resubmit them.

**I sent an article to a magazine and it came back without a rejection slip. Somebody had just crossed out the editor's name in my query letter and scrawled, "Read the magazine!" Isn't this rather insulting?**

Apparently, you hadn't looked at a recent issue and learned that the editor you were addressing the submission to no longer worked there—a serious error on your part. The comment "Read the magazine!" may also indicate that the editorial slant of the magazine has changed and the type of article you were submitting is no longer appropriate. It's very important to look at recent sample issues of a magazine in addition to reading the market requirements for the magazine.

**I sent a query to an agent who was mentioned specifically in a writer's magazine for her openness to new writers. I received a form letter that said she was "no longer taking new clients." What's going on here?**

The agent is probably overwhelmed with queries and submissions after being mentioned in that magazine, so she has probably decided to start turning new prospects away. Or, this could be her polite way of informing you that she didn't like your work well enough to represent it.

## INTERPRETING REJECTION PHRASES

After you get rejected a few dozen times, you might discover that agents and editors tend to use the same old phrases over and over again when turning down your work. Here are a few of the most common and what they might mean.

- *Doesn't fit our needs* usually means that you've targeted the wrong agent or editor for your work—your work doesn't fit in its genre, style, tone, or approach. If you know without a doubt that the material you sent is a perfect fit, then your work probably lacked sufficient quality or didn't suit the editor's needs on that particular day. Doesn't fit our needs could also mean that your topic or focus is too strange/esoteric or too cliché/overdone.
- *Doesn't have sufficient market appeal* means that your work lacks marketability or salability. Perhaps the market for your work is too small or indistinct or weird. Or maybe your work lacks punch—it's not different enough, unique enough, or special enough for people to take notice.
- *Just couldn't get excited about it* means exactly what it sounds like. If someone makes this comment about your fiction, it usually reflects the lack of a compelling story or hook or character.

- **The writing doesn't stand out** probably means your writing lacks a voice, or your story is boring, unoriginal, or uninspired.
- **Not fresh enough or original** is similar to *the writing doesn't stand out*. For fiction writers, perhaps your plot line is too cliché, your characters are too common, or your story is not special enough or compelling enough for publication. In a competitive market, your story has to stand out and have unique qualities, in addition to being well-written.

Remember, even if an editor or agent gives a specific reason for the rejection (that you understand), that doesn't mean she's interested in seeing the work again. If she is, she'll invite you to resubmit.

## WHERE TO FIND OUT MORE

### BOOKS

*The First Five Pages*, by Noah Lukeman, contains essential information for any novelist wondering what triggers rejection in the first five pages of a manuscript.

In *The Resilient Writer: Tales of Rejection and Triumph from 23 Top Authors*, you can read all about how best-selling authors deal with rejection, and glean tips about how mere mortals can survive as well.

In *No More Rejections*, Alice Orr, a longtime agent for successful novelists, gives advice on making your fiction manuscript rejection-proof (almost).

### WEB SITES

Rejection Collection (www.rejectioncollection.com) is a Web site devoted to collecting writers' rejection letters; good inspiration and comfort.

# 8

# How do book
# publishers work?

One day, it finally happens: A publisher accepts your manuscript for publication. For first-time authors, it can be one of the most exhilarating days of their lives, but also terrifying when they realize how much they *still* don't know. What does a fair advance and book contract look like? How much say does the author have on the book title and cover? What should an author expect from the publisher's marketing and publicity department? This chapter addresses the most common questions writers have after they've found a publisher for their work—or sometimes even before.

**Once a writer submits her final manuscript to the publisher and it is accepted, what part does she play in the production process?**

First of all, you'll likely be asked to make some revisions, or at the very least read the copyedited manuscript, clarify any vague statements, and respond to any challenges of fact. Then you may have to read either galley or page proofs (the typeset copy) to check for errors on the part of the typesetter or to make last-minute corrections. If you wrote an illustrated book, the publisher may have you review the layout to proofread the captions and compare them against the illustrations to be sure they match.

You may also be asked to provide or proofread the contents page, the glossary, and the bibliography, if any, plus the acknowledgments, and the copyright and permissions page. The jacket copy and your biographical information may be provided for your review as well.

If your book is nonfiction, you may be responsible for providing an index. Usually the publisher will hire the indexer at the author's expense (this could cost as little as a few hundred dollars or more than a thousand, depending on the length of your book), and the indexing cost appears as a deduction on the first royalty statement.

These are things you *may* be asked to do. Each publisher works a little differently, but you should be provided guidelines by your editor that clearly state what's expected of you at each stage of the development and production process.

### What advice do you have for a writer submitting her contracted manuscript to her editor?

Be patient. You'll probably be anxious to hear what the editor thinks of your manuscript and want feedback right away. While your editor will work as quickly as possible to review your work, keep in mind that your editor is most likely juggling a dozen other projects in various stages of development and production. When you first submit your manuscript, ask when you might expect to hear back, and don't check back on a response until after that time.

### Why do I have to revise according to an editor's suggestions? My work is written exactly how I want it. How do I know an editor's criticism is valid?

Important information

Writers who are new to the business sometimes consider an editor's requests for revision a personal affront, when in reality the editor is only trying to get the best possible manuscript for her market. Editors know what works for their audience, and have the experience and expertise necessary to objectively criticize work. If you don't want to revise your manuscript to the editor's style or suggestions—and you could be right—you can always withdraw the work, if it comes to that. But there's a good chance you will never get your work published if you don't learn to take constructive criticism from editors.

Authors who have been in the game a long time and have published dozens of books are typically the most open to revision suggestions. Some beginners find this fact paradoxical, but it isn't once you consider that seasoned authors have attained a level of professionalism and experience that's taught them to respect the editor's eye.

Both magazine and book editors are eager to help you achieve your best efforts. If there are occasional misunderstandings along the way, the writer should not overlook the editor's essential goodwill toward her work.

### What's a trade book?

A trade book is a hardcover or paperback title distributed mainly through retail bookstores. Trade books can be novels, works of nonfiction, or children's books.

### Why are some books published in hardback and others in paperback?

It used to be that most paperbacks were reprints of hardcover books, but today you can find original fiction and nonfiction issued in paperback. You may hear the term *trade paperback original* in reference to books first published in paperback. Sometimes, if these books become best-sellers, they will come out in a hardcover edition later. Best-selling books that were released in paperback first include *Bright Lights, Big City*, by Jay McInerney, and the Pulitzer Prize–winning short-story collection *Interpreter of Maladies*, by Jhumpa Lahiri.

Paperback originals have long been perceived by industry insiders (and authors) as being of less value or importance, but this stigma is fading as everyone realizes that readers are much more likely to give a new author a shot if the book costs fourteen dollars and not twenty-four. Still, publishers and authors often prefer hardcovers because they offer a better profit than paperbacks (even if they sell fewer copies), and they offer authors a higher royalty percentage. Authors receive a lower royalty percentage on paperback editions because the publisher's profit margin is lower for paperbacks.

### What's the difference between mass-market paperbacks and trade paperbacks?

The difference can be defined in terms of size, price, distribution, and the royalties the author receives. Mass-market books are sold in drugstores, airports, and supermarkets (that is, in the mass market), as well as in bookstores, for low prices; they are published in a single size, designed to fit paperback book racks and to be conveniently carried. Trade paperbacks are larger, cost more, and are distributed mainly in bookstores and department stores.

**If my publisher decides to release my book as hardcover, will the book also be released in paperback?**

Many publishers make what is called a hard/soft deal, meaning that the house will first print the book in hardcover and, if the book sells well, reprint the book in paperback. Occasionally, though, your publisher will sell those reprint rights (paperback rights) to another house. It used to be that hardcover publishers and paperback publishers were distinct and separate, but many have merged, or started to publish in both formats.

**Should I find an expert to write an introduction for my nonfiction book?**

An introduction by an expert does lend more authority to a nonfiction work, especially if you are not a known quantity in the field. Usually the publisher (or even your agent) will assist you in securing someone to write the introduction or a foreword.

**Are book introductions and forewords paid for, or are most of them complimentary? I'd like to ask a well-known author to write the foreword for my book. Will she expect payment, and if so, how much should I offer her?**

Many are complimentary, but people who write forewords and introductions are sometimes offered an honorarium. If offered, the size of the honorarium depends on several things: the length of the material required, how well-known or in demand that person is, the complexity of the material to be written, and how "big" (or important) your own book is. Rates range from a couple hundred dollars to thousands. Much depends on the author's personal interest in your book and how well you're connected to her, if at all. In some cases, the publisher will pay the person who writes the foreword or introduction, or costs may be split between publisher and author.

**Will I have any input on the cover design for my book? What about the title?**

When a publisher accepts a book, it usually reserves the right to decide on the title and cover design, but you can make suggestions to your editor after the book is accepted. Do not offer to design your book (or have your friend or family member design your book), and do not send amateur mock-ups

Important
information

of what you think the cover should look like. (During the querying and submission process, *never* send mock-ups of the cover design; it's a red flag that you might be a controlling or difficult author, or at the very least one who doesn't understand the publishing process.) Most publishers work with their own graphic designers, who understand the style and sensibilities of that particular house. You can usually trust them to make the right cover and title decision for your book; they've been in the business longer than you, and they know what sells books. However, if you feel the cover design (or title) conveys the wrong idea or feel for what you've written, raise your concerns with your editor.

**I've seen quotes from well-known people on the jackets of books, commenting on the book's excellence. How do I solicit similar endorsements for my book?**

Garnering blurbs or testimonials from famous people is usually the job of the publisher's publicity department, but if you decide to go after some yourself, all you need to do is fashion a polite letter requesting an endorsement, and send it along with a copy of your manuscript or the page proofs, which the publisher can provide you.

The problem for most beginners is that they don't know how to find the address or contact info for famous authors. If you're unable to find that information online or through your publisher, then send your request in care of the author's publisher. (Most publishers have a specific address to use; check their Web sites.)

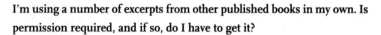

**I'm using a number of excerpts from other published books in my own. Is permission required, and if so, do I have to get it?**

See chapter seventeen for more information on fair use.

If your excerpts go beyond the limits of fair use, then you will have to write the publishers of those books for permission. Major publishing companies have a permissions department and specific forms for permissions requests, and obtaining permissions almost always involves some type of fee. Your contract with your book publisher likely holds you responsible for securing necessary permissions and paying any related fees. If you run into prohibitive or unreasonable fees, discuss the situation with your editor.

**What is a book packager?**

A book packager is a middleman who supplies books to publishers. She may supply the books in any form from raw manuscript to bound copies. The packager usually signs a contract with a publisher, then signs a different one with the writer based on what she thinks she can get the writer to do the work for, and what the writer thinks she's worth for that particular job. Some packagers pay the writer a flat fee; others split the advance and royalty with the author.

## YOUR CONTRACT

**Is an author required to furnish a large sum of money before her book is published?**

No. Trade and academic publishers assume all regular production costs and usually pay the author an advance (see the next question for more on advances). You only pay to publish if you sign with a vanity, subsidy, or print-on-demand publisher (see chapter twenty-nine).

**What is an advance, and when does the author receive it? Does it have to be returned if the book doesn't sell?**

An advance is a sum of money a publisher pays you before the book is published, in partial consideration for the time and effort you expend in producing the work. Often, the advance is a gauge of how well the publisher thinks the book will sell; advances are usually computed as a percentage of a book's estimated first-year sales. When sales begin, the amount of the advance is deducted from the author's royalties before any payment is made to the author.

Ideally, the author's contract with the publisher should state that the advance need not be returned if it exceeds royalties collected. A contract should also ideally either forbid the publisher for asking for the return of the advance if she decides not to issue the book, or state that the advance will be repaid only after the book is placed with another publisher.

Advances are usually paid in installments; for example, the author might receive one-half of the advance when she signs the contract, and one-half when she delivers a complete manuscript. The amount of the advance will vary with the type of book, the author's writing ability and reputation, the type of publisher, and the specific book idea.

## FLASHBACK QUESTION

**I have never learned how writers arrive at the total number of words in a manuscript. Can you tell me?**

Count every word on five representative pages; divide by five to get an average number of words per page, then multiply that average by the total number of pages in the manuscript. When counting words, abbreviated words count as one word, as do the words *a, the,* etc. Type the approximate number of words in round figures, such as "2,700 words" (not "2,693 words") in the upper right corner of page one.

There is a faster method that will estimate your manuscript's word count. Many production editors at book and magazine publishing companies consider the "average" word length to be six typed characters, when taking into account the number of short words, such as articles and prepositions, balanced against the longer words present, even in children's books. To estimate the number of words in your manuscript, count the number of characters in a full line of type; multiply by the number of lines on the page; multiply again by the number of pages in the manuscript; and divide by the magic number, six. The result will be a fairly accurate count of the words in your story or article.

[Editor's note: Do not attempt this at home unless you want a headache! Use your word processor's word count feature.]

**A book I've written has been accepted for publication. How long will it be before I can expect to receive royalties?**

For starters, it probably will be at least a year before your book is published. After your book goes on sale, your first royalty statement will probably arrive six to eight months later. (Publishers usually send royalty statements every six months.) It may take longer than six months for your book to earn out its advance; you can't start earning royalties until the advance is completely earned out, which means there's a chance you'll never receive royalties if your book doesn't sell.

### What do standard book contracts and royalties look like?

There is no standard book contract; terms vary depending on the type of book, how it is sold, the track record of the author, and other factors. The Authors Guild recommends that authors negotiate for royalty percentages on trade hardcover books of 10 percent of the retail price on the first five thousand copies, 12.5 percent on the next five thousand, and 15 percent thereafter. Publishers of textbooks and other specialized nonfiction books, however, often base their royalty percentages not on the retail price but on the publisher's net receipts—that is, the retail price less the bookstore or wholesaler discount.

Frequently asked question

Royalty contracts offered on paperbacks vary widely, but you might expect 6 percent on the first twenty thousand copies and 7.5 percent thereafter. Mass-market original paperback royalties are often 6 percent on net copies sold—the number of copies distributed minus the number of returns. Paperback reprint rights are usually split fifty-fifty between the author and original hardcover publisher, which means that the author's royalty would be only 3 percent on a paperback reprint. Heavily illustrated children's books may split a 10 percent royalty (based on either retail price or net receipts) between author and artist.

If you don't have an agent to negotiate your contract, you should thoroughly research book contracts or retain a lawyer to help you. A number of resources are listed at the end of this chapter.

### What are subsidiary rights, and how should they be handled in my contracts?

Subsidiary rights involve the licensing or selling of a book in part or in whole to another party. These rights include paperback reprint rights; book club rights and book club editions; dramatic, radio, television, and movie rights; foreign reprint and foreign-language translation rights; audiovisual production rights; novelty or merchandising rights; and serial rights. The author and publisher divide profits from subsidiary rights, and the original contract specifies how profits are split and who has the right to make subsidiary sales. Authors Guild guidelines suggest that established authors negotiate for at least 80 percent of the earnings on British editions of a book, 75 percent on other foreign reprints, 50 percent on paperback and book club sales, and 90 percent on sales to movie and television production companies. These terms should be discussed and agreed upon by author and publisher and included in any book contract. Actual earnings will, of course, depend on the success of the publisher or author's agent in selling the rights to the book.

### Should I hang on to my subsidiary rights?

Ask yourself what you hope to gain by keeping them. Most authors cannot sell such rights themselves and must rely on the publisher or agent to sell them on their behalf. If you don't have an agent, there's little harm in giving the publisher a specified period of time to sell the subsidiary rights, but you should expect to share the proceeds, as indicated in the previous question. If you're working with an agent, she will advise you on what's best for your individual case.

### If a publisher sends me a contract and I don't agree with certain parts of it, what is the proper procedure?

Contact the person who issued the contract by phone or e-mail and discuss the changes you want. (If you handle the negotiation by e-mail, outline your objections and the publisher will look it over and make her decision.) If you cross out objectionable portions, then sign and return the contract without discussion, you'll certainly get your point across, but this practice usually doesn't work. Negotiation is almost always necessary.

### Do textbook publishers have a standard royalty schedule? Does the same royalty apply to textbooks as to books in the trade division?

Textbook publishers do not have a standard royalty or the same royalty schedule as trade book publishers. College textbook royalties may vary from 8 percent to 19 percent of the net price the publisher receives, while elementary and secondary text royalties may be only 3 percent to 5 percent, depending on illustration costs and the amount of staff work that must be done by the publisher.

**I have to provide photographs and other artwork for my book, but doing so is going to be a significant expense. Will the publisher pay, or at least help me collect the art?**

Your contract with the publisher will determine who absorbs this extra expense and responsibility. Usually, authors must provide all materials needed to publish the book, and the advance is meant to cover the costs of doing so. But publishers work in different ways; always check with your editor to find out the standard procedure.

**I sold a novel about fifteen years ago, and the contract gave the publisher a sixty-day option on each of my next two novels. She has rejected my second novel since that time, and I'm almost finished with my third. Do I still have to submit it to her first, after all this time? What if she puts the same clause in the new contract?**

Although fifteen years have passed, you are still required to submit the third book to the publisher to satisfy the terms of the contract, though you may want to check with a lawyer about the wording of your option clause. In answer to your second question, *don't sign* a contract with such a clause in it. Option clauses bind the author, not the publisher; this is why the Authors Guild recommends deletion of the clause from a book contract. Also, some option clauses state that the publisher can buy your second book for the same price she paid for the first; obviously, if the first book is a surprise best-seller, the writer would be able to sell the second book for a lot more money, and would come up the loser in a deal like this.

If you must agree to some sort of option clause, limit it to thirty days. That's long enough for a publisher to make up her mind. The option clause should indicate that the terms are negotiable at that time. Additionally, the option clause time period should not be keyed to publication date of the first book, since this may hold you up on the next book. You should be free to submit a new proposal or manuscript anytime after the first book has been accepted by the publisher.

**My friend says her book contract has a clause that states the manuscript "must be acceptable to the publisher in form and content," and that if it isn't, she must return the advance she was paid. Do most contracts have this clause?**

Yes, although there are variations in the wording. Some clauses require the return of the advance only if the manuscript is sold to another publisher; others require it whether or not the manuscript resells. The Authors Guild recommends a rewording of the clause: "The Author shall deliver a manuscript which in style and content is professional, competent, and fit for publication." This rewording helps protect authors when a manuscript is subjectively pronounced unacceptable. Publishers may find manuscripts unacceptable for many reasons: Perhaps the author didn't deliver what her outline promised, and refuses to revise. The market may have changed, and the publisher is dissatisfied more with the terms of the bargain than the manuscript itself. The publisher's lawyers may have concluded that publishing a controversial book would put the house in danger of lawsuits. All of these reasons help courts decide the good faith of the author or publisher if a clause calling for the return of the advance is invoked.

**My royalties to date have been very low. How can I find out the number of copies my book has sold?**

Your royalty statement should show the actual number of copies sold. The only way to verify the actual number of books sold by a publisher would be to access its accounting records. Some book contracts have a clause that permits the author to bring her certified public accountant to the publisher's office to check the sales records and accounting procedures. Even if your contract does not have such a clause, you still have the legal right to request such a review, provided you are willing to go to the expense of hiring a CPA. Royalty examinations can cost several thousand dollars, so only an author with sales sufficient to warrant such an audit should engage a CPA.

**My publisher says my book sold in well, but suffered heavy returns. What does this mean?**

Book publishing works primarily on a returnable basis, meaning all products "sold in" to bookstores can be returned at any time for any reason for full credit. If a bookstore is unable to sell your book, it will take it off the shelves and return it to the publisher.

**After a contract has been signed and the publication date set for my book, what do I do if the book isn't released on that date?**

Whether publication postponements are prompted by factors outside of or within a publisher's control, they do happen. Production schedules are often juggled when the schedules for unexpected manuscripts and potential best-sellers clash with lower-priority books or problem manuscripts that need work. There should be a specific time of publication inserted in your contract—usually a certain number of months after receipt of an acceptable manuscript. After you've delivered your manuscript, keep in touch with your editor by correspondence. Don't hesitate to ask, "What is the schedule for my book? When should I expect to receive the copyedited manuscript?" If the answers are vague, and the time of publication as stated in the contract passes without production of your book, remind the editor via e-mail, and follow with a phone call, if necessary. If you feel the delay has become unreasonable, you can legally reclaim the rights to your book and try to sell it to another publisher.

## MARKETING, PROMOTION, AND PUBLICITY

If you thought getting your book published was the tough part, wait until it comes time for your book's release. Many unfortunate first-time authors have an unwelcome wake-up call when they realize that publication does not equal money, readership, or visibility. With more than 175,000 new titles being published every year (and about 3 million available in the English language), how will your one book break through the noise of the everyday?

Marketing, promotion, and publicity strategies are beyond the scope of this beginner's book, but every wise beginning writer—especially those wishing to write books for living—will start thinking about how to reach their readership and sell books, even before writing the first word. If your first book fails to sell, a publisher will not be interested in your second.

**My publisher didn't promote my book at all—no advertising, no book signings, nothing. What can I do to prevent this from happening again?**

The most important thing a publisher can do for your book is distribute it to the trade and specialty markets. Your publisher has sales reps that pitch your book for placement in chain and independent bookstores and in specialty or mass-market outlets (think Wal-Mart, airport stores, groceries, and any other place you find books for sale). The publisher will add your book to its catalog, which is sent to booksellers nationwide, and will also send it to prepublication review outlets such as *Publishers Weekly* and *Library Journal*. Most publishers will also send review copies or press releases to appropriate magazines, newspapers, and Web sites.

Authors often express frustration when the publisher makes no additional investment in advertisement or book tours and signings, but for that type of marketing and promotion, the costs often outweigh the benefits. These days, the biggest marketing and promotion dollars often go toward A-list authors and titles. So if you're a new author, midlist author, or "small" author, you might not receive much marketing support. And there's not much you can do about it.

**How can I support the sales and marketing of my book?**

Start with the assumption that your publisher will do nothing but act as a distributor for your book. It will make sure the book is available for purchase; you, the author, will drive readers to the stores to make the purchase.

Start preparing for your book's release ahead of time—at least three months before. There's a wide range of things you can do to help your book's sales and marketing—in fact, entire books are devoted to the topic. One of the most popular references is *Guerrilla Marketing for Writers*. A few other resources are mentioned at the end of this chapter. Plan ahead what you're going to do and how much you're going to invest; the wisest authors often invest a portion of their advance money back into their book's marketing and promotion. However, don't make the mistake of thinking that marketing and promotion must be expensive to be effective. Some of the best things you can do—such as creating a Web site for your book—are free. You only need to have the energy, enthusiasm, and *time*. And that's why many authors give up after a while—they prefer to invest their time and energy somewhere else. But a book's marketing and promotion period never really ends until the book is out of print.

With any luck, your publisher will assign your book to an in-house publicist, who will contact you about marketing and promotion plans and may solicit your input on how to reach your book's target audience. If you don't hear from a publicist (or there is no publicist), let your editor know of your promotional efforts. An author who is proactive in her book's marketing and promotion is much more desirable than one who waits for the publisher to make the first move.

**Should I hire an outside publicist for my book?**

If you can afford it, yes. A 2006 study found that authors who had outside help sold an average of 10,000 copies of their first book and earned royalties averaging $55,000, while writers who depended solely on the efforts of their publishers sold 4,500 copies and saw royalties of $25,000. The majority of authors who hired an outside firm said they would do so again.

A publisher will not be offended if you hire your own publicist (or marketing firm), who will work in tandem with the publisher to make sure there isn't duplication of effort.

**Would it be possible for me to have my book, now out of print, published with another house?**

Yes. As long as rights have reverted back to you, you're free to approach other publishers with your book. If the publisher has not reverted rights, but the book is off the market, write a letter requesting your rights back. Your contract should have a clause detailing exactly how and when the reversion of rights occurs. If the publisher has a large inventory of books, it will be reluctant to revert rights until the stock is depleted, even if sales have slowed to a snail's pace.

# WHERE TO FIND OUT MORE

## BOOKS

*Agents, Editors, and You*, by the editors of Writer's Digest Books, covers the basics of the book publishing process.

*Kirsch's Guide to the Book Contract*, by Jonathan Kirsch, is incredibly useful if you're attempting to decipher or negotiate your book contract.

*Putting Your Passion Into Print*, by Arielle Eckstut and David Sterry, provides great information on how to get published, but even more valuable information on how to work with your publisher before and after your book's release.

*How to Get Happily Published*, by Judith Appelbaum, is a popular guide to the book publishing process, though it's becoming dated (it was last revised in 1998).

*Guerrilla Marketing for Writers*, by Jay Conrad Levinson, Rick Frishman, and Michael Larsen, is an excellent guide for authors who need ideas on how to market and promote their books.

*1001 Ways to Market Your Books*, by John Kremer, is another valuable compendium of book-marketing advice.

## WEB SITES

Buzz, Balls & Hype (www.publishersmarketplace.com/members/BkDoctorSin) is a blog from M.J. Rose that focuses on how to generate buzz for your book.

Marketing guru John Kremer offers www.bookmarket.com, a site that will guide you to the many resources available to help you market and promote your book. Look for his blog, too.

# How can I write a successful novel?

After ten years of writing, Janet Evanovich decided to get serious about getting published. She had three novels written, all of which had been submitted to and rejected by dozens of publishers and agents. So she decided to abandon those projects and try genre writing. Her first effort was rejected, but her second manuscript was accepted, and she was on her way to becoming the best-selling author of the Stephanie Plum mystery series.

Becoming a published novelist is mostly a matter of talent, persistence, and luck. First, you have to write very well—well enough to stand out against the competition—and then you have to send and resend your material until it reaches someone who appreciates it as much as you do. It takes drive and determination, and many years of dedication to the craft. Most first efforts don't find publishers; it's your second, third, fourth, or even tenth effort that finds a home.

This chapter can't possibly answer every novel writing question a beginner has, but it introduces you to the most common issues and topics that concern novelists. To develop confidence as a novel writer, it takes practice, and maybe a few fiction-writing technique books to help you identify your weaknesses and show you how to improve.

## QUESTIONS OF GENRE

**In my quest to submit my work, I have stumbled across a problem. I'm having trouble placing my work into a category. What is the difference between commercial, mainstream, and literary fiction?**

In general, fiction is divided into literary fiction and commercial fiction (also called mainstream fiction). There aren't any hard and fast definitions for one or the other, but there are some basic differences, and those differences affect how the book is read, packaged, and marketed.

Literary fiction is usually more concerned with style and characterization than commercial fiction. Literary fiction is also usually paced more slowly than commercial fiction. Literary fiction usually centers around a timeless, complex theme, and rarely has a pat (or happy) ending. Good examples of literary fiction are books by Toni Morrison and John Updike.

Commercial fiction, on the other hand, is faster paced, with a stronger plot line (more events, higher stakes, more dangerous situations). Characterization is generally not as central to the story. The theme is very obvious, and the language not as complex.

The biggest difference between literary and commercial fiction is that editors expect to make a substantial profit from selling a commercial book, but not necessarily from selling literary fiction. Audiences for commercial fiction are larger than those for literary fiction. Tom Clancy, John Grisham, and Stephen King are all prime examples of commercial fiction authors.

One of the easiest ways to determine whether your work is literary or commercial is to ask yourself, "Is my book more likely to be read in college English classes, or in the grocery checkout line?"

### What is a genre novel?

The term *genre* is generally used to describe fiction that has certain expectations and conventions; some specific genres are romance, mystery, horror, science fiction, fantasy, and westerns. Genre novels must adhere to the styles, conventions, and tropes of their category in order to meet readers' expectations. For example, readers of mysteries assume any novel in that genre will start with a crime or threat of a crime, provide clues and possible motives throughout the story, and conclude with a resolution of the problem (the criminal being brought to justice, the evil plan being thwarted). Readers of romance expect to encounter a hero and heroine who feel intensely attracted to each other, undergo some sort of conflict that complicates their relationship, and resolve that complication so the romance can flourish (and, often, result in marriage). In order to understand the conventions of each genre, you should read several books in that category and note the similar structures, plot devices, and character types within them. (See appendix one for a list of major fiction genres.)

**I have dabbled in creative writing for many years but have never published anything. I am ready to get serious. Are there particular genres of fiction that are easier for new writers to break in to?**

Before looking into which markets are easiest to break in to, first consider what you enjoy reading, what you enjoy writing, and what you write well. The single most important factor determining whether you succeed (and get published) is the quality of your writing. Ultimately, if you want to get published, a good story well written is key. If you're passionate about your subject matter, that level of engagement will come through in your story, and your enthusiasm can help you get through the tough patches when you lack confidence, inspiration, or fresh ideas.

If you must look strictly at marketability, the romance genre would be the place to break in. Statistics from a 2004 Romance Writers of America study show that romance novels comprise 55 percent of paperback book sales in the United States, and 40 percent of all fiction sold is romance. (Comparatively, the mystery/thriller genre comprises 30 percent of all fiction sold, and so-called general fiction comprises about 13 percent.) Within the romance genre, contemporary romance is the most popular subgenre, with 1,438 titles (of 2,285 romance titles) published in 2004. So statistically, contemporary romance offers the greatest opportunity to break in. But again: Write what you love, and write the best book you can, and worry about publication later.

**My novel crosses a number of genres—I call it a romantic thriller fantasy that will appeal to readers in a number of genres. But I'm told by editors that I have to stick with one genre. Why?**

Frequently asked question

You may be able to find a publisher willing to take a risk on your cross-genre book, but most agents and editors look for stories they can easily target to a specific audience. Without a firm categorization, your book is a difficult pitch to store buyers, and it's a difficult sell to readers. While you may think crossing genres makes the audience bigger, the market usually proves that interest in cross-genre books is limited—unless you find yourself in the midst of a cross-genre trend. (At the time of this book's publication, literary fiction was fond of incorporating fantasy or supernatural elements, such as in *The Time-Traveler's Wife*, by Audrey Niffenegger.) It's best to push the boundaries of a genre—and stay well within it—rather than struggle to find a publisher for a cross-genre work.

When pitching a cross-genre work to an agent or editor, you can increase your chances of success by aligning it with the one genre that's at the heart of your story—or by identifying the one audience that would be most interested in it. (Does your novel appeal mostly to romance readers, mystery readers, science-fiction readers, etc.?)

### What is a novel-in-stories?

A novel-in-stories is a book-length collection of short stories that are interconnected. (One of the very first examples of this genre is *The Canterbury Tales*; a more recent example is *The Girl's Guide to Hunting and Fishing*, by Melissa Bank.) A novel-in-stories overcomes two key challenges for writers: the challenge of writing a novel-length work, and the challenge of publishing a book-length work of unrelated short stories. (Few publishers are willing to publish a short-story collection from an unknown writer.) So, the novel-in-stories helps you sell a story collection like you would a novel—as long as the interconnected nature of the stories is strong and acts as a compelling hook. Another advantage to novels-in-stories is that they afford you the opportunity to publish pieces of your novel in a variety of literary magazines, which might attract the attention of an editor or agent. (Editors and agents often troll literary publications looking for new talent to publish or represent.)

## CRAFT AND TECHNIQUE

### What is a protagonist?

The protagonist is the main character of a story, the one the author spends the most time exploring or developing and the one whose conflict moves the plot along. The protagonist may also be the story's first-person narrator, although this is not always the case.

## What is point of view?

Point of view refers to the perspective from which the story is told. There are three traditional points of view:

**First-person narration.** The narrator—often the protagonist—tells the story from his perspective (using *I*), and the information given to the readers is filtered through this character. Examples are *The Adventures of Huckleberry Finn*, by Mark Twain, and *The Catcher in the Rye*, by J.D. Salinger.

**Third-person omniscient.** The story is narrated by an all-knowing voice that does not belong to any one character but instead gives readers access to the thoughts, feelings, and motivations of all characters. The narrator refers to the characters using third-person pronouns. Examples are *The Old Man and the Sea*, by Ernest Hemingway, and *Brave New World*, by Aldous Huxley.

**Third-person limited.** The story is narrated by a removed voice that does not belong to any one character but focuses on a single character and only gives the readers access to the thoughts, feelings, and motivations of that focused character. The narrator refers to the characters using third-person pronouns. An example is *Of Mice and Men*, by John Steinbeck.

There's also second-person point of view, which is rarely used and a tough one to make work. For a successful example, see *Bright Lights, Big City*, by Jay McInerney.

Many books use different points of view for different chapters or sections, but this is difficult to do in a seamless and unobtrusive way for readers.

## What are the various advantages of writing in first and third person?

First-person viewpoint involves only one character (presumably your protagonist) and permits close reader identification. The disadvantage is that all other characters must be developed strictly through their actions and dialogue *as observed by the protagonist*, which can be difficult and limiting.

Third-person omniscient viewpoint allows you to get inside many characters' heads and explore multiple viewpoints. You can also tell or show things that would not be known to any of the characters. In the case of third-person limited viewpoint, you can show the way your protagonist perceives and reacts to events throughout an entire novel, and make him very well rounded and demanding of reader sympathy.

To choose the best point of view for your story, you might try writing several different passages, each with a different point of view and central character. Play around and see if anything fits. Don't be discouraged if this exercise makes things worse; many great novelists come to realize the "right" point of view only after putting many months of work into a manuscript.

**I'm writing a novel about two central characters. How do I decide which to use as my viewpoint character?**

If you're using third-person point of view, you can include the viewpoints of both. When both of your central characters become viewpoint characters, you can more easily develop subplots and suspense, as well as the personalities and histories of those characters. Care must be taken to switch viewpoints only at scene changes—never within a scene (unless you're an absolute master).

**Important information**

**I keep reading warnings not to switch viewpoints in the middle of a scene, but I can't seem to find out how to detect accidental shifts. What's wrong with switching viewpoints, anyway?**

The reader needs time to shift gears as the viewpoint of the story changes; switching viewpoint frequently creates an effect similar to having several people speaking to you at once. Confusion, not understanding, is the probable outcome. Also, consider: Through how many viewpoints do *you* see the world? Only one, of course. You cannot see into any mind other than your own; you can only know as much about other people as is indicated by their actions and what they tell you.

You can detect a shift in viewpoint by counting the number of characters who share their thoughts or opinions within a scene. Remember: If you're sticking to one viewpoint per scene (which you should), then you should relate only one viewpoint character's thoughts, feelings, or observations. Keep in mind that revealing a character's thoughts and feelings doesn't always take the direct form of *Sally thought* or *Sally felt*. A viewpoint is present in any statement of a thought or observation, like "How had the apartment become so filthy and disgusting, especially Jack's room ..."

Viewpoint is one of the most complicated aspects of fiction writing, sometimes difficult even for advanced writers to grasp. If you're committed to writing novels, then you should read up on viewpoint—*Characters, Emotion & Viewpoint*, by Nancy Kress, would be a good start.

**I am writing a novel about a fourteen-year-old ballerina. She is telling the story. I am concerned about reader identification. Will adult readers identify with a leading character of this age?**

It's rare, but adult readers can identify with younger heroes and heroines. But look closely at your work: Are you really writing young adult fiction? YA novels can be just as complicated and meaningful as adult work, and there's no disadvantage to writing for that market. It can sell as well as adult fiction, and a publisher might issue and market your novel within that genre anyway, whether you think of it as young adult fiction or not.

**Editors tell me my dialogue passages are too long, but I'm only telling it the way it is in real life. What's wrong?**

You're probably doing too much in the way of "telling it the way it is in real life." You must refine your dialogue so that you present the reader with only the *essence* of reality. Conversation in real life is never as pointed as writers present it in fictional dialogue. Readers will be bored by dialogue that recounts the polite rituals and trite conversations that are a part of everyday life. Compress and focus your dialogue so that your characters get right to the point when they talk. All dialogue should either advance the plot, characterize the people, or both. If it doesn't do these things, it's not effective or necessary.

**My writing teacher says dialogue has to do more than just let characters talk. What does he mean?**

Besides the fact that good dialogue positively affects pacing—makes a novel easier to read by relieving the reader from long descriptive passages—it also effectively characterizes and adds to the reality of the speakers. It can take the place of long, tedious character descriptions. What a character says about himself and how a character speaks about others should give clues to his personality, emotions, attitudes, opinions, and desires. In addition to revealing character, good dialogue must also advance the plot by giving information that heightens conflict or by building tension between characters.

## FLASHBACK QUESTION

**Must a novel include sex in order to sell to a publisher these days?**

No. Many novels are published each year that have little or no sexual activity in the plot. A glance at the bookshelves and any of the major best-seller lists reveals many books that rely on plotting, characterization, and style rather than sex. The novels of Michael Crichton, for example, are diverse in setting and style; they contain little, if any, sex. If you don't feel comfortable putting sex into your novel, and if you don't feel it advances the plot or deepens the characters, there's no reason to include it.

**An editor said my exposition in the first chapter is too long. Can you tell me how much exposition I should have?**

You've heard the old writing directive *Show, don't tell*; think of exposition as the *telling* part of writing—the scene-setting explanation that provides back story, context, or description. The reason writing instructors caution against too much telling is that readers are generally more interested in and engaged by *showing*. For this reason, economy of language in exposition is key: Everything in your exposition should have a purpose, whether it is to give tone or mood, to describe the setting and time, to characterize, or to provide necessary background. One thing beginning writers often forget is that background information doesn't have to come in the first paragraphs of the novel. The reader doesn't need to know what you're telling him, and you're likely to lose him quickly if you start with a long, uninteresting history. However, if you start off with an interesting situation that grabs the reader's attention, he will *demand* explanation. Then breaking into the flow of the plot is more easily justified.

**I've heard editors say how important it is for a character to be well rounded. What makes a character well rounded?**

Well-rounded characters are distinctly individual; you come to understand their motivations, flaws, emotional traits, and other distinctive qualities. These can be related through a character's actions, his reactions to situations and other characters, dialogue, and also through narrative. A flat character, in contrast, usually carries only one distinguishing trait or might act predictably or according to stereotype.

**A friend read the first draft of my novel and suggested that I write a prologue. When writing a novel, is it necessary to have a prologue?**

Unless your audience will be confused by the details of your story, there's no need to include a prologue in your novel.

**How important is research in the novel?**

Many beginning writers know a novel is a work of imagination, but seem unaware that the factual material in a novel must be as accurate as that in a nonfiction work. The fiction writer uses the same research tools as the nonfiction writer—particularly sources on the period he is writing about, whether he's writing a Regency romance or a novel set in 1930s New York. And the research must be carefully woven into the story, not dropped in awkwardly in a way that interrupts the flow. Study good novels to see how research is integrated, or read interviews with novelists to see how they approach it.

Identifying research needs is a very project-specific task. The best time to do this is during the initial outlining stage. As you add each scene, make a note of any research required to complete that step. Managing the results of your research requires good note-taking and leaving yourself a retraceable path back to the source. For information gleaned from printed sources, make a photocopy of the material itself and be sure to note the source title, publisher, publication date, the page numbers (if they don't appear on the copy), and where you physically located the source. Keeping this information right on the copy will help you document your work and locate the source again, should that become necessary. If you're doing research online, print out relevant pages and make sure that the Web site appears on your printout. Bookmark any sources you think you'll return to often.

**What kind of planning should I do before I start to write a novel?**

Planning methods vary greatly among writers, who often modify their systems as they gain experience and maturity. Some are satisfied with a brief summary of the plot, the character's conflict, and the resolution. Others may put together as many as fifty or a hundred pages of detailed charts of action, character, and environment sketches. (This is usually referred to as outlining.)

Writers who advocate outlining say that it cuts down on wasted time and endless revision because you understand your characters at the outset and can produce a logical plot. But writers against outlining say it inhibits creativity and inspiration, and even prevents them from finding the true line through the story. You'll have to decide for yourself what makes sense for you. Perhaps it would be useful to begin with an outline but give yourself permission to go off script and revise your original outline if you get new and better ideas once you start writing.

**What makes up a chapter in a novel? How do I separate scenes within a chapter?**

Exactly what and how much goes in to a chapter is up to the individual author. Chapter divisions are an author's means of organizing the major events and developments in his novel, and can provide easy transitions in time, place, or point of view. Many writers (and agents) like to have a cliffhanger at the end of every chapter that keeps people reading and on the edge of their seat.

Changing scenes within a chapter can be accomplished by a simple paragraph change, using a transitional phrase like *The next morning, she....* Or it can be accomplished by leaving blank lines between paragraphs, a technique especially helpful when the scene change also involves a change in viewpoint.

**What are some common beginner mistakes that I might learn to avoid?**

In *Writing for the Soul*, Jerry Jenkins points out a major mistake that plagues nearly every beginning writer: including too many details of ordinary life that don't contribute to character or plot. For instance, if your character backs his car into a garbage truck, just state it. There's no need to lead up to it with your character's movements to leave the house, walk to the car, open the door, slide in, turn the key, etc.—unless these movements are highly unusual and somehow make a significant contribution to character. Otherwise, cut to the chase and don't go overboard on the *showing*. (Writers, after hearing *Show, don't tell* one too many times, can err in the other direction.) Jenkins also points out how ordinary life scenes, even if written well, fall into cliché territory that you're better off avoiding. He advises, "Don't begin with the main character waking to the alarm clock; don't allow your character to describe herself in the mirror; don't make future love interests literally bump into each other at first meeting."

At the sentence level, most writers go overboard on the adjectives and adverbs. Instead, you should favor concrete nouns and action verbs. A book like *The Elements of Style* can teach you and show you what this looks like.

### What about flashbacks?

It's best to avoid flashbacks, because they prevent the story from moving forward. But carefully considered and implemented, they can add texture and meaning. Look to some of the resources at the chapter's end to learn how to handle them effectively.

## WORKING WITH IDEAS

**I've got a couple of good ideas for a mystery, but I'm not quite sure how to go about getting them into novel form. What should I do?**

First, learn the techniques, style, and conventions of the genre, and read widely from classic mysteries (Arthur Conan Doyle, Agatha Christie) to contemporary bestsellers (Sue Grafton, Harlan Coben). You want to understand what popular writers are doing, though it would be a mistake to closely imitate them—you're not likely to sell your mystery unless it has a fresh voice or approach.

Many mystery writers find detailed plot outlines to be useful, but be careful that you don't become so wrapped up in the intricacies of the puzzle that you neglect to build a strong theme or well-rounded characters. Like all fiction (and most nonfiction), your mystery must have a human element to it.

Some basic elements of mystery stories are described in *Writing and Selling Your Mystery Novel* by Hallie Ephron and *How to Write a Damn Good Mystery* by James N. Frey.

**I have had a novel in mind for almost ten years. My insurmountable problem is one of skillfully covering many years without confusing the reader. What should I do?**

Decide exactly how many years the story really needs. If the same basic story can be told in five years rather than fifteen, by all means choose the shorter period. Remember that, for dramatic purposes, you can telescope events that might, in real life, be spread over a long period.

Regardless of how much time the story spans, you must be discriminating in your choice of detail. Don't include anything that does not keep the action moving forward toward the climax. Avoid all irrelevancies and descriptions for description's sake. Develop important incidents in full scenes. But information of minor significance can sometimes be handled by brief transitional summaries that link the highlights together. Flashbacks can help a story make a time leap, but this technique should be used sparingly because too much hopping back and forth between the past and present can wreak havoc with readers' time sense.

**I have a very broad-stroke idea for a story. Can you share some tips as to how to evolve concept to story line?**

One of the best quick-stroke plotting tools comes from the 1945 (yes, 1945) *Writer's Yearbook*. It's what author John Nanovic calls the Triple-O method. For every story concept, identify in one or two words these three things: object, obstacles, outcome. If you can't name all three, you don't have a story; if you can, you have the backbone of your plot.

## QUERIES AND SUBMISSIONS

**I have a novel in the works, but it is months from completion. When should I send query letters to publishers? Is it ever too soon to send one?**

See chapter four for more on queries.

With your first novel, don't send a query letter to agents or editors until the work is complete. You need to be able to demonstrate that you are capable of finishing a novel. Many writers can craft a strong fifty or one hundred pages, but can't go the distance, which is why agents and editors in general aren't interested in a first novel until it's done.

## SYNOPSES AND OUTLINES

**Some of the agents I plan to query ask for a synopsis. What is a synopsis and why does an agent need one?**

A synopsis is a complete summary of your novel that's supposed to help sell it. Synopsis length varies tremendously, so you should try to find out the agents' preferences on length before sending one. If in doubt, make yours about one to two pages single spaced, or three to five pages double spaced, and go from there. (If you find yourself writing three or four different lengths of synopses to please three or four different editors, consider it good practice for your writing skills.)

What makes synopses so difficult to write (at least for most authors) is that the shorter ones require you to leave out the majority of the story and usually quite a few characters. To make them lively and interesting, the synopses are generally written in present tense, third person; they should read almost like a novel and carry the same tone (humorous, dark, mysterious, etc.) as your actual manuscript. They rarely feature dialogue.

A basic synopsis will give the opening hook, sketch out the key characters, describe the plot's high points, concentrate on the core conflict, and reveal the ending. Evan Marshall, in his book *The Marshall Plan for Getting Your Novel Published*, says "To achieve conciseness, you must write as clean and tight as you know how. Don't do what many writers do and try to keep boiling down your actual novel again and again until it's short enough. Instead, learn to write in a synoptic style—read a section or chapter of your novel and simply retell it, as you might describe a great book or movie to a friend."

Like query letters, synopses should not include editorialization, such as "in a thrilling turn of events" or "in this heartbreaking scene."

**Are an outline and a synopsis the same thing?**

The term *outline* is often used interchangeably with *synopsis*. Sometimes, though, an editor or agent is looking for a chapter outline when he asks for a synopsis. A chapter outline makes each chapter its own story and takes a few paragraphs to describe each chapter. Never submit an outline unless an editor asks for it. (Fewer and fewer want them these days.)

**I am writing a novel, and realized a long time ago that it may be too long to publish as one book. In a heartrending decision, I managed to separate my novel into four smaller books. Do I need to finish the entire work (all four books) before I query an agent for the first of them?**

Your first book should be strong enough to stand alone without the other three, and if it's complete, you can begin querying right away. It doesn't hurt to have all four finished, but as long as you have one finished and outlines of the rest of the books in the series, you should be OK.

**I've written twelve novels. My agent proposed them. All rejected. I've done everything possible to make them look polished. Still rejected. Is the industry overcrowded?**

Agents and editors are always looking for excellent writing; however, editors are under increasing pressure to find the "perfect" manuscript—one that requires little work and that will earn huge profits for the publisher. So the writing world isn't overcrowded as much as the publishing world is very picky. The reasons that a publisher might reject your book are legion. If your book's genre doesn't quite fit with the publisher's other books, if your manuscript needs too much editing work, if your book's concept isn't very marketable, your manuscript will be rejected. These are but a few of the reasons an editor will turn down a manuscript.

While the industry isn't exactly overcrowded, you do have to compete against other authors (both published and unpublished) for coveted spots on a publisher's list. The demand for high-quality work—with no allowances for second-best—might be the reason for your work's rejection. Just because your work is polished, doesn't mean it's compelling. Or your work could be before its time (or behind the times). It's hard to know unless your agent tells you the reasons the editors rejected your work.

**I've heard that it's impossible to sell a book longer than 100,000 words. Is this true?**

There's some truth to the fact that the longer your manuscript, the more challenging it is to sell it. Publishers prefer novels that are in the 80,000- to 120,000-word range, depending on the genre. Once you start getting into the 150,000-word or 200,000-word range, an editor or agent is going to think twice before making an investment.

Word count becomes even more crucial when writing in a genre with rigid conventions, such as category romance. Publishers that issue romance series have strict limitations on how long each book can be, so you should write to fit their specifications and not consider yourself an exception.

**I'm an unpublished novelist and don't have any fiction-related writing credentials to mention in my query letter. What should I say about myself if I lack publications?**

Frequently asked question

If you have any writing education, or any way to reveal the seriousness or quality of your writing, you can mention those factors instead. Maybe you have a degree in writing, took a writing workshop under a noted author, or have won awards. Or perhaps the manuscript you're shopping around is actually the sixth unpublished novel you've written—that's actually a positive thing because agents and editors know that you learn, grow, and mature each time you finish a novel-length manuscript. Another tactic is to mention any experience you have that relates to the novel you're writing. For instance, if you're pitching a legal thriller, and you have a legal background, you definitely want to mention it. But the best remedy for writers with no quality credentials is to summarize their novel in a way that sounds unique, interesting, and compelling.

**How much detail should I get into when describing my novel in the query letter?**

Not much. The agent or editor only needs a taste of your novel's plot and protagonist to know whether he wants to read a partial or complete manuscript. Most successful novel queries are only a page long, single spaced. The description of your novel should take only a couple of paragraphs, and no more than half your query. The very best queries contain a mini-synopsis that isn't more than a couple hundred words. In *Writing the Breakout Novel Workbook*, agent Donald Maass says, "Long plot summary overwhelms the person getting the pitch."

According to Maass (a literary agent who represents novels exclusively), your mini-synopsis should describe your protagonist, your protagonist's problem/conflict, the setting, and the one thing that sets your novel apart from all the rest. He warns, "So many novels sound ordinary and unoriginal, like I have read them before. Probably I have. There are no new stories, after all, just new ways of telling them. And *that* is what I'm interested in. What is your new angle on it? What is the twist or turn in your novel that no one sees coming? Yes, give it away! Why are you saving it?"

**What are some major mistakes that people make when writing novel queries?**

Don't put so much hype in the letter that you come across as amateurish. Predicting your book's climb up the best-seller lists, comparing yourself to Stephen King, or claiming you've got the next *Da Vinci Code* on your hands—all of these tactics will only put off the editor or agent. Similarly, refrain from editorializing the description of your novel. The agent or editor shouldn't have to be told your novel is thrilling or romantic or heartbreaking. Your description should *show* or *reflect* these qualities.

Also avoid caps, exclamation points, and exaggeration, as well as adjectives, superlatives, and anything more than a word or two on your theme. Keep a professional tone and avoid acting like a salesperson. Concentrate on the *story*, and you'll win over agents and editors.

Final word of warning: Don't claim your mother (or child or spouse or friend) absolutely loves your work. (However, if you have an endorsement from a best-selling author who loves it, mention that!)

**Is it OK to compare my writing style to that of another author?**

Agents and editors disagree on this point, but one thing's for sure: It's not to your advantage to compare yourself to a mega best-selling author. The best comparisons are those that indicate your writing style, your story's themes, or the overall feel of your work. Sometimes it's better to mention specific book titles that evoke the same style as yours, or to mention authors that would be familiar to the agent or editor you're querying. (It's wonderful if you can compare your work to a book that the agent or editor recently represented or edited.)

**Is it OK to include the first chapter or so with my query?**

Unless the submission guidelines ask for that first chapter (or more), don't include it. However, if you think your first five pages are really outstanding, there's no harm in slipping them in with your query letter. (But no more than five!)

## WHERE TO FIND OUT MORE

## BOOKS

*Writing the Breakout Novel* and *Writing the Breakout Novel Workbook*, by Donald Maass, provide excellent instruction on how to write a novel, for both beginning and advanced (published) novelists.

*The First Five Pages*, by Noah Lukeman, helps you discover how agents can spot a manuscript's flaws in the first five pages, and learn how you can fix those flaws in your own work.

*The Plot Thickens*, by Noah Lukeman, is a follow-up to *The First Five Pages* and concentrates on effective plotting for your novel.

*Novelist's Boot Camp*, by Todd A. Stone, offers more than a hundred brief lessons on how to improve your novel; excellent for first-time novelists.

*The Complete Handbook of Novel Writing* is a compilation of the best articles on novel writing from *Writer's Digest* magazine, *Writer's Market*, and other sources.

*How to Write a Damn Good Novel*, by James N. Frey, is a longtime favorite of writers that focuses on the basics of storytelling.

*Your First Novel*, by Ann Rittenberg and Laura Whitcomb, is a guide for first-time novelists, written by an agent and author team.

*The Marshall Plan for Novel Writing*, by agent Evan Marshall, offers a very detailed, systematic plan for writing your novel, complete with worksheets, tables, etc. Great for people who love to outline and do a lot of preplanning.

The Elements of Fiction Writing series and the Write Great Fiction series by Writer's Digest Books focus on specific elements of fiction writing, such as character, plot, dialogue, setting, and description. Invaluable if you find yourself struggling with a weakness in a particular area of fiction writing.

# How do i sell my
# nonfiction book?

Writers do their best work when they write what they love. Unfortunately, love is sometimes not enough when it comes to writing and selling nonfiction books—you have to understand what will sell and how to sell it. This chapter will help you understand how to bring about that transformation.

### Do you have to be an expert on something to get a nonfiction book published?

Usually some level of expertise is necessary to produce a successful nonfiction book, especially for fields such as health, self-help, or parenting, where no one will trust your advice without recognized credentials. Your background must instill trust in the readership. (Would you, as a reader, trust a healthcare book by an author with no medical degrees or experience in the healthcare field?) However, some types of nonfiction, especially biographies, historical surveys, and creative nonfiction/memoir, can be written by anyone who has good research skills plus organizational and writing abilities.

### In writing a nonfiction book, is it advisable to try to first publish single chapters as magazine articles?

Previously published articles can certainly be used to sell a book idea. They show the editor your abilities and that your idea is a marketable one. If you do sell your book chapters as articles first, make sure you don't sell all rights to the material. One warning, however: Some book manuscripts are rejected because they are simply a collection of articles. A successful nonfiction book has a definite focus and thread of continuity that runs from beginning to end. After the book is published, you might want to write related articles—or sell excerpts—to help promote it.

### What is narrative nonfiction?

Narrative nonfiction tells a true story using fictional techniques and is meant to be entertaining. An example of narrative nonfiction is *Seabiscuit*, by Laura Hillenbrand.

### What is prescriptive nonfiction?

Prescriptive nonfiction usually gives advice, rules, or directions on how to do something or achieve something. The book you're reading now is prescriptive nonfiction. Usually there is less emphasis on writing or literary quality in a prescriptive guide, and the emphasis is on the quality of information or instruction. The book sells based on the benefit to the reader, like losing weight, making money, or knitting a sweater.

### Do I have to write the manuscript first before querying agents and editors with my nonfiction book idea?

For the majority of nonfiction book ideas, you should prepare a book proposal first. A book proposal argues why your book idea will make a salable, marketable product, and if the editor is convinced by your proposal, she'll offer you a contract and advance to write the book. (Remember: The opposite is true for first-time novelists; you always complete the novel first, then query and receive a contract.) The querying and submission process for book proposals is the same as fiction; you send a query, then submit your book proposal if invited, though some agents or editors will take a book proposal on first contact. Check their submission guidelines.

Sometimes, it's better to complete the manuscript first. If you're an unpublished writer, you may be better off completing your book first so that agents and editors see that you're able to pull off your idea successfully. Another consideration is whether or not your nonfiction book will primarily inform or entertain. If you're writing a prescriptive nonfiction book meant to inform, then you're selling it based on the quality of your idea, its market potential, and your expertise; having a completed manuscript is of less importance. If you're writing a memoir that will succeed based on its literary merit or entertainment value, then it becomes more important to have a completed manuscript that shows your writing strengths and ability to construct a narrative.

**I published my own nonfiction book, and now I'd like to query commercial publishers about a second edition, but how can I approach them about this idea?**

There are two ways you can approach this. One way is to submit a copy of your book to several publishers along with a concise description, its market potential, and the sales record you achieved on your own. Include any other information likely to convince them to invest in your project (such as your marketing plan), as well as copies of notable reviews and special promotional contacts you may have.

If your book didn't sell many copies, and you consider your self-publishing attempt a big mistake, then don't send a copy of the book. Query the publisher as if it were a new project, and if your manuscript is requested, send a print-out of the word-processed manuscript (not the typeset book)—as well as the proposal.

**Do I need an agent to sell my nonfiction book?**

It depends. Consider these factors:

1. Are you writing a book that you believe has significant commercial value?
2. Do you want to publish with a New York house, or does your project merit a large advance (at least $20,000 or more)?
3. Do you need the expertise and knowledge of an agent to get your proposal into the right hands?

If the answer to any of these questions is yes, then you probably should look for an agent.

Usually, projects that don't require agents include scholarly works that should be published by a university press; regional works that are likely to be published by a regional or independent press; a work with little commercial value; or a work that has a specialized audience and would work well with a specialized press. For many specialized or niche books (which include scholarly or regional works), you're often better off approaching publishers on your own, particularly if those publishers are small and specialized themselves. Of course, always check to make sure the publishers you're querying take unsolicited queries and submissions.

## THE BOOK PROPOSAL

**If I have a completed nonfiction manuscript, do I still need to write a proposal to accompany it?**

Yes, it's a smart idea. The editor or agent will want to know your target market for the book, your marketing platform and promotion plan, and any other information that shows why your book will sell.

**How long is a book proposal and what should it contain?**

Important
information

Book proposals vary in length, format, and content, depending on the project; a strong proposal will cover, at the very least, these areas:

Target market. Who's the audience for your book? How big is that audience? What evidence do you have that your book will sell to that audience? Editors and agents look for quantifiable proof that a market exists for your book and that it will sell. If you're an expert in a particular field, and you know your market well, this may be a very easy task. But if you don't have a clear idea of your audience, or if you've been generalizing your market as "everyone who likes a good read," then it's probably time to do some market research. Look for studies, reports, magazine and newspaper articles, books, and anything else that shows your book idea can be sold and marketed successfully to a well-defined audience.

Competitive title analysis. What books currently on the market are similar to yours? What are the strengths and weaknesses of these competing titles? Why is yours different, better, or unique? Many editors and agents will know the biggest competitors to your book, but they need to hear from you why your project is a needed addition to the market. Show how your book fills a gap or brings something new to the table. It could relate to content, presentation of content, format and packaging, comprehensiveness, price, illustrations or special features. Your book must have a special angle or hook that sets it apart from the other books on the shelf. Why would someone choose your book over a competitor's?

**Author bio.** You must convince agents and editors that you're the perfect author for the book. Don't simply attach a resume; tailor your bio and background to the book idea you're proposing. Show how your expertise or experience has given you the perfect platform from which to address your target audience. If you have no background or expertise in the subject area you're proposing to write about, you have a tough battle ahead. Look for other strengths that may help give you credibility or sell books: established connections to experts or to your target audience, a strong online presence or following, and previous success in marketing and promoting yourself and your work.

**Marketing plan / marketing platform.** Your marketing platform is your unique space in your field that allows you to market, promote, and sell your book. It's your reach into the marketplace, including your personal and professional network, your Web site, your e-newsletters or e-mail list, your regularly published articles or columns, your positions within national or regional organizations, speaking engagements, media experience, and so on. A strong marketing plan details how you plan to make your audience aware of your book and should build upon the strengths of your platform. For instance, "As president of the National Widget Guild, my book will be featured in the monthly Widget Guild newsletter that reaches 50,000 readers."

**Chapter outline and sample chapters.** If your manuscript is not complete, you'll need to include a chapter outline that describes your book's content. You should also include a sample chapter or two. Make sure to write a chapter that showcases the very best material in your book and not something like the introduction or first chapter.

After you have all of these elements ready, you should write an overview (several pages long) to begin the proposal; it should tie together the most persuasive or important elements of your proposal and summarize why the book is needed, who the market is, and why you're the perfect author for it.

As mentioned before, length can greatly vary, but even the most simple proposal usually runs a dozen pages, longer if an extensive outline or sample chapters are included. Very detailed proposals can run one-hundred pages or more.

Proposal writing is an art, and the best ones demand careful research, careful writing, and careful revision. Be sure to read a good sample proposal or two before embarking on your own. *How to Write a Book Proposal,* 3rd edition, by Michael Larsen, has several proposal examples, not to mention excellent and in-depth instruction on writing a compelling book proposal.

## FLASHBACK QUESTION

**Who is the patron saint of writers?**

The patron saint of authors and journalists is St. Francis de Sales (1567–1622), Savoyard noble, Bishop of Geneva, Doctor of the Church. He preached that everyone, however busy, could have a spiritual life. He authored two masterpieces of religious writing: *Introduction to the Devout Life* and *Treatise on the Love of God.* The ideas expressed in his works were instrumental in developing the Roman Catholic emphasis on loving God as well as fearing him as a judge. His Feast Day is January 29 and two of his oft-quoted sayings are: "You can catch more flies with a spoonful of honey than with a hundred barrels of vinegar," and "What is good makes no noise. What is noisy does no good."

**I think I have a good idea about my audience, but I'm not sure how to collect meaningful information about them or the market. What kind of information should I be looking for?**

Here are some questions that should help spark some ideas.

As far as your potential market, what's your book about and what's at stake here? How serious is the problem or issue? How far-reaching? Usually you can find news articles online through simple keyword searches, or ask your librarian to help you research information on your topic.

Who's affected by the issues in your book? What age are they, how much money do they have, what's their education level? Where do they shop? What organizations or clubs do they belong to? Where are they likely to live in the country? In what type of setting? Is your audience growing or dwindling or stagnant? Does the economy affect your market? Does technology affect your market? Offer any facts or figures that show trends favoring your book sales.

### How much thought should I put into the book title? I hear that publishers just change it anyway.

While it's true that the publisher will likely change your book's title, you should still create an effective title that captures people's attention and identifies the book's audience, benefit, or purpose. Usually, you want your book title to be positive and empowering, and to convince book buyers that it will solve their problems or otherwise benefit their lives.

### Can I include clippings, illustrations, or photos along with my proposal?

Yes, include any supporting materials, as long as they look refined and professional. You can attach them at the end, and include a page serving as a brief table of contents if you have more than a few supporting documents. Or, if using a pocket folder, put the main proposal on the right-hand side, and put your supporting documents on the left-hand side.

### How can I find out the sales of competing titles?

You can try to interpret Amazon rankings or look at a book's reprint record (on the copyright page) to determine its popularity or endurance, but you won't be able to find its sales numbers. Publishing houses do have access to an online resource, Nielsen BookScan, that gives sales information that's said to account for about 70 percent of a book's sales. But this resource is not available to the general public; publishers pay very high subscriber fees to get access.

If you're trying to figure out what the best-selling books are in a particular category, check how many copies the chain bookstores keep in stock on the shelf; more than one or two copies at a time is the mark of a fast seller. Also, sometimes a high number of Amazon reviews can tip you off to a particularly favored or popular title.

**While my nonfiction book proposal is circulating among publishers, may I sell parts of it as magazine articles?**

Yes, you can sell parts of your book as magazine articles; it is not likely to affect the chances of getting your book published and may even help a little. Just make sure that you're not selling all your rights, but first rights. (You should ensure that in any case.) If you do subsequently find a publisher, make it clear to them, before signing a contract, that portions have been previously published.

You should not sell portions of your book as magazine articles after you're contracted with a publisher unless you receive permission. Usually your book contract stipulates who has the right to sell serializations, and how the proceeds will be divided between publisher and author.

## TROUBLESHOOTING YOUR BOOK IDEA

**My nonfiction book was rejected by an editor who said it wasn't authoritative enough. What does that mean, and how can I solve the problem?**

The editor might mean that you have not researched the topic adequately, or that you have not used your research wisely. Or he might be saying that you are not qualified to write about the subject and would lack credibility with readers.

If you lack credentials or qualifications to write your book, you could try finding a well-known expert in the field to endorse your book or write an introduction. You could also include more material in your book from experts (interviews, quotes, and other references).

**What are some other common rejection reasons for a nonfiction book?**

Many prospective authors (usually beginners) don't bother writing a book proposal, especially if they have a completed manuscript—or they write a few pages describing their book without any discussion of the target marketing or their marketing platform. Never assume your project is the exception to the rule because of its compelling or timely nature, and don't submit your idea to numerous publishers without any care or attention. Example: "I know that ABC Publishing House doesn't usually consider books in this subject area, but this is such a compelling book, I thought you should see it anyway." A few other tips:

- Pitch only the book you know has a firm and identifiable spot in the marketplace. Don't assume that the editor or agent will make exceptions for your project, or that someone will figure it out later. Unfortunately, excellent proposals sometimes get rejected because the book's market is just too small or niche for a publisher to pursue.

- Don't skimp on the competitive title section—editors can tell when you haven't done your homework. (Also, knowing the competition and its strengths/weaknesses should help you better write your own proposal.) Whatever you do, don't claim there are no competitors to your book. If there are truly no competitors, then your book is probably so weird it won't sell.

- Editors of nonfiction aren't looking to acquire finely written manuscripts; they're looking to acquire a powerful selling handle. Your proposal should deliver a promise of a book that will fly off the shelves and make the publisher a profit. (Exception: Editors of narrative-driven nonfiction, such as memoir and popular biography, do look at the writing as the first consideration, though the selling handle still matters just as much. It's no good to have great writing on a subject no one is interested in.)

- An incredibly common problem with many book ideas is that they're too general and broad, without a unique angle or hook. For example, if you wanted to write a book on losing weight and titled it "How to Lose Weight Fast," it would be much too generic to interest anyone. Or if you wanted to write a book on how children can cope with parents who have Alzeihmer's, you would need to find a special angle or unique hook that sets the book apart from the many competitors already on the shelf.

- Similarly, many aspiring writers want to do a book based on their own personal experience of overcoming a problem or investigating a complex issue, without any expertise or credentials. Sometimes such books are thinly disguised memoirs, written more for the author's psychological benefit than for a reader's benefit. Remember: Just because you experienced it doesn't mean you can write a salable book about it.

## MEMOIR

**I've written a memoir about my military service. It includes 280 letters to my mother, illustrations of the times, and my recollections. I wrote it for my family, but friends say it warrants publication. What course should I follow to find out?**

Many people who write life stories or memoirs—which are of primary interest to family and friends—decide to self-publish with a print-on-demand (POD) company. There are a couple of reasons for taking this approach. First, you can publish your work right away, and you don't have to go through the time-consuming process of looking for an agent or publisher who might reject your work because it's not marketable enough. Second, going the POD route is relatively inexpensive and will allow all friends and family, as well as future generations, to cherish your life and history in a lovely book that can be kept on the shelf for years to come.

However, if you think your work might be marketable to the general public, and you're willing to spend some time writing a book proposal and looking for an agent, you may want to consider the traditional publishing route.

### How do I know if my memoir is salable or marketable?

It's probably safe to assume that your memoir is not salable unless you're confident of several things. First, your writing must be outstanding. If your memoir is your very first book or very first writing attempt, then it may not be good enough to pass muster with an editor or agent. Second, you must have a compelling and unusual story to tell. If you're writing about topics that affect thousands and thousands of people, that's not necessarily in your favor; Alzheimer's memoirs or cancer memoirs, for example, are very common, and will put you on the road to rejection unless you're able to prove how yours is unique or outstanding in the field. Third, you must have a marketing platform. If you have a way to sell your memoir, on your own, without a publisher's help, then you're more likely to be attractive to an editor or agent.

**What's the difference between autobiography and memoir? When reviewing publisher and agent listings regarding what they specialize in, I often see biography/autobiography and memoirs as separate topics. To me, they're basically the same.**

It's true that in some general contexts, *memoir* and *autobiography* can be used interchangeably. However, when publishing houses note a difference, they're making the following distinction: autobiography focuses on the writer's entire life, whereas memoir focuses on a certain aspect of it. As Susan Carol Hauser explains in *You Can Write a Memoir*, autobiography focuses on the chronology and timeline of a life. Memoir takes in-depth look at one or more themes in a life, rather than an in-depth look at an entire life.

## WHERE TO FIND OUT MORE

## BOOKS

*How to Write a Book Proposal* by Michael Larsen, now in its third edition, has instructed writers on how to craft nonfiction book proposals for more than twenty years.

*Write the Perfect Book Proposal: 10 That Sold and Why*, by Jeff Herman and Deborah Levine Herman, offers ten examples of book proposals and why they succeeded.

*Nonfiction Book Proposals Anybody Can Write*, by Elizabeth Lyon, is another helpful resource on the craft of book proposals.

*Thinking Like Your Editor—How to Write Serious Nonfiction and Get It Published*, by Susan Rabiner and Alfred Fortunato, is a publishing insider's look at why certain nonfiction ideas get accepted and why others don't; most of the book is devoted to the craft of nonfiction and working with an editor and agent.

# 11

# How do i write and sell articles?

The wonderful thing about magazines is that there are just so many of them—by some counts, more than twenty thousand in North America alone. The terrible thing about magazines is that there are just so many of them. Each of them has a different audience, a different style, and a different voice—and different requirements of their writers.

The trick to selling your work to any of these magazines is matching the article to the magazine. In other words, to sell an article to a magazine, you have to do a little market research. Professional writers recognize that magazines are as individual as people are, and that they have to know what stirs readers' interests and what bores them. This chapter will cover the ins and outs of how to do that effectively, and what problems you might encounter.

## TYPES OF ARTICLES

**How many different kinds of articles are there?**

Dozens. Articles most commonly published today include interviews and how-to, personal experience, inspirational, humorous, investigative, personal opinion, travel, technical, and new product articles.

- How-to pieces teach the reader how to do something, such as find a job, build a bookcase, or fix a leaky faucet. They usually focus on step-by-step instruction, and sometimes include photographs or illustrations.

- A personal experience piece relies upon the writer's personal experience to entertain and inform about a larger issue applicable to everyone (e.g., finding reliable child care).
- An inspirational piece is meant solely to inspire and motivate the reader by telling of a challenge overcome or a lesson learned. Sometimes the word inspirational also refers to pieces of a religious nature.

The other popular article types—interview, humorous, investigative, personal opinion, travel, technical, and new product—are fairly self-explanatory. As with all article types, their focus and slant should closely match the interests and attitudes of the magazine's readership. For more instruction on different magazine article types and how to write them, read *The Writer's Digest Handbook of Magazine Article Writing*, edited by Michelle Ruberg.

**In college we wrote what teachers referred to as essays, but I don't see many markets for essays. What's the difference between an essay and a magazine article?**

An article is usually based on facts uncovered in research and/or interviews and manifests itself in forms like the personality sketch, the investigative report, or the how-to. It will have a particular slant, but any opinion will be backed up with quotes, anecdotes, and statistics. While they are often entertaining, articles are usually meant to educate and inform.

In its original sense, the essay was meant to express opinion, to be persuasive, or to be interpretive. It is marked by a more personal treatment of the subject matter, which may or may not interest a wide audience. Although an essay may require research, the information is used along with subjective ideas, whereas an article remains fairly objective. More recently, newspapers have printed interpretive essays. These pieces are really extensions of the news story, analyzing the background of a political event. Editorials, humor pieces, and inspirational articles could all be considered essays.

**What is a feature?**

The term feature usually refers to those articles appearing in a magazine that are not columns or part of a regularly appearing department. Feature articles run longer than columns and department pieces, get featured on the cover, and are grouped together in what is called the editorial well, which is at the magazine's center.

### What is new journalism?

New journalism is a school of article writing that uses fiction techniques to relate an event or story that is factual; it's a form of journalism that also involves the writer's own feelings about his subject, as opposed to what is termed objective journalism.

### What is a think piece?

A think piece is usually an article that has an intellectual, philosophical, provocative approach to its subject.

**I have known some very ordinary people who have done some very unusual things in their lives. Is there a market for articles about these people? It seems I only read stories about famous people.**

Your stories may not interest editors of major magazines, but they may very well sell to local newspapers and possibly to a specialized consumer magazine or trade publication. The only way to find out is to look through *Writer's Market* until you find some magazines interested in buying the human-interest nonfiction you want to write. Make sure you study a magazine thoroughly before you decide to query or send a manuscript to its editor.

**An editor said that he thought part of my article would work better as a sidebar. What does he mean?**

Sidebars are short articles that accompany longer features. They're boxed off and titled separately from the rest of the article and may even be set in a different typeface. Sidebars are used to add information to the article or to take an in-depth look at a topic that is related to the main article, but is too tangential to be included in it. For example, an article on a papal visit to the United States might have a sidebar summarizing the city-by-city heavy security precautions. Other kinds of sidebars include historical notes, tables of statistics, and how-to's.

**What subjects are taboo in magazines?**

It depends. Magazines with taboo topics often mention them in their submission guidelines. You just have to do your research. Try the magazine's Web site or *Writer's Market*.

## MATCHING ARTICLE TO MARKET

**Is it better to have a specific market in mind when writing an article, or to write the article first, then look for a market for it?**

Frequently asked question

It is usually better to write with a specific market in mind so that your writing will match the publication's style and tone, and be directed toward its particular readership. Writers trying to earn a living as freelancers study potential markets before starting to write; this increases potential sales. However, you can write an article and then look for a suitable market. Make sure you carefully research the market before you submit anything. Editors do not appreciate writers who bombard them with material that is obviously not aimed toward their audience.

Most experienced freelancers will query a market before writing an article specifically for it, and write only on assignment—that is, they only write articles that have been assigned to them based on a query.

**How do I obtain sample copies of magazines not sold locally?**

First, check the magazine's Web site and see if there's any way to order sample copies online, or look for a general e-mail address for inquiries. If there's no way to contact the publication via e-mail or through an online request form, try calling the customer service number, if it exists. As a last resort, snail mail a request to the magazine, along with a SASE, and offer to pay for a sample copy. Some magazines charge, others don't.

**How can I find back issues of a magazine?**

Check the magazine's Web site. Most of them explain how they handle back issues of their publication. If the Web site doesn't turn up anything, look closely at the fine print in the magazine's masthead. Most explain how you can order back issues either by phone or snail mail.

**What is meant by the slant of a magazine article?**

A writer slants his article when he specifically gears it to a particular magazine's audience. Finding the proper slant demands in-depth market study to determine the subject matter and style an editor is interested in, and the kind of audience his magazine is intended for. Carefully review several issues of a magazine you wish to write for, analyzing the articles. Are there mostly opinion pieces? Factual features? Personality profiles? What's the tone of the articles? How about the average length? Close observation of the advertisements will give you an idea of the average age and socioeconomic status of the readers, as well as some of their hobbies and interests. By studying the market, you'll be able to present an editor the kind of article he wants, thereby greatly increasing your chances of making a sale.

**I have an idea for an article that would be perfect for a home decorating magazine. However, I found that the magazine published a similar article several years ago. Does this mean it won't be interested? Should I try other magazines instead?**

You can still query the magazine, but emphasize your piece as an update of the previous article, or suggest new ideas and angles. Many magazines must cover the same topic in many different ways in a very short time; for instance, *Cosmopolitan* has at least one article about how to improve your sex life in every issue, but its angle or hook is different every time. Find a unique angle or hook to your idea that will distinguish it from other pieces that may have recently run.

**Where can I find a listing of markets where a beginner can break in?**

Look for magazines with smaller circulations and lower payment rates. While the editors will not be less demanding about the quality of material they accept from freelancers, you may not have as much competition.

**What are literary magazines?**

Literary magazines (or journals) are small-circulation publications that print political, literary, and often unorthodox material that might not otherwise be published. They represent creative writers interested in fine literary quality and are read by writers, editors, and students of literature.

Since these publications make little or no profit, payment for published work is usually no more than a contributor's copy or a subscription to the magazine.

**Is there some way I can find out about upcoming community and corporate events that I can use as possible subjects for freelance articles?**

Large companies, universities, and nonprofit groups schedule a variety of events that can be grist for the freelancer's mill. Most public relations departments of large organizations maintain mailing lists and notify interested persons of upcoming events. Convention and visitor bureaus of large cities can also inform you when special-interest groups and professional organizations will be holding conventions in your area. All you have to do to start receiving information is contact the organization and ask—as a professional freelance writer—to be placed on its mailing list.

## COMMON ARTICLE PROBLEMS

**I've done very little writing, but I'd like to write an article about working mothers—especially those with small children. I know several in my neighborhood and am impressed by what they manage to accomplish in a day's time. But whenever I begin to write, I quickly run out of things to say—after only a page or two. What's my problem?**

It seems that you have a fairly solid interest in your subject, so your problem might be a lack of ample research. Have you really talked to these women about their trials, the advantages and disadvantages of their two-career situation? Another problem may be that you do not have a clearly developed angle for your article. Instead of merely making random comments on how working mothers cope, you could perhaps better interest your readers by including specific tips on how they could manage their own time better, secure cooperation of other family members, etc. A writer who knows enough about his subject will never be at a loss for words: Ideas, anecdotes, facts, and angles will come easily. Begin by formulating a solid outline, and strive for smooth transitions between ideas. Take plenty of time to plan, research, and write your piece; rushing things will result in disorganized and unclear writing. And it's a good idea to write such a piece with a particular publication in mind. That way, you can tailor your story to the magazine's style, tone, and readership.

**An editor rejected my article, saying he uses a more anecdotal style in his magazine. What does that mean?**

Used in article writing, an anecdote is a brief human-interest story illustrating a point. Although each anecdote is complete in itself, it should be relevant to the purpose of the article. Anecdotes can serve to hold reader interest by breaking up a lot of factual material. They can be used to add insight to the personality of someone discussed or featured in an article, to act as a transition from one topic to another, or to provide a "grabber" of a lead in a news or feature article.

A good interview will easily yield anecdotes. Ask your subject open-ended questions like "What person influenced you most in life and how?" or "What was your greatest opportunity?" or "What do you consider the most important decision in your life?" Through such inquiries, you will learn much about the forces that guide and shape the person. If you are writing about someone not available for interview, talk to people who know him and get them to discuss incidents involving your subject, and his personal characteristics.

Often, writers use anecdotes stemming from personal experience, which can be appropriate and useful, but don't overdo it. It only takes a couple of anecdotes before you're writing an article that's more about yourself than the topic at hand.

**Do the anecdotes I use in my articles have to be true?**

If you're going to mention people's names, then you'd better stick to real-life facts; but if you want to make up an anecdote to illustrate a point, then you might preface it with something like: "It's the sort of town where something like the following could easily happen ... " or "There's a rumor going around that ..." This way the point can be made without giving the erroneous idea that the incident actually did take place. The secret of good anecdotes is witnessing a real occurrence and describing it in such a way that your interpretation gives it new dimension and significance.

**I sent an article to a magazine and got back a rejection with the comment "Too general—no peg." What does that mean?**

It means that you did not concentrate on one specific aspect of your topic, and the article was too general for the audience of that magazine. Most article ideas lend themselves to several pegs, each one of which could be developed into a separate article. For instance, an article on buying a computer could be geared toward the needs of a college student, a family with children, a self-employed businessperson, a teacher, or a corporation—five different article possibilities (or pegs) that could end up in five different magazines, each with a different audience.

## WORKING WITH EDITORS

**When a magazine published my article it was completely changed from my version, although they used my facts. Does this mean they didn't like my writing and only wanted to use my research? I know they needed to shorten it, but I was surprised to see it changed so much from the way I submitted it.**

An editor will often change syntax, clean up grammar, and rearrange ideas to make an article clearer and more easy to read. If the article is longer than the specified number of words, it will be cut. Editorial space is limited. The editor may be forced to do a lot of rewriting, even though the article may contain valuable information, because he knows that it does not conform to reader expectations or the personality of the magazine—editors edit to make you sound better relative to the rest of the magazine. You can avoid severe editing of your work by studying the slant and style of the magazine to which you are submitting. Look closely at the printed version of your article and analyze the reasons for changes. And it wouldn't hurt to drop the editor a note and ask why the changes were made. He will probably be frank with you, and you may learn something from the experience.

**I've written a magazine article for which I've taken some photographs as possible illustrations. How do I submit a manuscript-photo package?**

If you've already been given an assignment, and the editor is expecting the photographs, then choose a couple of your best shots and include them with your manuscript. If he's not expecting the photos—or if you're simply querying or submitting on spec—then don't send the photos; just let the editor know they're available.

**I sold a piece to a magazine, and it was a year before it was published. When it was published, they spelled my name right, but that was about all. The style was hacked apart until there was no style. What's more, facts were altered, so the reader was bound to get an impression different from what I intended. How much can my story be edited or changed without my permission?**

Ethically, an editor should discuss any significant changes with you, especially if they affect the intent of your piece. Some editors will show galley proofs to authors; others will not. You might ask to see galleys at the time the piece is purchased. If you see galleys and don't like what is there, you can ask to have your original meaning restored or the manuscript returned to you for submission elsewhere. But be sure you aren't mistaking tight editing for changes in meaning, as beginning writers sometimes do. Most of the editor's changes are to make the story more readable—not different.

**An article I recently sold was heavily edited, distorting the meaning of some of the opinions and quotes contained in it. Can I ask for the right of article approval on any future sales?**

It might not be a good idea to make such a request in your query letter, since such preconditions might turn off the editor. The question can be raised when you submit your article; simply state that if the editors make any changes—in terms of content, not copyediting revisions—that you would like the opportunity to see the final edited copy before publication.

**Can a magazine change the title of my story?**

Just as the editor has the right to make editorial changes, so too does he have the right to change your title. Some editors might consult you first, but titles are changed routinely for a variety of reasons. If the editor changes your title in a way that distorts your meaning, you certainly have cause to complain.

A magazine editor assigned an article to me, based on a variation of an idea I queried him about. When I got into the actual research, I found the article wasn't going to produce what the editor was looking for. There just wasn't enough solid information available to support the editor's thesis. What's the best way to handle this?

Let the editor know right away what the problem is. The editor will either abandon the idea and pay you a kill fee, or suggest some contacts who may be able to supply you with what the editor is searching for. Editors, as well as writers, sometimes have to admit that a certain idea has to be temporarily abandoned.

Is one editor liable for another editor's commitment? When an editor assigns something to a writer or offers payment for a manuscript, then leaves the magazine staff, is the replacement editor liable for that assignment or payment?

There are no rules on this one. Often it depends on the terms of departure for the editor. If he is fired, chances are his replacement or his former manager will want to disregard his editorial thinking—perhaps that was the reason for his dismissal. If he was promoted or transferred, or if he otherwise departed on good terms, there is likely to be more transitional grace, and old projects and commitments may be honored. The writer should summarize the situation in a letter to the new editor, including copies of all correspondence. The new editor then will be in a position to judge whether he wants to keep the writer on assignment or kill the idea. Whether a kill fee will be paid depends on whether a kill fee was part of the original agreement and how far the writer has gone with the idea. Most editors will be fair with the writer. But when a magazine staff changes, it is often because the publisher is unhappy with earlier staffers—and it can signal a new editorial direction for the publication.

What does it mean to be a contributing editor?

Contributing editors are writers who regularly sell articles to a magazine. Being named as a contributing editor usually gains the writer no additional money or special favors, but is prestigious in that it indicates that the writer knows how to successfully (and repeatedly) write for and sell to that magazine. It also gives him more visibility, in that his queries, suggestions, and manuscripts are given red-carpet treatment (they are read sooner and acted on more quickly than unsolicited mail). Contributing editors have more clout when arranging interviews, and the title may give the writer more credibility when he wants to break in to other markets.

**What exactly does a magazine correspondent do? How can I get a job as a correspondent?**

Magazine correspondents usually work on assignment, conducting interviews, making phone calls, and doing all sorts of other research for articles that are sometimes initiated by the magazine and written by staff writers. The results of this legwork are usually submitted as a research report and are incorporated into articles of larger scope. The correspondent may also be able to initiate, research, and write articles of his own for the magazine. He's in a better position than the regular freelancer, because his editors know the quality of his work and are more willing to consider it for publication.

To get a job as a correspondent, you usually must have a substantial track record as a writer and be able to demonstrate a wide knowledge of and interest in the subjects you write about. These jobs are normally obtained with a particular magazine after the writer has had several pieces published in that magazine.

**What do editors call the small descriptive phrase or sentence that usually appears under the main title of an article?**

Some editors call it a subhead, and others a deck. This phrase or sentence is designed to pique the reader's interest in reading the article or story by telling just a little bit about the subject matter.

## MARKETING YOUR WORK

**Is there any danger a writer might get too many articles going at the same time?**

Planning your production time—whether you are a part-time or full-time freelance writer—is important. If deadlines are too close together, you may be inclined to rush through an article without sufficient research, eliminate some important interviews, or turn out a draft that really needs better organizing and rewriting. You will be judged by your readers and editors on what appears under your byline, so give only your best effort to each assignment.

**I have written a human interest article that I think would be perfect in the Sunday supplement magazine in our local newspaper. How many weeks in advance should I make my submission if I have a particular Sunday in mind?**

It would be wise to submit your piece several months (or more) before the date you would like to see it published. This gives the editor plenty of time to make a decision concerning your article, and, if it is accepted, to ask for revisions or prepare accompanying artwork.

Writers should consider lead time (the time between submission and publication) when writing articles that are time sensitive. For a monthly magazine, you should submit your work no less than five or six months in advance of the issue date. A magazine's lead time for seasonal articles is usually listed in *Writer's Market*.

**I've written several articles for local newspapers and magazines, but I'm not sure I can write a national-interest article. How can I write something that will sell to a national publication?**

Many topics of local and regional articles can be expanded to fit the needs of national publications. By examining how a local story relates to a national trend, or by using it as an example of that trend, a writer can create an article that will be attractive to a national magazine. Of course, you'll have to supplement your local information with related examples from national sources, which you'll have to uncover through research. You should also contact persons involved in the subject at a national level, obtain their viewpoints and comments, and add their quotes to your story.

**I've come up with several ideas for articles, but I don't know enough about the topics to write about them. Do magazine editors purchase story ideas, or will writers more knowledgeable in a specific area buy the rights to use my ideas?**

It may surprise you how little the average writer knows about a given topic before he begins to write about it. With some research and interviews with knowledgeable sources, you can learn enough about your subject to intelligently write the article yourself.

That said, magazine editors only purchase queries that pitch a written (or soon-to-be written) article, not ideas that will later be written by someone else. Writers who specialize in specific fields of information usually have so many ideas of their own that they don't purchase from others.

**How can I find addresses of the daily and weekly newspapers to which I can submit articles of regional interest?**

*Editor & Publisher* magazine publishes the *Editor & Publisher International Year Book*, an annual directory containing a comprehensive list of all the dailies worldwide and all the community and special interest U.S. and Canadian weeklies. The yearbook is available by mail or online at www. editorandpublisher.com.

## TRAVEL WRITING

Frequently asked question

**I just discovered the travel-writing field and am very excited about it. How can I get started in this field?**

One way to get started in travel writing is to do some short travel features aimed at local newspaper and regional magazine markets. It helps if you have a general knowledge of newspaper and magazine article writing and some experience in freelance writing. If you're new to writing, check out *Travel Writing*, by L. Peat O'Neil.

At the beginning of your career, you will have to finance your trips out of your own funds. Later, when your name becomes known for travel pieces, the publications you write for will often pay your travel expenses. Payment depends on the newspapers, books, or magazines you write for and the degree to which you sell reprints of your articles.

You shouldn't quit your job to become a travel writer. You should work as a freelancer in that field until you have established enough credit with magazine and book editors to enable you to support yourself entirely from your writing income.

**I want to do an article that will involve some travel expense to a nearby state. Will an editor reimburse me for these expenses as well as pay me for the article?**

If you are fairly new to the business of freelancing and have not built up many writing credits, you will probably be expected to cover extra expenses yourself—but it never hurts to ask! Expenses may include travel, extensive research, photography, photocopying, and the like, and should be negotiated prior to accepting the assignment. An established writer can often get an advance from the editor to cover expenses, and, when writing on assignment, may even get a flat-out expense-paid trip to wherever he needs to go. If you do have to cover your own travel expenses, keep receipts, and remember that travel expenses can be written off with your other business expenses as a tax deduction. Take full advantage of every trip by taking notes, being observant, taking photographs, and following leads that will open and enhance other writing projects, too.

**I'm planning a trip to the Middle East next fall and am interested in doing some magazine article writing while I'm there. Is there any way I can get some assignments before I leave?**

Unless you've written many articles in the past and editors know your name and your abilities, you probably won't be able to secure any definite assignments. However, if you are able to suggest in detail some of your ideas in a query letter, you may find a couple of interested editors who will consider your work on speculation. Make sure your ideas have sharply focused angles; general suggestions such as "I'd like to do an article about modern Arabia" will only label you as a novice and will yield few interested editors.

**In a travel writer's newsletter I saw a reference to a fam trip. What does this term mean?**

Fam trip is an abbreviation for familiarization trip, a trip a public relations agency for a country, hotel, or airline arranges so travel agents, travel editors, and travel writers can visit and become familiar with the amenities offered by the host country or firm; the PR agency and its client hopes that these trips will lead to subsequent travel articles and business. Transportation and lodging costs might be paid for travel agents and offered at a considerably reduced rate for editors and writers.

---

## FLASHBACK QUESTION

**I'm taking an extensive trip through the British Isles this fall and will be writing several articles for some newspapers that I have served for years as a correspondent and feature writer. I also plan to write some freelance travel features, which I hope to sell to one or more magazines or wire services. How does a traveling freelance writer handle work like this from abroad?**

It is customary for freelance writers submitting to markets from abroad to send a self-addressed envelope addressed to them at the point they next expect to be. Usually they enclose an International Reply Coupon, which can be bought in European post offices to cover return postage from anywhere in the world. If you'll be dealing only with American markets, of course, you can take U.S. postage with you to affix to your self-addressed envelope. You might want to consider submitting queries on your features rather than complete manuscripts, since the publications may want a different slant than what you have in mind.

---

## CONTRACTS AND PAYMENT

**How much money can I expect to earn from a typical magazine article sale?**

What magazines pay freelancers depends largely on what they can pay (in terms of circulation and advertising revenue), the length of the article in question, and the reputation of the writer. Paychecks can vary from a few dollars to thousands of dollars. With some publications, the fee paid is standard, and with others it is negotiable. Check the market listings in Writer's Market for the specific rates various magazines will pay for freelance material.

**Should I set a price for my articles, or does the editor set the rate of pay? How do I determine my own pay scale?**

Most magazines have a certain rate they pay writers, and they make an offer based on those standard rates. If you're a new writer and have never sold anything to the publication before, you can't expect to get more than that. Remember that sometimes, especially early in your career, a byline is more important than a check, since it bolsters your confidence, builds your reputation, and may lead to other sales.

If you're a well-established writer and think you might be able to negotiate a better rate because of your experience and value to a magazine, go ahead and suggest a higher rate than standard. What payment you finally receive will depend on your previous record, the locale, and your ability to negotiate.

If you are just getting started as a freelance writer, don't try to do too much bargaining with an editor. Take what he offers and give him the best piece of writing you can. If he wants you to rewrite, do it. It is important that you get quality work published. When you feel you have made enough sales to warrant it, you can begin to negotiate or set rates.

**What happens when an article is accepted by a magazine? Does the writer get a check in the mail, or are there preliminaries to go through?**

The writer is customarily notified of acceptance through a phone call or by e-mail. You may have to sign a contract, and you may be asked to make revisions or review proofs. If the magazine pays upon acceptance of an article, you will receive payment shortly after it is accepted. If the magazine pays upon publication, you'll have to wait longer.

**What do the phrases *payment on acceptance* and *payment on publication* mean?**

Important
information

Both refer to the time the publisher begins the check-writing process. *Payment on acceptance* means the check is ordered after the editor accepts the article as ready for publication (that is, after the writer completes any necessary rewrites). The article may be filed and not edited or published for a period of time, but that does not affect the writer's payment.

*Payment on publication* means the check is not ordered until after the piece appears in print. At a newspaper, this is generally no more than a few days or weeks. The writer may not even notice a delay in receiving his check. At a monthly or quarterly magazine, however, publication may lag months—even years—after acceptance (depending on the size of the editor's manuscript inventory).

### When a story is accepted with payment on publication, is payment to the writer assured?

Payment on publication is risky, though it is sometimes necessary to the beginning writer trying to get established. There is never a guarantee that an article will be published or paid for when it's accepted. Sometimes editors change their minds, and the piece is eventually returned to the author, neither used nor paid for. Most publications, though they may take a long time to actually publish the piece, will pay after publication. It doesn't happen too often that you don't get paid, so it's worth the risk if you want to get published. In the case of new markets, you have the risk that the magazine may fold (discontinue publication) after one or two issues are published, and you'll never be paid. If a magazine folds, you will not be paid, but you are free to submit that material to other markets.

### What does *payment in contributor's copies* mean?

*Contributor's copies* is a term that means copies of the issue in which the contributor's work appears. A magazine that pays in copies (as it is also phrased) offers writers no other remuneration than a copy of the magazine in exchange for the right to publish a work. This is why they are less elegantly called nonpaying markets.

### What does it mean when a publisher listed in *Writer's Market* says he'll accept a writer's work on spec?

When an editor responds to a query letter by offering to look at the proposed work on speculation (*on spec* for short), he means he's interested in the article idea and will consider the finished article for publication. In his response, the editor will usually indicate a deadline, the desired word count for the article, and the terms of payment if it's accepted. However, agreeing to look at the work on spec in no way obligates an editor to buy the finished manuscript. Since an agreement on spec does not guarantee a sale, some freelancers will only write an article on assignment, with the editor giving a firm commitment to purchase the finished product; but beginning writers should celebrate an invitation to submit an article on spec. Often the editor will buy the finished manuscript—if it meets editorial specifications and is submitted within the time specified.

**What's a kill fee, and when is it used?**

Important information

A kill fee is a fee paid to a writer who has worked on an assignment that, for one reason or another, was not published. For example: A writer is asked (assigned) to write a 3,000-word article, but after he does the research and writes the 3,000 words, the editor decides the piece will not be published after all. The writer is then given a percentage or a flat fee as a kill fee. The amount of a kill fee is usually flexible, and depends on the publication's policy. It's rare for an editor to offer a kill fee to a writer whose work is not familiar to him or to a writer who hasn't previously worked for him. The writer is, after receiving the kill fee, permitted to submit the manuscript to other markets for possible sale. A writer should not expect to receive a kill fee unless this provision is specifically covered in the original assignment.

**I want to submit a how-to article to a magazine that pays by the word. The problem is that I spend much more time on the charts and diagrams that accompany the article than I spend on the actual writing. In fact, my articles often contain very little copy. What should I do?**

The magazine will most likely consider payment for graphics separately from that for the article itself, depending on the quality of the graphics. Often, an editor must have his staff redo the artwork. You might write and ask this particular editor for an answer to your question.

**I submitted an article to a magazine that ceased publication with the issue in which that article appeared. I was never paid for the article. Can I submit it to other publications?**

Since the publication never paid for your article, although it was published, you are legally free to use it elsewhere. Be sure to inform the editor who buys the article of the circumstances under which it was originally published.

**After submitting a 2,000-word article to a magazine, I received a letter of acceptance saying the editor was buying 500 words of the article at five cents a word, with a check for twenty-five dollars enclosed. Is this a usual procedure?**

A publisher who is not able to use a full article may offer to buy a part of it from the writer. If the writer accepts, then he agrees to the terms. The balance of the article can be sold by the writer, since he still owns the rights to that material.

**What is the difference between selling one-time rights and first North American rights?**

If you sell first North American rights to a magazine, you are guaranteeing that it will be the first publisher of your article in the United States and Canada, but you are not restricted from selling it to other North American publishers after that initial publication (or to publishers on other continents before publication). One-time rights can be sold to any publication, regardless of whether it's the first to print the story, but that publication can't run the story more than once.

**Once in a while I sell a story that the magazine pays for, yet I never see it in print—even though the editor said he would send copies of the issue containing it. What's going on?**

Sometimes magazine editors forget to send copies of stories they published to the original authors. Write a note to each of the editors asking for a copy of your story, if it has been published. In some cases, editors leave or editorial policies change, and although stories are bought, they are not used. Many magazines keep a large inventory of manuscripts, so your piece may not have run. Be patient.

**What's the going rate for a magazine column?**

What a magazine will pay a columnist varies greatly with the size of its circulation and the eminence and expertise of the writer. A small magazine might pay a couple hundred dollars (or less), while a large-circulation magazine may pay thousands. Although payment is usually on a per-column basis rather than per word, the editor will usually specify desired column length. If you have an idea for a column for a small magazine, send a query along with a half-dozen sample columns to the editor, explaining why you think the column would benefit his readers.

**Will a magazine's libel insurance protect me from libel suits for articles I write?**

It depends on the publisher. Many major magazine publishers have libel insurance that can be applied to a freelancer at the discretion of the publisher, and in most cases the publisher will extend coverage to protect the writer. But if the publisher feels the writer has been negligent in preparing the material, he may decide to let the writer get himself out of the situation. Many publishers have no coverage for freelance writers.

If an article involves investigative reporting and/or a potential lawsuit, a freelancer should consider asking the magazine about freelance insurance when negotiations are underway for such an assignment. The writer should ask the publisher the circumstances under which he would be covered if his article caused any libel action. But don't count on a publisher's insurance bailing you out of hot water if you haven't properly researched and written your article. Accuracy is still the best insurance against libel.

**My magazine article was published four months ago and I haven't received payment for it. What recourse do I have? How can I get the editor to pay me?**

Frequently asked question

If the magazine's policy is to pay on publication, you might expect to receive payment within sixty days after publication. You should never be expected to wait longer than ninety days. If you still haven't received a check, send a follow-up letter requesting the specific amount of payment. Give the editor all the details—whether the manuscript was submitted on speculation or assignment, the date of original submission, the date and title of the published piece. If that doesn't work, you can try appealing to a publication's accounting department or senior executives.

In a worst-case scenario, write the Better Business Bureau. Also, send a letter with all the above-mentioned information to *Writer's Market*, which will notify its readers to be wary of dealings with this publication. You might also try the National Writers Union. There is no additional recourse but to sue—which can result in a net financial loss because of legal fees, unless you can take your case to a nearby small claims court.

## REPRINTS AND RESELLING

Freelancers who discover the magic of multiple markets and reprint sales often also discover the difference between being a working writer and a working, selling writer. Reselling is often the best way to achieve the maximum return on a minimum investment.

**What rights to my story should I sell to a magazine so that I may also sell it to a number of other magazines?**

Although most editors will specify the rights they want to purchase, you might be successful in negotiating the rights purchase. Try to sell one-time rights or first rights, which leaves the whole gamut of reprint and second rights open for you.

**How do I indicate in my query that my article submission has been previously published?**

Simply offer reprint rights and give the name and date of the publication in which the material first appeared.

**Many magazines buy first or second rights—I know what first rights are, but what are second rights?**

Second rights mean simply that an editor buys (typically for a lower price than you originally received) the right to publish an article, story, or poem that has already appeared in another publication.

When a publisher buys first or second rights, it usually means he will consider material that has been sold before as well as original material. Some editors want to buy both first and second rights—which is the right to publish the manuscript first, and then reprint it either in another publication, in an anthology, or in the same magazine several years down the road (when the audience is new). If the publication does want to purchase second rights in addition to first rights, restrict the rights it buys to nonexclusive second (or reprint) rights, so that you can sell the article again as well.

**I sold first and reprint rights for an article to a magazine. Can I sell reprint rights to another publication, or must I wait until the first magazine has used its reprint rights?**

It is permissible to sell reprint rights to the second publication. The only exception would be if you sold the first magazine exclusive reprint rights for a certain period of time. Then you would have to wait until the article was reprinted before reselling.

**If I sell first rights to a magazine article, does a certain amount of time have to pass before I sell reprint rights to a second publication?**

Unless otherwise specified in your contract, the piece you sold may be resold immediately after the first publication publishes it. Actually, you can sell reprint rights any time after you sell first rights, but the second magazine may not publish the article until the owner of the first rights has done so.

**What will I get paid if my article is reprinted in another publication?**

Assuming you sold only first rights to the original publisher, the reprint publisher will either make an offer or ask the writer to suggest a fee. This payment will be a per-word rate or a flat fee, which could be, for example, 50 percent of what the publication would pay for an original article.

**Can I reuse the basic research for one article I sold to a magazine by rewriting and reslanting the original article, adding additional interviews and quotes to it, and selling it as original material to another magazine?**

Research always belongs to the writer, and you are free to rewrite, reslant, and resell articles based on that research as many times as you can. In fact, you owe it to yourself to try for as many sales as possible. Look for different angles, different spins you can give your research to write an article for another publication. One caution: Don't send rewritten articles to publications with slants similar to the one you originally sold to, unless they accept reprints or material from competing markets.

**Under what conditions may I not resell a work?**

You may not sell a published work to another publication if you sold all rights to the piece to the first publication. If the first-rights purchaser has not yet published your manuscript, then you can only sell second rights to a publisher if he agrees to hold off his publication until the holder of first rights has printed the work. You cannot sell a piece that was written as work made for hire. Some people find old pieces of writing and try to have them published under their own name; even if the piece of writing in question is not covered by copyright and is in the public domain, this practice is ethically wrong.

**A public service newspaper column I write in connection with my job has the potential to become a regular syndicated feature. After it has been printed for the purpose of my job, can I sell it elsewhere?**

Companies generally feel that the writing produced as a part of a person's job falls under work-for-hire category and belongs to the company rather than to the writer. However, it's possible that you might be able to work out an agreement with your employer allowing you to have outside use of the material.

**A magazine article a publication rejected was slanted so specifically that I can't find another market. How can I make the article marketable elsewhere?**

Change the slant. Although your particular arrangement of the facts in your article isn't salable to other magazines, revision and rewriting could make it suit the slant of another publication. For example, an article about stress tests with a slant toward executives could be sold to an airline magazine; with the same research, another article could be written for a sports magazine, with a slant toward how stress tests can improve sports performance. In any rewritten article, open the piece with the specific tie-in to that magazine's readership. Amplify the point with extra quotes and information you've gathered through additional research.

## FROM MAGAZINES TO BOOKS

**A magazine published my children's story. I'd now like to offer the story to a book publisher. What's the procedure?**

You can do this only if you've retained the book rights to the story. Check the contract you signed with the magazine. (If the magazine bought all rights, you might negotiate for their return.)

**I wrote and sold a series of short biographical pieces several years ago. I now have the opportunity to expand them into full-length books on the subjects. Do I have to contact the original publisher and get permission?**

You should be able to expand the shorter pieces into more comprehensive biographies, since the facts and specifics of each person's life are not copyrightable. You won't have to contact the publisher for permission unless you intend to use a large portion of the earlier works verbatim and you sold more than first rights—or if you wrote the earlier works as part of a work-for-hire contract.

Several times in the course of my writing career, newspapers have written me for permission to reprint my articles. I've always given my permission, but I've never been paid for this use of my material. Should I request payment when this happens, or should I just be content with the publicity?

If you've never brought up the subject of payment, that's why the newspapers haven't paid you! As long as you give permission without asking for payment, the newspapers aren't going to volunteer to pay you.

I have contributed a great deal of material—free—to our local natural history group's mimeographed magazine. Is it permissible to sell some of these articles? If so, is it necessary to tell the prospective buyer the details about how it has been used?

You are free to make whatever use of it you wish. It would be ethical to advise prospective buyers where and when the articles first appeared.

**In such magazines as *Reader's Digest*, do the editors select the articles from perusal of various magazines, or do authors submit printed articles they believe are suitable for reprint?**

Editors usually select the articles for reprinting, but an author may submit tearsheets to bring his material to their attention. For a magazine's editorial requirements, see its Web site.

**I have sold some verses and articles to a British magazine and would like to sell them to American publications also. Can I still offer first North American rights? Should I mention that these items have already been printed in Britain?**

Yes, you can sell to American publications, but check your British contract—there might be restrictions. Tell the American publications of the previous sale.

**For several years I have edited a newsletter for a club (I am a member). I may want to gather all the material and publish it in a small book. Each issue is published with the notice "Permission to reprint material from this newsletter is granted provided proper credit is given." May I legally gather and print my material without permission from the club? I intend to make it clear that the material came from the newsletter.**

Yes, you can. But in the interest of good relations, you'll probably want to mention it to the other members.

**I recently sold a novel idea for a party invitation to a leading children's magazine. Do the rights purchased by the magazine prohibit me from selling the invitation elsewhere—to a greeting card company, for instance?**

That depends on what the terms of your agreement were. If the magazine bought only first or one-time serial rights, you can resubmit. If you don't know what rights the magazine bought, drop a note to the editor and clarify this point before you submit your idea to another company. Although ideas themselves cannot be copyrighted, the particular presentation of the idea—in this case, a party invitation—is covered by copyright.

**One of my stories was published in a nonpaying magazine. Can I sell it to a paying magazine?**

Yes, but the fact that your first "sale" was to a nonpaying magazine does not change the fact that you granted the nonpaying magazine first rights. A publication can still acquire rights to your manuscript without paying you for them—your compensation was publication.

**A magazine that recently folded had accepted several of my pieces. The pieces were never published. Can I remarket them?**

If the material was not paid for, you are free to market it elsewhere. If, however, the magazine paid for the work, the company that owned the magazine may choose to sell the rights to publish to another investor, who may resurrect the magazine under its original or other name. The deciding factor, then, is whether the material was purchased. If it was, contact the magazine owner and request that the rights be reassigned, in writing, to you.

## WHERE TO FIND OUT MORE

### BOOKS

*The Writer's Digest Handbook of Magazine Article Writing*, edited by Michelle Ruberg, is a comprehensive guide to the craft.

*The Complete Idiot's Guide to Publishing Magazine Articles*, by Sheree Bykofsky, Jennifer Basye Sander, and Lynne Rominger, has the weight of New York literary agent Sheree Bykofsky's experience behind it.

*How to Publish Your Articles*, by Shirley Kawa-Jump, is a solid guide for beginners.

*The Best American Magazine Writing* is an annual collection of the best articles from magazines across the U.S.

## WEB SITES

MediaBistro (www.mediabistro.com) offers news, advice, and tips primarily for freelance writers at magazines. The best info is subscriber-based, but well worth the money.

# HOW DO I START A
# FREELANCE CAREER?

Freelance writers who think only in terms of articles, stories, poems, or books often overlook hundreds of other opportunities for using their writing skills, many of them in their own backyard. If you've been walking too narrow a path as a writer, broaden your horizons with some of the other ideas suggested in this chapter. The range of writing opportunities open to you is limited only by your imagination.

## GETTING STARTED

**For many years, I've had a deep-seated desire to write, and I'd love to break in to the field and make enough money to support my family. How much money can I make freelancing?**

A lot of money can be made by freelancing, but most writers receive fairly little income while they perfect their writing and marketing abilities. There are hundreds of full-time freelancers who make good livings but who started slow—freelancing on the side while holding down a day job. Your best bet is to begin with magazine articles, since the market is large and varied, and fodder for articles is everywhere.

**How long does it take to become a competent, professional freelancer?**

There's no good answer to this question. Writers, even established ones, are continuously developing their skills, improving their style, and learning more about their writing, their markets, and the world. In that sense, you'll never stop striving to better yourself. A good test of your competence is whether your work is being accepted by publications or book publishers you respect. Being unpublished doesn't necessarily mean you don't have writing skills, but sales will probably make you feel more like a professional writer.

### What are the advantages and disadvantages I might face as a full-time freelance writer?

There are many advantages to being a full-time freelance writer. You are your own boss. You control your working hours and, in a sense, the amount of money you make. You practice as a profession the thing you enjoy most. You may have much more opportunity to be creative than if you worked as a staff writer. You choose what you want to write about, and get paid for learning something new through research. You can work at home, and if you're a parent, you can save on childcare expenses. In addition, the research involved in writing can bring you into contact with interesting, stimulating people.

On the other hand, most writers face innumerable rejections (and no income) before making their first sale. To avoid losing faith in yourself and your career at this stage, it helps if you are thick-skinned, self-confident, and persistent. Unlike a job in a company, freelance work does not bring regular paychecks in regular amounts. Further, you are responsible for collecting your own payments. You receive no fringe benefits, such as the insurance and retirement benefits that company employees receive. Being self-employed, you must spend part of your working time on administrative tasks like bookkeeping and filing income tax and social security forms.

Writers usually work alone, and this can be a disadvantage (depending on your personality), especially after a number of days without contact with your colleagues. If you're married, it's best to have a spouse who approves of your career and all it entails, since your irregular working hours and irregular income will affect him or her.

### How are professional writers able to write enough to stay afloat?

Most writers are obsessively attracted to their work; that is, they have an inner urge to write. Professional writers find that the satisfaction their writing brings is enough to outweigh the deadlines, rejections, and other problems they face. On a more practical level, self-employed writers know that if they don't write, they don't eat, so they structure their work as though they had a regular job working for an employer. For example, self-employed writers begin at the same time every day (but not necessarily in the morning), produce the same number of words or pages each day, and establish a place (at home or away from home) to be used exclusively for writing. In addition, they make their working hours known to friends and family to minimize distractions. Finally, professionals get maximum mileage out of the work they produce; they resell articles, use one session of research to fuel two or more related pieces, and employ other tactics to maximize results.

**How much should I earn as a writer before I can feel secure enough to quit my job and become a full-time freelancer? Can writers really make a living freelancing?**

Frequently asked question

It's safe to start thinking about becoming a full-time freelance writer when your freelancing income over a period of several months equals or is greater than the salary earned on your regular job in that same time period. Plenty of writers have succeeded after breaking away from regular full-time employment, but the road to success isn't easy. You'll be better off if you enter into the venture with your eyes wide open to the disadvantages that you'll face. If you quit your job, you'll lose your steady income and all fringe benefits, like health and life insurance, retirement security, and paid vacations. You must also be prepared to discipline yourself to eight or more hours at the keyboard every day. It's not poor writing skills that defeat so many full-time freelancers, but a lack of economic preparedness.

Start planning your switch to self-employment about a year in advance. Begin to cut down on your spending, try to accrue about six months' income in your savings account, and, several months before the break, begin to step up your editorial contacts and magazine sales. A clear view of the difficulties to be encountered in the first months, some penny-pinching, and a lot of hard work are the keys to succeeding in the field of full-time freelance writing.

**I'm not making as much money as I had hoped I would as a freelance writer. Can you suggest other sources of income that might utilize my skills as a writer?**

There are many part-time, seasonal, or one-shot opportunities that will help you during the lean periods of your writing career. For example, a local advertising agency may need someone to write an annual report or do other types of staff-related work for clients. If your town is large enough to attract a convention, you might find out if any groups need someone to staff the press office and act as a liaison with the local media. Are there any local printers in need of competent writing, copyediting, or proofreading for themselves or their customers? If you've had enough experience, you might consider teaching journalism at the high school or community college level.

The first place you should look, though, is online. Many freelance opportunities can be found in your local area or across the globe—these days, it doesn't matter where you are located, as long as you can do a quality job by the deadline. See the end of this chapter for Web sites to help you get started.

## NICHES

**How does a writer get started in theater and movie criticism?**

Start locally with a publication that doesn't have a staff critic. Don't expect to make much money (if any!)—do it because you love it.

**Do I need special training to write book reviews?**

You don't need special training, but you should know how to write interesting, brief reviews that editors will want to publish. Most local newspapers pay little or nothing for reviews, although the reviewer gets to keep the book. When contacting book review editors to see if they can use your work, enclose a sample review you've written of a relatively new book.

**Do the publishers of comic books buy freelance material?**

Different comic book publishers have different policies concerning the purchase of freelance material. Usually the editorial staff determines current needs, then assigns a story to a writer and designates its length.

Beginners in the field often start by writing for fanzines—small, often amateur productions.

**How can I get my comic strip published?**

You can submit to newspaper markets yourself, or you can market your work to various national syndicates. It would probably be best to try to sell your strip to noncompeting local markets first. When submitting to a newspaper or syndicate, you should have finished art samples to submit and perhaps six months of ideas to carry on the strip.

**Is there a market for freelancers interested in researching and writing other people's family histories? I'd like to try that kind of writing, but where do I find potential customers?**

Most of the market for writing family histories comes from the elderly, so you could try placing ads in local newsletters to senior citizens, or on bulletin boards in places you know they gather. If you make yourself known to area museums, librarians, and historians, they can refer inquiries to you.

**Where can I find names and addresses of entertainers needing comedy routines?**

Watch for rising young entertainers on TV comedy shows and contact these newcomers in care of those programs. You might also subscribe to *Variety*, the show-business newspaper that mentions the names and places where lesser-known comedians appear. Write the performers in care of the clubs where they appear.

**I think I would do well as a technical writer. What steps should I take to break in to the field?**

While the goal of creative writing is to entertain, the primary goal of technical writing is the accurate transmission of information. Technical writing, then, can be described as putting complicated information into plain language in a format that is easy to understand. The tone is objective and favors content over style. (This does not mean, however, that you should present the subject in a formal, stunted style.) Above all, technical writing should be concise, complete, clear, and consistent. The best way to achieve all these is to make sure your writing is well organized.

By far the biggest area for technical writers is the computer industry, though there are a wide variety of possible assignments, including preparation of customer letters, utility bills, owner manuals, insurance benefit packages, and even contracts (some states have laws requiring that contracts and insurance policies be written in simple English). In any technical field, writers who can bridge the gap between the engineers who design things and the customers who use them are in high demand.

Technical writers do not necessarily need formal training in the areas they cover. To the contrary, one of the greatest talents a technical writer brings to a project is the ability to take a step back from the technical details and see the subject from a different perspective than the engineers, scientists, and experts. Thus, a technical writer becomes familiar with a subject by interviewing experts, reviewing drawings, studying specifications, and examining product samples.

Technical writers themselves often shy away from the term *freelance writer*, preferring to be known instead as independent contractors or consultants. This probably has a lot to do with the fact that technical writers work mostly with corporations, where the term *independent contractor* sounds more impressive. It's very important to establish and maintain a high degree of credibility when working with firms.

The number of ways to enter the technical field are as varied as the people entering it. If you're cold-calling large companies, you'll want to contact the manager of technical communications or the manager of documentation. Local employment agencies may also be of service.

If you lack experience, build a portfolio by volunteering to write material for a nonprofit organization, or offer to help your colleagues prepare reports and presentations. If you are interested in pursuing this type of work, it is probably a good idea to join the Society for Technical Communication (www.stc.org), where you can network to gain contacts in the industry. Many businesses hire writers from the STC talent pool.

National Technical Employment Services (www.ntes.com) is another good source of work. It provides job listings for contract employees nationwide through its weekly newspaper, *Hot Flash*. The annual subscription rate also includes a quarterly directory of companies as well as a "shopper index" that publishes information about contractors seeking employment in this field.

Some books that might help you learn more about this field include *The Elements of Technical Writing*, by Gary Blake and Robert W. Bly, and *The Tech Writer's Survival Guide*, by Janet Van Wicklen.

## What qualifications does a person need to write advertising copy?

There are two main reasons that an advertising agency or PR firm might hire freelance help. Sometimes expertise is needed, such as in writing about engineering, medicine, accounting, etc. Or the firm must produce a large volume of collateral material, and find themselves in need of freelance help when the workload gets too heavy. This collateral material can take the form of a postcard, brochure, or direct-mail piece. Sometimes a company will look for someone who can shepherd a project from conceptualization to production. Other times they may only need simple copywriting.

Some large- and medium-size organizations may have their own in-house creative department in need of occasional (or not so occasional) assistance. Hospitals are especially open to freelance help because federal cutbacks and outside competition have forced them to walk a financial tightrope.

To land freelance assignments with an advertising agency or public relations firm, you usually need hard experience writing ad copy. However, a willingness to study what's already been produced and for whom, and to hit the streets asking for business, could get you copywriting jobs in a number of different areas. Small businesses, nonprofit groups, and industries that don't have advertising agencies usually rely on outside help for their advertising, and although they pay less than the big ad agencies, they are more willing to work with an inexperienced person.

To learn more about how to start writing copy for corporations, businesses, and organizations, consult two of the best-selling guides for copywriters: *The Well-Fed Writer*, by Peter Bowerman, and *The Copywriter's Handbook*, by Robert W. Bly.

## How can I get started in ghostwriting?

When a book is ghostwritten, the person whose name appears on the book as primary author does little or none of the actual writing. She is merely a source of information—providing content, background, information, and (hopefully) credibility. Typically, this person is a celebrity or someone well respected in her field of expertise. While she has the experience and the name recognition that can make for a best-selling book, she lacks professional writing credentials. As a result, the so-called author relies on a more experienced writer—a ghostwriter—to put her ideas into book form.

The ghostwriter gathers information for the book by interviewing the author, and will often conduct her own research and interview several other sources as well for background material. While each collaboration is different, the author usually will review the manuscript and possibly edit it for content. For their part, ghostwriters may be credited as a co-author or get no visible credit at all.

The arrangement that a ghostwriter walks into is inherently more complex than the typical relationship between a writer and publisher (which is already complex enough). It's easy for misunderstandings to arise between the so-called author and publisher, with the ghostwriter being caught in the middle. In one sense, the ghostwriter is a translator—taking what the author has to offer and trying to deliver what the publisher expects. The best way to diffuse potential conflict is to clearly map out in writing what each party expects from the arrangement.

There are a number of ways to break in to ghostwriting. One is to seek out a rising star in sports, entertainment, business, or politics. Publishers are often in search of new talent and new celebrities. Armed with a collaboration agreement and the right amount of talent, you can sell your services to a publisher.

Very often, successful executives or entrepreneurs look for writers who can help them self-publish a book of their own. The finished books are then distributed through their businesses to clients, co-workers, and relatives. This is a great way to get work and hone your talents, and possibly even make a name for yourself.

**What are the markets for translations of foreign stories, articles, and books?**

Few magazines are interested in translation material, but U.S. book publishers often issue translations of previously published foreign works (and vice versa). To find U.S. publishers of foreign works, look in *Writer's Market*.

**I speak and read French and found a marvelous short story in a foreign magazine. I'd like to translate and sell the story to an American magazine. How do I do it?**

If you have a facility with another language and would like to submit a translation of a foreign short story, you must write to the publication in which the story first appeared and get permission from the author and the publisher to do your translation. Whether you would be required to share payment from tthe American publisher with the original author and/or publisher depends on what arrangements you make with them. It's always best to clarify this point before you approach any American editor, so there is no delay if she is interested in your idea.

**What qualifications do I need to write greeting card verse?**

You need nothing more than the ability to study existing greeting card material and to provide appropriate copy to greeting card editors. Greeting card verse sells best if your ideas are original and carry a me-to-you message in a conversational tone. Enthusiasm is important, since writing verse for greeting card publishers is not as easy as it might seem. Companies that publish greeting cards can be found through the WritersMarket.com subscription service.

**Are recipes copyrighted?**

Simple lists of ingredients cannot be copyrighted, but the directions for how to make something from those ingredients can be copyrighted.

**A friend of mine says hobby magazines are a good place to start getting published. Are they?**

If you have ever designed a pattern for an embroidery project, made your own Christmas tree ornaments, or built a home darkroom, then craft, hobby, and handyman magazines might want to hear how you did it, step by step. Since these how-to articles are relatively simple to write (and you probably already subscribe to magazines that buy such pieces), many beginners find them an easy way to get started writing.

Then you can move on to articles that require more research, organization, and writing skills.

**Some authors rewrite unusual news stories to submit to other markets. Are there laws against using and reusing ideas culled from newspapers?**

News items are facts open to anyone's interpretation, but feature articles usually have a specific angle or slant, and involve the research, selectivity, and interpretations of the individual writer. The expression of these elements is protected by the overall copyright on the paper or by the syndicate, if it is a syndicated feature. You may write a new article using the *facts* of the story, or use the original item to suggest a new slant and new research—in short, a new article.

## FREELANCING FOR BOOK PUBLISHERS

**Do publishers use freelancers to index the books they put out? How can I get started in work like this?**

Ideally, a book should be indexed by an expert, preferably the author herself, but many authors are not interested in learning this specific and tedious skill, so the publisher assigns the index on behalf of the author. You must have experience to get indexing assignments. To have been an editor or librarian helps. To learn more about the profession, visit the American Society of Indexers at www.asindexing.org.

**What's the difference between copyediting and proofreading?**

A copyeditor deals with a manuscript before it is typeset. She makes sure the manuscript makes sense and reads well. Names and facts are verified, which means that a copyeditor must have some background in the subject her editing assignment covers. She looks for consistency in spelling, abbreviations, and numbers, making sure they comply with the publishing house standards.

A proofreader usually compares typeset page proofs with the original manuscript to make sure that nothing is omitted, added, or changed. She also makes sure that the typesetter has followed specifications for typeface, style, and margins. The proofreader must be on the lookout for mistakes in the original manuscript.

### Are there book publishers who hire freelancers to do copyediting and proofreading work?

Larger publishers usually have freelance work available—check listings in *Writer's Market* or *Literary Market Place* (*LMP*) to locate publishers who produce one hundred or more books per year. These houses are probably your best prospects for work.

Whenever you apply for freelancing projects, specify the fields in which you have enough background to be able to edit someone else's writing. You may be asked to take a test to prove your skills. To learn the basics of copyediting and proofreading, you'll need to take a class or workshop to get started; try visiting the Web site of *Copy Editor* newsletter (www.copyeditor.com) or MediaBistro (www.mediabistro.com) to find workshops online or in your area.

### I write nonfiction, proofread, and edit copy. How can I advertise my services?

There are many ways to advertise your editorial services, both in print and through the Internet. You can have brochures printed describing your services and mail them to businesses or organizations that require editorial services (most businesses need some form of editorial services, whether it's editing menus or writing company newsletters). You can also post business cards in public places, including university and library bulletin boards. It may also be worth your time and effort to run classified ads in your local newspapers and in writers magazines.

The Internet is probably the easiest way to start. Look at sites such as:

AllFreelanceWork (www.allfreelancework.com)

Elance Online (www.elance.com)

PoeWar (www.poewar.com)

SunOasis (www.sunoasis.com)

The Write Jobs (www.writejobs.com)

WritersWeekly (www.writersweekly.com)

You can also post your résumé on various listservs and bulletin boards (places online where people chat, interact, and post messages).

Although you might not be directly promoting your editorial business, you can make yourself and your services familiar to the public by becoming involved with organizations as a volunteer, or by accepting public-speaking engagements for businesses and organizations.

## FILLERS

**What is meant by filler material? What is it used for?**

A filler is any of a variety of short pieces of writing, including tips, anecdotes, short humor, recipes, proverbs, household hints, unusual trivia, brain teasers, puzzles, insightful quotes, and news clippings. Although editors originally used them to fill empty spaces at the ends of columns, fillers are now often used as regular magazine features. Because they are short and focus on one point, fillers are good practice for beginning writers and give novices a greater chance of being published.

One can find ideas for fillers anywhere, from daily reading to strange road signs. Everyday experiences often provide humor or helpful tips, but you may have to look hard at what's going on around you to see something worthwhile for publication. If you think you might like to write fillers, study the fillers in several magazines to get an idea of what editors are looking for, and go to it!

**Some magazine editors say they buy anecdotes. What is an anecdote?**

An anecdote is a short narrative slice of life, a description of a particular incident, usually biographical, autobiographical, or stemming from something the author has observed. Anecdotes may employ humor, dialogue, or unexpected endings to share insight or illustrate a point. Successful anecdotes will evoke laughter, surprise, sympathy, or some other emotional reaction on the part of the reader. Due to their brevity, they work quite well as fillers. Here is one of many good examples that can be found in *Reader's Digest*: "A woman who works for the state of Louisiana got a call from a man who paused when she told him the name of her agency. He then asked her to repeat it again. 'It's the Governor's Office for Elderly Affairs,' she told him again. There was another pause. 'For gosh sakes, sign me up,' he said. 'I didn't do too well when I was young.'" (This anecdote came from Smiley Anders of the Baton Rouge *Morning Advocate*.)

When writing an anecdote, make sure that your narration is uncomplicated and free from extraneous detail. Since description has to be short, every word used should be essential to the picture. The impact of the anecdote comes with a good punchy ending.

### What is a newsbreak?

A newsbreak is a newsworthy event or item. For example, an opening of a new retail shoe store in a town might be a newsbreak for a shoe trade journal that publishes news items of new openings. Some publications (such as the *New Yorker*) use newsbreaks in a different sense—that is, to indicate a typo or an error in reporting that appears in a printed news story. Such newsbreaks—followed by tongue-in-cheek editorial commentary (known as a tag line)—are bought from contributors and used in the *New Yorker* and other publications as filler items.

### Is it okay to submit identical fillers to several markets?

There's no reason why you can't, as long as you don't submit identical fillers to markets with common audiences. Editors of magazines with similar readerships don't want to see a filler they just bought from you published in a competitive magazine. You may want to indicate that the material is going to more than one publication at the same time by noting "This is a simultaneous submission to publications with differing readership."

**I have written several anecdotes and other fillers, from my own personal experience. How can I find magazines that might be interested in buying these fillers?**

Successful marketing is a combination of writing what you want to write and what magazine editors want to print. Read *Writer's Market* to find magazines that publish what you'd like to sell (anecdotes, for example) and then look at copies of those magazines to help you get a feeling for the style, content, and audience they cater to. Knowing what an editor is looking for before you send in your work will save you from the quick rejection you'd get if, for example, you sent your personal anecdotes to a political magazine that only publishes bureaucratic bloopers as fillers. Your chances of making a sale will be greatly enhanced if you are careful about deciding where to send your work.

**How much money can I hope to get for my published fillers?**

Depending on the magazine, the filler, and how it is used, the average payment can be nothing at all (except maybe free product), to a hundred dollars or more. Magazines that place a lot of emphasis on filler items, such as *Reader's Digest*, pay several hundred dollars for a published item. See *Writer's Market* for payment rates of other magazines.

**Several months ago I sent a few jokes and a puzzle to a magazine. I have heard nothing from the editor so far. What kind of reply can I expect from the editor, and how long should I wait before inquiring?**

Although some editors may hold a filler for six months before using it, if you have not received any sort of acknowledgment within two months, you should not inquire, but rather send your piece elsewhere. Due to the large volume of fillers that many editors receive, replying to individual contributors is often impossible. If you do receive a rejection slip, it may be very dry and to the point, or it may encourage you to keep trying.

**I have written several hundred original epigrams and poetic proverbs that I believe are good. Would it be more profitable for me to submit them in manuscript form for book publication or in small lots to magazines?**

Since it is usually easier for a beginner to sell to a magazine than to a book publisher, it might be to your advantage to send these fillers to magazine markets. If possible, try to retain book rights so that eventually you can publish them as a collection in book form.

**I am just getting started as a writer and have submitted some children's sayings and anecdotes to bring in a little extra income. Some of the material in them would fit well in a couple of larger pieces I am working on. Is it okay for me to incorporate these fillers into my other work?**

Unless you sold the magazine all rights, the magazine has claim only to the first publishing of your work, and you are free to reuse it at any time. If the magazine bought all rights, you would have to request the editor's permission to reuse the material.

## GOING ONLINE

Ten years ago, freelance writers had to rely on market directories, personal contacts, and a bit of luck to find new opportunities and projects. Today, the Internet probably provides more opportunities for freelance work (and research and ideas) than you'll ever be able to pursue. It does take a critical eye, though, to ferret out the quality projects and information. Here are a few tips to help you get started.

**Where do I find writing opportunities online?**

When talking about online markets, we can divide the opportunities into several categories.

**Print publications.** Most traditional magazines have online counterparts that publish original content. To find out if a print magazine does publish original online content, check its Web site or submission guidelines.

**Electronic publications.** Online-only publications may not pay as much as print publications (or may not pay at all), but they can provide a beginner with good experience. Some online-only publications that pay for content are listed in directories like WritersMarket.com.

**E-newsletters.** Many electronic newsletters accept content from freelancers. Check with the editors and see if they accept freelance material.

**Corporate Web sites.** It's easy to research companies and businesses that might need freelancers; those that are known for hiring freelancers usually have information posted especially for them.

**Freelance writing sites.** The most popular sites for freelancers contain market information or postings from people looking to hire writers and editors. The largest circulating e-newsletter for freelancers is Writers Weekly; sign up at www.writersweekly.com.

### What's the difference between writing for the Web and writing for print?

People read copy differently on the Web. They read more slowly, they scan, their eyes bounce around the screen. As a result, you must adjust your writing style to suit. Keep your writing focused and brief. If you drone on too long, readers will be tempted to click away. Break longer sentences into shorter sentences, and break stories into chunks, with catchy subheads.

## FINDING A WRITING CAREER

Being a full-time freelance writer is a challenge, and many writers opt to use their writing skill to bring home a regular salary. People who seek full-time writing or editing jobs usually traverse one of two routes. They attend journalism school, or they acquire a good liberal arts background. There are exceptions, of course: Some start out in science and wind up in scientific or technical publishing; others turn from teaching to corporate communications.

### What can a beginning writer do to get a job on a small newspaper staff?

Try to place some freelance features with the newspaper you'd like to work for, so the editor can see that (1) you know what a good feature is, and (2) you write well. You can also try supplying the editor with news items from a section of the newspaper circulation area that is not well covered. Show samples of your work that are similar to what the paper publishes.

**I'd like to work on a newspaper but am having trouble finding any openings. What other similar career choices do I have?**

The corporate world is always looking for people to edit and write company publications or run the PR machine. Charitable and nonprofit organizations also need grant writers, media people, and people with good communications skills. As long as there are words, you can find jobs. To fully explore your career options as a writer, take a look at *I'm an English Major—Now What?* by Tim Lemire. Even if you aren't an English major, this book can help you use your writing skills to find a career.

**What are the advantages of working for a magazine versus working for a newspaper?**

One of the major differences is that newspapers work against much shorter deadlines than magazines; deadlines are often a matter of hours for a newspaper as opposed to weeks or months for a magazine. A writer who doesn't work well under this kind of pressure is better off working for a magazine. The difference in deadlines means that magazine writers have a chance to develop their ideas into more in-depth articles, and newspaper writers must be concerned with quick, up-to-the-minute reporting.

**What kinds of jobs are available in the book publishing industry?**

Although duties vary with the size and scope of each publishing house, the jobs most often available are for editorial assistants, production assistants, and publicists. To learn the basics of book publishing jobs and the range of opportunities available, visit www.bookjobs.com, a site sponsored by the Association of American Publishers.

When looking for work in a publishing house, read the job postings at the *Publishers Weekly* site (www.publishersweekly.com), MediaBistro (www.mediabistor.com), and PublishersMarketplace (www.publishersmarketplace.com). The job descriptions and requirements should give you an idea of how much experience you need and what skills are expected.

# WHERE TO FIND OUT MORE

## BOOKS

*The Well-Fed Writer: Financial Self-Sufficiency as a Freelance Writer in Six Months or Less*, by Peter Bowerman, provides helpful insight into how to earn money from corporate clients.

*The Wealthy Writer: How to Earn a Six-Figure Income as a Freelance Writer*, by Michael Meanwell, gives thorough information about the highest-paying freelance opportunities many freelance writers overlook. It offers invaluable tips on how to run your writing business, from marketing yourself to outsourcing work when you become too busy to take on every job you're offered.

*Make a Real Living as a Freelance Writer: How to Win Top Writing Assignments*, by Jenna Glatzer, is an excellent guide for novices considering the freelance life.

*Ready, Aim, Specialize! Create Your Own Writing Specialty and Make More Money*, by Kelly James-Enger, is a good guide for someone who is interested in a very specific subject area, like technology, business, or science.

*The Renegade Writer: A Totally Unconventional Guide to Freelance Writing Success*, by Linda Formichelli and Diana Burrell, tells you how to break the traditional rules of freelance writing, with style and panache.

*The ASJA Guide to Freelance Writing: A Professional Guide to the Business, for Nonfiction Writers of All Experience Levels*, by Samuel G. Freedman, includes contributions from members of the American Society of Journalists and Authors (ASJA) and will instruct you on all aspects of the freelance business.

## WEB SITES

Absolute Write (www.absolutewrite.com) offers writing instruction and keeps tabs on upcoming contests and deadlines. Delivers two free e-newsletters, one specifically on markets, and has excellent message boards (Absolute Write Water Cooler).

WritersWeekly (www.writersweekly.com) is a popular place to learn how to make more money freelancing, and to find new opportunities.

Writing-World (www.writing-world.com) is hosted by author and freelancer Moira Allen.

FreelanceWriting (www.freelancewriting.com) is a collection of resources for freelancers.

# 13

## How do i conduct effective research?

American playwright Wilson Mizner said, "When you take stuff from one writer, it's plagiarism; but when you take it from many writers, it's research." Today's writer-researcher has at his fingertips not only the traditional resources of books, magazine articles, and directories of experts' names and addresses, but a host of new resources on the Internet that can save him hours of tedious manual searching.

It's been said a good writer doesn't have to know much; he just has to know people who do. Learning who these people are, how to find them, and what to ask them are among the basic tasks of a freelance or nonfiction writer. Fiction writers, too, need to verify facts presented in their works, maintain historical accuracy, and sometimes even discuss the personalities of their characters with psychologists. No matter what the subject of your article, story, or book (or even your poem), there's probably a source available that can help you add insight and authority to your manuscript.

### Where should I start my research?

To find the most comprehensive up-to-date information on practically any subject, start with the Internet, where valuable resources await. Even if the information you need is not available online (or not verifiable online), you can search for the organizations, companies, libraries, museums, and other experts who can help you find or confirm that information. Basic starting places: The U.S. government site FedStats (www.fedstats.gov) features many government statistics and reports on specialized topics, and RefDesk (www.refdesk.com) is an essential bookmark for most researchers and librarians.

Second to the Internet should be the public library and librarians. Many accept phone calls from patrons asking research questions, so long as the questions are specific and can be answered quickly. Libraries at large universities are likely to have more resources available than your local library and are usually open to the public.

Other sources include businesses, organizations, and professional associations. Businesses routinely make information available through their public relations offices, and many trade associations and organizations can give you information or steer you to an expert in your topic. Most associations and organizations can be found online, and an individual association site will offer detailed information about the association and the services it offers.

### How can I find contact information for authors and/or well-known persons for requesting interviews?

Book authors can generally be reached by contacting them through their publicists; the publicist's contact information (and specific instructions for contacting authors) can usually be found on the publisher's or author's Web site. The best way to locate contact information for anyone else is through an Internet search.

### How can I get quotes from experts?

If you're having trouble finding an expert on your topic—say you need someone intimately knowledgeable with the effects of deforestation but don't have any contacts—use one of the many reference Web sites, such as ProfNet (www.profnet.com) or RefDesk, to find the right people. Also, JournalismNet has a page dedicated to finding experts online at www.journalismnet.com/experts. If you already have an expert in mind, you should contact him by regular mail or e-mail, explain the subject matter of your article and the magazine for which you're writing, and ask your questions. Also, ask the experts to suggest other people who may be able to help you in your research.

### How can I contact the author of a magazine article I recently read?

You can either write to the author in care of the magazine in which the article appeared, or you can e-mail the author directly. If you choose to write the author in care of the magazine, you can find the address of the magazine's editorial office on the magazine's masthead or contents page. Some publications have their subscriptions fulfilled at a different address, so be sure you write to the editorial address, not the circulation or advertising address. Most editors will forward mail addressed to contributing writers, but will not give the home addresses of their contributors.

If you prefer to e-mail the author, check his bio at the end of the article for his e-mail address, or try an Internet search.

### What's the difference between a primary source and a secondary source?

A primary source—or primary research—provides the writer with original, firsthand information. A primary source can be the writer's own experience and observation; another person (such as an interview subject); or personal papers, correspondence, diaries, or manuscripts relating to the person or subject being studied. Primary research is closer to the subject, and therefore preferable to secondary research, which is based entirely on what others have written in newspapers, books, or magazines about the primary sources. For instance, if your topic is former president Bill Clinton, a primary source would be a letter written by Clinton. A secondary source would be a book or article written *about* Clinton. If you use only secondary sources, you run the risk of a source's research being inaccurate or containing misquotations or other errors. Secondary sources should be used for gathering supporting information and background material for an article.

### In doing a round-up article in which I quote the opinions of several different people, should I obtain the consent of the individuals included when the information is not obtained by interview?

While it probably isn't necessary to obtain permission to quote brief opinions from published sources, it's usually best to verify published quotes to avoid repeating another writer's error.

I'm writing a piece that requires a lot of research, and I don't know how to keep all my notes and sources straight. Is there a solution?

Every writer develops his own system of organization, so there is no right way to prepare your research. But it's important to develop *some* system to keep you from wasting time.

Generally, you'll want to think through your article's requirements or elements from beginning to end and decide what kind of information you'll need—such as statistics, advice from experts, and illustrative anecdotes. Make a list of pertinent questions that must be answered in the course of the article, as well as secondary questions that are beneficial but not crucial. Decide what your probable sources are, and list them in the order in which you should consult them. Adjust your research plans to fit your schedule (how much time can you spend on this article?); budget (is the publisher covering any of your costs?); and the scope of the topic. Do your homework early, break everything into very small tasks that are easy to complete (and won't overwhelm you), and adhere to a schedule. As you gain experience, your system of research will develop and you'll gain confidence and increase your ability to cut your research down to size.

## FLASHBACK QUESTION

In doing research in libraries for story material, copying long passages is a slow laborious job. Is there any known method that is faster?

Talk to your local librarian about the availability of copying machines (such as Xeros) or perhaps about photostating the material you need.

When I'm finished researching an article, I have so much raw material I'm overwhelmed by the sheer bulk of it and don't know where to begin. How can I distill my research to a manageable size?

Most writers develop a very personalized way of dealing with research, but here's a step-by-step plan to help you get started. First, reduce the bulk of material you've gathered by getting rid of resources you aren't going to use anymore and taking notes on any material you've gathered from various publications, instead of keeping those entire magazines and newspapers on your desk. Next, decide what information is essential to your article, and what's only tangentially related to your topic, filing the latter for future use. Then divide your material into subject categories. Some writers use highlighters to code the information, while others use card file folders, but many writers cut or copy and paste bits of information into computer files for saving or filing. (When you do a lot of copying and pasting into electronic documents—especially when you're taking copy from the Web—make sure you keep careful records of where the material came from; sloppiness can lead to plagiarism or just plain chaos when you're attempting to attribute sources.)

**What are databases, and how can they be useful to a writer?**

A database is a large collection of specialized information organized for rapid search and retrieval, and can save a writer tremendous amounts of legwork. One of the most well-known databases is LexisNexis (www.lexis-nexis.com), which houses the world's largest collection of public records, opinions, legal documents, news, and business information.

The best databases are rarely accessible for free; you usually have to go through a library or university computer (or have a library membership or student ID) in order to access them. Don't let that discourage you; the benefits will far outweigh any inconvenience you might encounter, especially if you're seeking particularly specialized information.

**I'm currently working on a novel set in the eighteenth century. How do I research it?**

Start your historical research with a relatively simple book on that period, or with a general history of the country in which you've decided to set your novel. Even if you're not writing about an actual historical figure, biographies can be a valuable source of information on the manners of the time.

To check on the customs, foods, clothing, and technology of the period, look for chat groups online or Web sites dedicated to the time period (in addition to any books). You're almost never the only one searching for information about a given topic, and you're likely to find someone generous enough to share the resources they found most helpful. If the Internet doesn't turn up anything useful, look to your librarian—he can be your best friend when in a time of resource need.

**I'm doing some research using turn-of-the-century books and material from state archives, including some family papers. Since the material is a hundred years old, can I use it in my manuscript? Would it be covered by copyright?**

The state archives should pose no problem for you if they aren't copyrighted. However, the family papers could possibly raise the question of invasion of privacy, if any members of the family are living. It would be a good idea for you to verify with any descendants whether they would object to your use of the material.

**I'm researching an article, and some of my sources disagree on several points. What can I do about this?**

One of the most difficult tasks in writing a nonfiction article or book is reconciling information received from different sources. In some cases, the writer's own research gives him enough knowledge about the subject to judge who is right. But other times, it becomes necessary for the writer to communicate the conflicting information to the conflicting sources, letting each answer the questions raised by the other. For example, if you were writing about the effects of cigarette smoke on nonsmokers, and two researchers gave you contradictory statements, you could call or write each and say "[Name], of [professional affiliation], disagrees with your position," quoting the other expert. Then ask, "Could you comment on that?" By including such comments in your finished piece, you allow readers to decide for themselves which source is credible. In some cases, both sources will be equally credible, and readers will come to the conclusion that enough research has not yet been done on the subject to reach a definitive decision.

**Is it possible to overresearch an article?**

When researching, it's usually better to wind up with too much information than not enough. The only way you can really overresearch an article is by using further research as an excuse to avoid actually writing the piece. In other cases, the trick is not to research less, but to use your research wisely. Sometimes you'll end up with a stack of material several inches thick, and you'll realize you can never use it all. That's when you must begin the long process of weeding out information, choosing only the material most pertinent to your topic. Material not used in the article might shed some light on another angle of the subject or provide human interest. That material might be developed into a sidebar, a short feature appearing within an article, providing more depth or additional factual information that would not fit well into the body of the article. You could also use the extra material to write another article on the same subject, using a different approach and slanting it to another, noncompeting magazine.

**Most books state on the copyright page: "No part of this publication may be reproduced, stored in or introduced into a retrieval system, or transmitted, in any form or by any means (electronic, mechanical, photocopying, recording, or otherwise), without the prior written permission of both the copyright owner and publisher." Does the warning mean I can't copy material for my private research without first contacting the publisher?**

If the photocopy is for your research only, and you do not intend to reproduce the copied page in your article, then using the copy machine is as legal as taking notes. However, if you intend to quote much of the material verbatim in your manuscript, you will need permission. (See chapter seventeen for more information.)

**Is there any way a library can find out if another library has a book I need?**

Yes, if your library has access to the Online Computer Library Center (OCLC), a service which links the information centers of more than fifty thousand libraries in eighty-four countries and territories. OCLC allows its members to locate, catalog, and lend library materials. It provides libraries with catalog card index files, helps them exchange information, and lends books to member libraries. OCLC's central office, in Dublin, Ohio, keeps the location listings of library material. Its database contains material in hundreds of languages and dialects, and OCLC adds more than thirty thousand titles to its file every week. Visit their site at www.oclc.org.

## ONLINE SEARCH

No doubt the Internet provides many wonderful shortcuts when conducting research. The challenge is sorting through a lot of junk to find meaningful information. Knowing a few good search sites and databases can save you a lot of time. A few helpful ones are listed below.

Cross-check information if you are not sure of the source. You can be fairly confident of the accuracy and fairness of information you uncover through academic, library, and government sites, but if you're looking at private or personal sites, always question the accuracy (even if several of these sites agree).

- Since 1995, RefDesk (www.refdesk.com) has been one of the best indexes of information available for free on the Web; every writer should bookmark it.
- AcademicInfo (www.academicinfo.net) is an online directory of twenty-five thousand handpicked educational resources.
- InfoMine (http://infomine.ucr.edu) is a database of scholarly Internet resource collections.
- LibrarySpot (www.libraryspot.com) includes a comprehensive listing of libraries, references, lists, and more.
- The American Library Association often issues a list of the best Web sites, which is always worth reviewing—visit www.ala.org.

## WHERE TO FIND OUT MORE

### BOOKS

Since 1995, *The Craft of Research*, by Wayne C. Booth, Gregory G. Colomb, and Joseph M. Williams, has served as an essential guide to researching effectively, then incorporating the research into your writing.

## WEB SITES

In addition to the sites listed above, try these:

The Librarians' Internet Index (www.lii.org) allows you to search only Web sites that librarians trust.

Robert Niles's home page (www.robertniles.com/data) offers a helpful lists of research sites, divided by categories of interest.

If you feel overwhelmed by Internet searches or don't feel you're very good at searching, try taking a free online tutorial offered by UC Berkeley, Finding Information on the Internet (www.lib.berkeley.edu/TeachingLib/Guides/Internet/FindInfo.html).

# 14

# HOW DO I CONDUCT
# A STRONG INTERVIEW?

It's been said that a good interview is just like a good conversation. That's not so. In a good conversation, it's polite for the folks involved to ask questions of each other and to listen with equal interest to the answers. It's a time for mutual discovery and communication.

But an interview is a lopsided interaction. The interviewee probably doesn't care much about the person popping the questions, and the interviewer is probably doing more than simply enjoying herself. Interviewing is, after all, work.

It shouldn't feel like work, however, and that's what the interviews-are-conversations theory is all about. If a person being interviewed feels as if she is talking to an old friend, the interview is more likely to produce powerful anecdotes, colorful quotes, and revealing information. Yet, before a source feels comfortable with an interviewer, the interviewer has to relax—a tough trick for many beginners.

In an effort to calm your nervous stomach, what follows are general guidelines for planning and conducting fruitful interviews.

## BEFORE THE INTERVIEW

### What is the protocol for arranging an interview?

For an in-person interview, phone or e-mail the subject for an appointment. If the subject does not return your calls, send a short note introducing yourself, requesting an interview, and telling her you will call on a specific date to set up a meeting. Be ready to be flexible on the date and time of the interview. You will need to accommodate your subject's schedule. For a phone interview, follow the same procedure—but be prepared to conduct the interview on the spot should your subject say, "How about right now?"

### What are the best places to conduct an interview?

Find a quiet setting where you can talk without frequent interruptions. Your subject's office—if she has one—can fit the bill, but may also be full of distractions. Office conference rooms, hotel lobbies and meeting rooms, libraries, parks, and quiet cocktail lounges are all good possibilities. Restaurants may prove too distracting to maintain the conversation (also, clattering silverware and the talking of other diners may render your tape recording indecipherable).

Frequently
asked question

### Should I query an editor before or after I ask the interviewee for her permission to be interviewed? And what should I do if I can't deliver an article because my interviewee wouldn't grant me an interview?

It is best to first get an editor's okay on an interview assignment before asking the subject for an interview. A subject is more willing to give you the time for an interview if she knows an editor is seeking the interview for her pages. But if a subject is willing to be interviewed without a commitment from an editor, you can also work that way. If a subject refuses to give you the interview, just drop a note to the editor and say that the interview was refused. Editors understand this. If a subject refuses the interview because you don't have an editor interested yet, then tell the editor this, also. She may then give you a firm assignment for the interview.

### How much research do I need to do for an interview?

The late historian Cornelius Ryan claimed that one of the rules of writing is "Never interview anyone without knowing 60 percent of the answers." He said that the person being interviewed has done her homework, so the writer should be equally prepared. Research is the best way to discover what you need to learn in the interview and the best way to learn it. It's always better to be overprepared than to run out of questions before you run out of time.

The main purpose of research is to enable yourself to talk and ask questions intelligently on any topic the interviewee raises. If you take the time to do your research, the interviewee can expect an intelligent discussion of the subject, which is always more interesting for an interviewee than talking to someone about a topic on which she is uninformed.

To research an interview, you will use many of the same techniques discussed in chapter thirteen. You should research the interviewee's background and any topics you think might be discussed. For a profile, prepare by interviewing around the subject, talking to friends, family, and co-workers to learn more about the person before you actually meet her.

Researching for an interview takes time, and you may not make use of even half the information you gather. But a thorough knowledge of the subject can help you craft good, specific questions and get the quotes that will make your work more lively and salable.

## OVERCOMING FEARS

**I am interested in writing magazine articles, but the thought of interviewing someone scares me. I know I have to interview to write successfully. How can I teach myself this method of gathering information?**

It is common for beginning writers to feel uneasy about interviewing. One way to combat this feeling is to begin writing about topics that will permit you to interview people you already know and with whom you feel comfortable. For instance, an article about how parents handle their children's problems would permit you to interview a variety of friends, neighbors, and relatives. If you live in a small town, talking to the local shopkeepers can give you information on how changes in economic conditions affect small business owners. Working on these types of articles will give you the experience of interviewing and help build your confidence for handling tougher subjects.

Interviewing is a skill that grows with time and practice. Remember that your job is to *listen* to the conversation and keep it flowing without monopolizing it. Prepare your questions before you interview and try to design them so that your interviewee will do most of the talking, and you will soon begin to feel more confident in your abilities.

**I'm a beginner with no credits. Why would an expert agree to be interviewed by me?**

An expert is only recognized as such by being visible and making her opinions known. That means, in part, being available to be interviewed. So it is in the expert's interest to be interviewed by writers. Most people you interview will be flattered that you're interested in their opinion and will not ask about your credentials. If they do ask, plainly state the article assignment you're working on, and leave it at that. Be confident and do not mention or apologize for your lack of experience. You'll be surprised at the number of "important" people who are willing to talk with you.

**I don't have any national publishing credits, but I've published in my local newspaper for a few years. I find interview subjects reluctant to speak to me because of my lack of credits. How can I change this?**

But you do have credits—in the form of your clippings from your newspaper experience. You can tell potential interviewees you've been writing for your local newspaper for years, or you can tell them you've done some research on them and would like to take a little of their time to make sure your facts are accurate. If you show confidence, you'll convince most people to consent to interviews.

After I finish research for an interview, is it necessary to write a list of questions before the interview takes place? How many questions?

By deciding on a particular list of must-ask questions, the interviewer makes sure she doesn't conclude the interview without obtaining all the necessary information for the article. However, the interviewer should pursue any interesting path down which her subject wanders; the list of prepared questions is a set of boundaries, rather than a hard-and-fast road map. In John Brady's *The Craft of Interviewing*, freelancer Edward Linn says, "The list of questions and the logical sequence invariably disappear very quickly. If they don't, you're in trouble."

To decide on a list of questions, first choose your angle—or let your editor tell you what she has in mind. Then look at your research and decide what you must learn from the interviewee. The number of questions you need will vary depending on the topic of the article, the interviewee, and in some cases, the amount of time an interviewee allows. The more questions you prepare, though, the better chance of leaving the interview with the essential answers plus additional interesting information.

Structure the outline of the interview to follow a logical course. You might open with easy, mechanical questions, such as those that would establish the interviewee's relation to or view of the topic, then move on to knottier questions or more thoughtful probes, such as asking what she thinks about someone else's particular criticism of her actions or point of view. At the end, ask "Is there anything we've not talked about that you'd like to comment on?"

## IN THE INTERVIEW

**What are some good techniques to remember when I'm conducting an interview? How can I make sure the interview is productive and interesting for both myself and the subject?**

First, try to build rapport with the interviewee. This serves two purposes: It not only makes your subject feel more at ease and more receptive to questions, it can help relax you and keep the interview flowing smoothly. Be a little formal at the start, rather than jumping into familiarity right away. (If you're doing an in-person interview, don't take liberties you wouldn't want a guest of yours to take, and remember that first impressions count, so dress professionally and avoid drawing attention to yourself.)

Don't talk too much at the outset. Encourage the interviewee to do as much of the talking as possible. Be flexible and follow the subject's lead.

If an answer is very general, don't interrupt, but follow it up. Follow-up questions not only secure specific details and anecdotes, they reveal a lot about the interviewee's personality and bolster rapport by demonstrating your genuine interest in what she has to say. Reciting an anecdote you have previously heard about the subject will often nudge the interviewee into providing further human-interest comments, in turn giving you a good anecdote to use to open or close your article.

Don't overlook your article's need for specific details, anecdotes, and examples. You must request these comments directly. Ask such leading questions as: "Can you tell me about the first time that happened to you?" and "Do you remember a time that strategy worked for you?" When a subject rambles or is unclear, place the onus on yourself by saying "I'm sorry, but I don't quite understand that last point. Could you explain it for me?"

**Sometimes when I'm setting up interviews for an article, I encounter people who are reluctant to talk about even the most innocuous of topics. The material isn't particularly controversial; they just aren't used to being interviewed and don't know what to do. How do I handle these shy interviewees?**

People may be fearful of being misinterpreted or shown in an unfavorable light. Sympathy to the subject's quandary, friendly understanding, and professional performance on your part can overcome barriers.

Scholars and physicians can be reluctant subjects, since many of them view publicity as unprofessional. When faced with this attitude, point out the need for public information in the subject's area of expertise. Your interest and sincere enthusiasm can be the catalysts that spark the interviewee into sharing her knowledge.

Persistence pays off. If you become a more or less ubiquitous presence around a busy subject, you may find that she will make time for the interview in her packed schedule. John Brady tells of tracking down author Jessica Mitford at a university seminar. By "hanging around a lot," he found the right time to get the interview; although her schedule was filled each minute of the seminar, he drove her to the airport and got the interview on the way. Recommendations from the friends and co-workers of reluctant interviewees can also be an aid to getting the time with them.

If none of these techniques work and the interview is necessary to the story, tell the subject that her comments are crucial to the story and she probably will appear in the article anyway, but you'd rather get her opinions firsthand.

**I'm not sure whether to take written notes or use a tape recorder when conducting an interview. What are the pros and cons of each?**

Both methods have their good and bad points. Tape recorders and digital recorders allow an interviewer to concentrate on conducting the interview and observing the interviewee and the surroundings. They allow you to ask more questions in less time and concentrate more on the replies you receive, listening for possible follow-ups. If the subject matter is at all controversial, a recorded interview is your proof that an interviewee said what she said in the context being quoted. If you must interview a subject in a situation in which it would be difficult for you to take notes, such as over lunch, a recorder can be a real lifesaver. However, there's always the possibility the tape recorder will malfunction when you need it most. Also, some interview subjects are uncomfortable with recorders and will not talk as freely as with someone who unobtrusively takes notes.

Also, most reporters caution against relying *too* much on the recorder; they suggest augmenting it with some note-taking. If you take notes, you can mark where in the interview a subject says something particularly provocative or relevant. Taking highlight notes is also insurance in case the recorder or tape breaks.

Keep your interview tapes and notes in a safe place after an article has been published. An editor may need them after publication if an interviewee claims, "I've been misquoted."

**I would like to use a tape recorder when I interview. Should I ask the interviewee beforehand if she minds, or should I simply plop it down without a word, turn it on, and proceed with the interview as if it didn't exist?**

It's more courteous to ask the subject first if she minds your using the tape recorder to make sure her statements are recorded as accurately as possible. Few interviewees will object.

**I have a gadget that records telephone conversations. When I conduct a phone interview, do I have to inform the person that she's being taped?**

Yes, that is always the safest course of action. Advising an interviewee that the conversation is being recorded for the sake of accuracy—and recording her agreement on tape—at the beginning of the conversation is the best defense against problems. No federal law prohibits taping of telephone conversations by either party as long as the taping is not being done for an illegal purpose.

## TOUCHY TOPICS

**How do I interview someone about information she might be reluctant to discuss?**

Making the cross into sensitive territory can be a delicate process. You know you need the information, but find it difficult to broach the subject without losing the interviewee's confidence. The tenuous path to sensitive information can be traveled only with patience and subtlety.

Each writer will find his own methods of dealing with each reluctant interviewee, but there are a few tried-and-true methods that will work in many situations. You could blame the question on someone else, as in asking an allegedly corrupt politician "There are those who claim you do some 'creative accounting' with the budget. Since you've heard these allegations, would you like to respond to your critics?" A playful approach—"Let me play devil's advocate"—can often place the question in a framework that makes it easier for your subject to answer. Prefacing a sensitive question with some praise for your interviewee can cushion the blow and make her more responsive.

Asking a question in a straightforward, matter-of-fact way, no matter how sensitive the topic, may elicit a response when all else fails. If the interviewee *still* does not respond, point out the gap in information and tell her that, in the eyes of the reader, silence can be more damaging, since it can lead to speculation on the answer.

The manner in which you cover sensitive material can influence how much information the interviewee will give you. If you do manage to extract a gem that has been under lock and key, don't make a big deal out of it; lack of restraint can cause your subject to say something like, "Oh, but maybe you'd better not print that." Just show normal interest, not wild delight that would worry or frighten your subject.

**When a subject wants to talk off the record, should I accept or turn her down? Do anonymous sources lessen the quality of an article?**

Within certain limits, using off-the-record sources can be helpful to a writer, but the writer should make sure she and her source understand the ground rules for their interview. There are two ways a source can talk off the record. She can request total anonymity, talking only to give the reporter background information; in such cases, the source is never to be quoted in the article. A source can also agree to talk "not for attribution." This means she is willing to give information for use in the article, but doesn't want her name mentioned; she can be quoted or paraphrased, but the material is attributed to "a source close to the scene," "a high-ranking official," "a veteran observer," or some other such tag.

Anonymous sources can provide the writer of an article with incisive, revealing information that she otherwise might not have been able to obtain. But there are dangers—identified sources make your article complete and credible. And anonymity can become an excuse for a subject to grind her particular axe without fear of retribution. Check what your anonymous sources tell you, and if a source gives you information, makes charges, or provides descriptions that she cannot document, ask her to go on the record.

**If I only have a few minutes of an interviewee's time, how can I get the information I need?**

A tight schedule makes an interview more difficult in a couple of ways. Not only do you have a time limit on getting the information, you must dispense with much of the preliminary conversation that can build rapport and good will with the interviewee. Cutting the chitchat must be done carefully, however; you don't want to seem abrupt or rude, which could affect the interviewee's receptiveness to questioning.

When you're interviewing under the gun, you should have your questions arranged in descending order of importance when the interview begins. This practice will ensure your getting as much pertinent information as you can in the time allotted. Take a gamble with your last few questions, making them more thought-provoking to interest the subject so she will permit the interview to run longer.

To supplement your brief notes, you can, at the end of the conversation, request a more detailed interview by e-mail (see later questions).

**I need the opinions of average people for several articles I'm working on. Do I just walk up to people on the street and ask them? Do you have to name them in an article, or are you not supposed to name them?**

Yes, many freelance writers just walk up to people at a shopping mall or other public place and ask if they can interview them briefly for some research material they are seeking. You can open the conversation by saying something like "I'm a freelance writer researching an article on [topic] for [name of magazine]. May I ask you a few questions?" Whether you name them in the article depends on how you write the article. For example, writing "Sally Jones, a twenty-year veteran teacher in inner-city schools, had this to say about merit pay increases in teacher salaries" might create more credibility than if you just referred to "One Chicago veteran teacher...."

**I can't afford to travel to conduct all my interviews in person. Can't I get the same information just as easily by phone or e-mail?**

Telephone and e-mail interviewing prevent you from observing your subject's mannerisms and surroundings; for this reason, in-person interviews are usually best. Interviewing someone by telephone is the next best option, especially when you need only one key source and the subject is too far away for you to meet her in person before your deadline. Interviewing by phone can also be necessary when many sources are scattered far and wide. The practice even has a couple of advantages over face-to-face questioning: many times, a subject will be willing to talk more freely if she can't watch you taking notes.

When interviewing by phone, always have your reference material nearby. If you use a recorder, advise the subject in advance. Remember the value of good telephone manners; be prepared to identify yourself and the publication for which you are writing, and also to answer some preliminary questions from a secretary or assistant to gain access to your subject.

At the end of the phone conversation, thank the subject and advise her that you might need to call again for follow-up questions, or to fill in any gaps you find after you've transcribed your notes. Be sure to give the interviewee your phone number so she can reach you with any additional information or afterthoughts about your article.

### So how about e-mail interviews? They're so easy and time efficient.

E-mail interviews can definitely save time, especially if you need to ask many people the same questions. For example, if you were writing an article on city spending on social programs and wanted to ask the members of the city council for their views, e-mail interviewing would be one way to get a lot of their opinions in a very brief time. This would also save you the expense of travel and long-distance telephoning.

To conduct an e-mail interview, first query your subjects. Your query should be personal, explaining the nature of your project and the name of the publication interested in your article. If you are contacting a number of people about the same issue, it's always better to personalize the e-mail query and the questions, based on what you know about your subject. Give your phone number, and tell interviewees to feel free to call you collect if a question needs clarification or talking to you is more convenient. Also indicate a deadline for response.

Examine the replies to see if follow-up questions are necessary or might provide additional, provocative answers, then e-mail the subject(s) with these questions immediately.

### What are the drawbacks to e-mail interviews?

Purists say that e-mail interviews don't count, because they remove spontaneity and also permit intermediaries (such as a PR person or assistant) to respond to questions without you knowing. If you do an interview via e-mail, you're giving control over to your interviewee. Answers become pat and predictable—processed. As the interviewer, it's your job to pick up on voice inflections, to push through vague nonresponses, to ask the smart follow-up questions, and to be open to the synchronicity of the interview as it unfolds. If you're corresponding via e-mail, then you're giving up all those opportunities.

Use e-mail interviews when you need to do quick surveys and gather lots of opinions in a short time—especially when you just need a general feeling for what the majority (or minority) thinks about an issue. E-mail is also a useful tool for corresponding after the interview—maybe to double-check a fact or to ask a quick follow-up question; but don't rely on e-mail as your primary method for conducting interviews. Remember, too, to not bombard your source with dozens of pre- and post-interview e-mails. Doing so is absolutely unprofessional, and your source will likely form an unfavorable opinion of you.

If you're profiling a major figure, or if the very life of your story depends on the success of a particular interview, then you should at least conduct it by phone. An in-person interview is mandatory if you're expected to deliver full, sensory detail about a person's behavior, manner, and appearance.

## SOURCE CONCERNS

### Should I ask my interview subjects to sign a release?

As a rule of thumb, no. If you identify yourself as a writer or reporter, and the subject agrees to speak with you, it is understood that she is consenting to the publication of her comments.

There are rare occasions—such as when your interview will involve extremely controversial or sensitive material—when you might wish to have the subject sign a release in which she agrees to the publication of her comments, gives you permission to edit the manuscript and sell it to an editor, and waives any right of inspection or approval of the edited manuscript.

### If I write a profile, must I pay the subject?

Not usually. The question will rarely arise if you're interviewing a local businessman for a trade publication or a friend or neighbor for a crafts magazine. If it does, you should tell the subject that publications don't pay interview subjects, although they may provide complimentary copies of the article when it is published.

However, some writers and editors have paid for certain interviews and consider the practice a good investment. When a freelancer receives a request for payment to an interview subject, she should discuss it with the editor who gave the go-ahead for the piece.

**I called to set up an interview for an article on which I am currently working, but the subject told me she'd only agree to see me if she could see her quotes before the article went to press. What should I do in a situation like this?**

Unless this particular interview subject is essential to your article, it is best to tell her "Sorry, professional writers don't do that." That said, there are a few times when it is necessary for a writer to allow her interviewee to see the manuscript before it is printed. When dealing with scientific, technical, or medical topics, the writer may need the subject to check the facts and figures to make sure they are accurate. If the interviewee is your key source, then it may be necessary to agree to her review of the manuscript to get the interview. But the writer should make clear to any subject with whom she has such an agreement that the article is submitted for the interviewee's correction of factual material, not for her approval. It should be made clear to her that she is only proofreading the quotes, and that any alteration of the manuscript may be done only by the editor.

**When I've interviewed thirty or forty people for an article, should I try to quote all of them, or at least as many as I can? Will they expect to be quoted in the article?**

Not all the people you interview will appear in the finished manuscript. Some will be poor spokespersons; some will be misinformed and therefore useless; others will not be able to shed any new light on the subject whatsoever. Unless you are interviewing someone you *know* will be a key figure in the finished piece, you should make clear to each subject that you are interviewing a lot of people in order to obtain background information (as well as quotation) for the article, and that not all sources will be mentioned. If an interviewee later objects to not being quoted in the finished article, you can always say that there was a problem with limited space or that the article was heavily edited. If you anticipate this response from an interviewee, it's professionally polite to phone the subject in advance of the article's publication.

---

## USEFUL QUESTIONS

Try out some of these questions to help you learn about a source's personality:

- How long have you been doing this?
- Why is your work important?
- What have you accomplished that makes you most proud?
- What mistakes did you make? What have you learned?

Try these questions to prompt interesting anecdotes:

- When did you make up your mind? How?
- When was there a turning point?
- When did it all begin?
- When did you decide to go ahead (or turn back)?
- At what point did things begin to go your way?

Try these questions to get the basic information about a situation:

- What were your (or your organization's) goals?
- What obstacles did you face?
- How did you find solutions to those obstacles?
- What would you have done differently?

Try these questions when interviewing people about other people:

- When did you meet?
- What was your initial impression of this person?
- How has that changed?
- When were you ever angry with this person?
- Why is this person's work (or actions) important?

Try these questions to dig deeper:

- What types of things concern you most right now?

---

> - What new projects are coming up?
> - What trends will affect your business?
> - How will the future bring changes for you (or your group)?
> - What would you change about your organization?

**I recently tried to interview a celebrity, but her press agent insisted on ground rules, telling me that there were only certain topics her client would discuss. What do I do when this happens?**

If you need the interview, you have little recourse but to accept the ground rules suggested. The rules are often self-serving and confine the interviewer, making it difficult for her to get the information she needs from her subject. However, while it may be necessary to agree to ground rules in order to get someone to grant an interview, the ground rules may not limit you in the interview itself. Your subject may simply be wary of discussing certain topics because of the way she has been handled by writers in the past. Once you begin the conversation, she may loosen up and discuss almost anything you wish. Agree to ground rules, and you may be surprised. Once your foot is in the door, the ground rules may go out the window!

**Is it unethical to print information that a source has labeled off the record or not for attribution?**

If you have taken information off the record or not for attribution, then you are obligated to keep it that way. Failure to do so can damage your reputation as a trustworthy writer and harm your chances of getting information from that source in the future.

**Can a person I interview for an article be sued by a third party she mentions in the interview? Can the writer be sued for what the interviewee said?**

The interviewee can be sued for libel or defamation by the third person. The writer and publisher of the interviewee's statements can also be sued. A writer, therefore, should not include such possibly libelous statements unless she can prove their truth if challenged.

**What opportunities exist for a writer who doesn't like to interview people?**

Conducting interviews by e-mail is an alternative to the in-person interview, and can be used to glean enough information from an expert or celebrity to develop a salable article. There are several kinds of magazine articles that don't necessarily require interviewing. Each of these can be completed with other types of research.

**The how-to article** demonstrates or explains to the reader how to accomplish something, such as woodworking projects or sewing different types of clothing. Illustrations or photographs are often an integral part of how-to articles.

**The service article** gives the reader information regarding the use or purchase of items, services, or facilities. An article discussing low-cost vacation spots or offering pointers on buying a used car would fit this category.

**The personal experience article** is designed to inspire, educate, or entertain. Writing about the experience of returning to college at age forty-five or making a career change are examples of this type of article. Your account of a personal struggle to get through a life-threatening experience or other conflict can also become a salable magazine article.

**The think article** analyzes facts, events, or trends as the writer perceives them. The writer presents informed opinions, drawing conclusions intended to persuade the reader. Think articles appear in newspapers on the op-ed page and in magazines such as the *Atlantic* and *Harper's*, where, of course, your opinions would have to be buttressed by those of experts you had researched in periodicals, books, and perhaps through personal correspondence.

Different aspects of **historical events** can be covered in a light manner for popular magazines, or through in-depth research for scholarly publications. Many editors indicate their lack of interest in "routine historical pieces," but a well-written historical piece related to a magazine's content can usually be sold, providing the slant is right and the approach is fresh and lively.

**The travel article** has two objectives: to inform the reader by way of facts, and to enlighten her by way of impressions. This type of article requires a certain amount of preliminary research, and the writer must be perceptive enough to see the less conspicuous elements of the place she visits, such as the people, customs, and atmosphere. Photos are an essential part of most travel pieces.

**The humorous article**, although one of the most difficult to write, can be one of the most financially rewarding. However, many writers of humor attain success only after years of experience.

**Is there any reason to keep interview notes and other research material after an article is finished?**

Many writers keep old research material for several reasons: They may need to answer questions from editors, readers, or other writers who request information on the sources of the research, or they may want to use the research for future articles. You should save material for at least a year, or longer, depending on the type of research and how much further use you may have for it. Some newspaper reporters involved in investigative journalism, on the other hand, have developed the practice of destroying their notes once they have served their purpose. This prevents the notes from being subpoenaed if the reporter is questioned about her sources in an investigative piece.

## WHERE TO FIND OUT MORE

## BOOKS

*The Craft of Interviewing*, by John Brady, was first released in 1977 and is still available. Excellent for beginning journalists, if you can get past the outdated nature of its research techniques and attitudes.

*The Art of the Interview: Lessons From a Master of the Craft* is by Lawrence Grobel, a famed *Playboy* interviewer, so it is rich in celebrity anecdotes if weak on the how-to. Gives a good glimpse of what an interviewer does.

*Creative Interviewing: The Writer's Guide to Gathering Information by Asking Questions*, by Ken Metzler, is an expensive textbook for serious journalists, and contains strong how-to on the craft of interviewing.

# How do i revise?

The headmaster of an elementary school once commented, "I see four kinds of writing: (1) just plain bad, (2) correct but dead, (3) incorrect but good, (4) correct and good." The beginner's search for that last ideal is often a struggle.

The most common advice given by agents and editors is: Revise, revise, revise. Revision is what separates the serious writers from everyone else; professional authors revise their work multiple times—sometimes dozens of times. If you expect to get anywhere in your writing career, find an effective method of revising your work. (Check Janet Burroway's *Writing Fiction* for the method taught to nearly every creative writing student.)

This chapter answers a few of the most common revision and style questions. For more detailed discussions, read two classic books: *The Elements of Style*, by William Strunk Jr. and E.B. White, and *On Writing Well*, by William Zinsser.

**What should I look for when revising my work? Is it possible to edit too much?**

The process of editing is one each writer develops on his own, through experience, trial, and error. There is no definite number of drafts you should write before you can consider the manuscript finished. There are, however, some techniques that will probably prove helpful.

First of all, if your schedule allows it, set the work aside for a few days. After the writing has had a chance to cool, errors and awkward phrases will jump out. Once you do look at the work, try to cut it. Eliminate anything that isn't essential, as well as redundancies, irrelevancies, statements that are too obvious, unnecessary words, and circumlocutions. (Don't worry about being too brutal; you can always put material back.)

Let the material rest again (for at least an hour or two), then read it aloud. This is probably the best way to discover awkward phrasings. If you stumble over something, fix it. Reading aloud also can tell you where you've cut too drastically, damaging the rhythm of the piece.

Assess the logical order of the remaining elements. Some writers use highlighters or colored pens to color-code the work's major elements to make sure the structure best suits the point they're trying to make. Next, check your word choices. Look for imprecise verbs and weak nouns that require too many modifiers. Finally, check for consistency of verb tense, verb agreement, punctuation errors, and misspellings.

It is possible to overedit. If, for example, you find yourself rewriting everything over and over, and seldom or never putting a manuscript in the mail, you might be using editing as a means of avoiding potential rejection. Most writers, though, are far more likely to be hurt by too little editing than by too much.

### What should I look for when revising a novel?

Look for the weaknesses that most often cause rejection: unsympathetic or flat characters, unrealistic dialogue, slow pacing, a boring beginning, lack of voice, and bad or clichéd writing. You're probably wondering: How do I know if I have flat characters or a slow pace or any of these weaknesses? Show your manuscript to people you can trust to give their honest opinion, and if they all give you the same criticism, that's a red flag. You can also consult these two excellent how-to books, which give examples of good and bad writing: *The First Five Pages*, by Noah Lukeman, and *Self-Editing for Fiction Writers*, by Dave King and Renni Browne.

One last option is to attend a writing conference or workshop that offers a session or course on revision. Sometimes these sessions are very interactive and feature hands-on editing; other times they're lecture-based. Either way, they can help you spot and understand your weaknesses in a fraction of the time it would take you working alone.

**What is a book doctor? Should I pay to have my book edited before submitting it?**

A book doctor (as opposed to a copyeditor or proofreader) will read your book, looking for big-picture issues that need addressing, such as development, structure or organization, and flow. (When reading novels, they look at plot, character, pacing, and other elements vital to lively and salable fiction.)

An editor you pay will be more objective than a teacher, writing group member, friend, or spouse. They can help you fix what's wrong with your novel, though they cannot guarantee publication. They also can't turn bad writing or a clichéd story into a best-seller.

Check the track record of the editor you wish to hire. He should have a background in the particular field of your manuscript (novels, plays, etc.) and should, if asked, be able to provide a sample of a former critique to give you an idea of the nature, extent, and content of the criticism provided. Usually, reputable book doctors or editors don't take on projects that they feel have no chance at traditional publication (if that's your goal).

Whether or not you should hire an editor is totally up to you, but most manuscripts do benefit from at least a line edit (or proofread) before submission. If an editor or agent has two manuscripts on his desk, and one needs a heavy edit, and the other looks polished and ready to go, it's not hard to know which one he'll prefer and be more likely to accept.

**I recently queried an agent with the first twenty-five pages of my work. He responded personally with a note that my submission needs the help of a good editor. He gave me the name, address, and telephone number of someone he recommends. My question is, how do I go about contacting the editor? Do I send a letter, or contact him by telephone? I'm not sure what the etiquette is.**

Send the editor a letter mentioning the agent's referral, and ask for some information, including a description of the type of editing he does, his rates, titles of books he's edited that went on to be sold to royalty-paying publishing houses, and references from other clients. Then, talk with those clients; ask them if they were happy with the editor's services. Determine if the type of editing that was done was the type you expect—was the work restructured, or merely read for stylistic, grammatical, and typographical errors?

Do understand that editors edit. They are entitled to a fair fee for what they do. But editors aren't agents, and don't sell your work. Also, understand that working with a particular editor does not ensure that an agent or publisher will represent or buy your work. Be leery of agents or publishers who promise to represent or publish you if you work with a specific editor.

**I need some advice on a manuscript I just finished. I'd like to consult a well-known author whose work I admire. What's the best way to approach him?**

It would be an intrusion to send the author your unsolicited work. Of course, you can always write and ask for his advice, but don't send your manuscript unless you've received permission first. Many well-known writers who speak at writers conferences set aside time for individual questions and informal criticism, so it may be better to ask your questions in those situations.

## STYLE

**When an editor or teacher talks about my style, what does he mean?**

Style refers to the way an author expresses his ideas. It's *how* he says something in his work, rather than *what* he says; style is form rather than content. Each writer's work has an individual style that's as unique as a fingerprint; this is true whether he writes novels, magazine articles, poetry, or plays. Good style need not be characterized by complex constructions and polysyllabic words; it *is* marked by a clear presentation and expression of ideas. A writer's personal style doesn't appear overnight. It takes time and practice to develop your own method of putting thoughts into words.

**Would you explain the term *depth* in the field of writing?**

Depth means many things to many editors. But perhaps the one interpretation they would all agree on is that a piece of writing that has depth has something important to say to readers. It avoids frivolity or top-of-the-head superficiality about the ideas presented; it requires thought on the part of the writer *and* the reader.

### How can I improve my style?

Each writer has his own personal style, his own way of expressing his ideas, so there are no set rules or guidelines for improving style. Style should be natural for the writer, acceptable to the reader, and appropriate to the content of the piece. Good style can only evolve and be refined through the practice of writing and the study of good writing.

To improve style, read widely and determine what is good about a particular piece of writing. Evaluation by either a writing teacher or a professional editor is also helpful.

---

## FLASHBACK QUESTION

I am a would-be writer; that is, I believe I could write salable material if I could only get rid of one great big fear—the fear of punctuation! Just how important is punctuation to the sale of a story or article? I have read and studied the English grammars until I can't remember the rules a minute after I've closed the book. I'm desperate when I can't remember the rule for using a semicolon, a period, a comma, or when to start a new paragraph. Are all writers expert grammarians? Should I let this fear stop me from trying to write?

You have let punctuation become more of a bugaboo than it really should be for you. Notice your punctuation in your letter; it's quite acceptable. Since you're allergic to books of rules, perhaps you would do better to work with the stories published in current magazines. Become aware of a function of punctuation by seeing how it's used in each case. By all means, continue to write and never let your fear of literary mechanics scare you off. If the talent is there, it will be recognized whether or not a comma is in the right place.

---

Several times I have come across the criticism of pedestrian writing. What is pedestrian writing?

The term *pedestrian*, when applied to writing, is definitely unflattering. It means the work is prosaic or dull. The Latin root *ped-* refers to the foot, and the usual definition of the noun *pedestrian* is "one who travels on foot," such as the common man (who presumably doesn't have a better way to travel). In connection with writing, the adjective means "common" or "ordinary."

**What does my writing teacher mean when he suggests that I loosen up my writing style?**

The statement implies that you should decrease the formality of your writing and strive for a style that is more casual and easier to comprehend. Conventional idioms, slang, contractions (*he's* instead of *he is*), common words, and shorter sentences can achieve an informal style. Loosening up your style gives your manuscript a more conversational tone and makes it easier to read.

**I recently read an article by a well-known fiction writer who said it isn't good to read other fiction writers. He stated that it confuses a writer's style and makes his work seem inferior. Is this true?**

That view is not generally shared by most writers who have one love in common—the love of reading. If reading the work of others confuses a writer's style, then such a style was probably not individual enough or rooted deeply enough to begin with. (However, many fiction writers do avoid reading fiction while heavily involved in writing their own work, to avoid outside influence or distraction.) A beginning writer should expect to go through several phases of stylistic expression before he establishes the one that is his own.

**At the bottom of a form rejection slip I received for an article, an editor had written, "Write more naturally." What does that mean?**

It probably means your writing is stilted. Stilted writing can arise when you use "difficult" words rather than simple words. Or your writing may be convoluted—too complex, wordy, or intricate to understand easily—and not straightforward. Anything that draws attention to the structure of your language, rather than your meaning, may not read naturally.

**A writing teacher said my writing lacked vigor. How can I make my writing more vigorous?**

Make good use of the active voice: not, "the car was stolen by Bob," but "Bob stole the car." Instead of depending on adjectives and adverbs, write with strong, specific nouns and verbs. Avoid too many qualifiers like the words *very*, *little*, and *rather*. Cut away unnecessary words. *The Elements of Style* offers many guidelines and tips that make writing more strong and lively.

**I seem to spend so much time on style that it takes forever to finish a manuscript. Is there such a thing as worrying too much about style?**

If you spend all your time worrying about *how* to say something, you may never get it said. While it is important to write clearly and with appealing style, too much concentration on the technique of writing can create a roadblock that prevents you from finishing a piece. It's more important and helpful to get finished pieces into the hands of editors than it is to spend endless time refining the same manuscript over and over again. If the content is good, an editor will probably iron out stylistic problems.

If a particular section of your article or story bothers you, it's best to leave it alone for a couple of days or even weeks or months. If you look at one piece for an extended period of time, you can lose all perspective and find fault with even your best work.

**Is it OK to use *he* when referring to both sexes, or do I need to use *he or she*?**

You should avoid *he* as a generic pronoun. The word *they* is often used as a replacement, although it can be grammatically incorrect. For instance, if your original sentence is "Everybody does what he likes," you could edit it to read: "Everybody does what they like." This usage is frequent in conversation, but technically incorrect (*everybody* is singular, but *they* is plural) and may be inappropriate in writing.

Another option would be "Everybody does what he or she likes." Used extensively, however, *he or she* can become awkward. Some writers shorten it with a slash, but this only results in an equally distracting *he/she* or *s/he*. In many cases, rewriting the sentence can eliminate the need for the pronoun. Book publishers vary in their styles, but one commonly accepted solution is to alternate *he* and *she* between chapters (as this book does).

**I've often seen *The Chicago Manual of Style* referred to by editors. Just what is it and where can I find a copy?**

*The Chicago Manual of Style* (sometimes abbreviated as *CMS*) is an extensive volume that details the manner of preparing a manuscript according to the style guidelines developed by the University of Chicago Press. It gives guidelines for capitalization, punctuation, italicization, and much, much more. It is not designed to help you develop your own writing style. The word *Style* in the title refers to the way a manuscript is set up for typesetting. Your editor will not expect you to know *CMS* style or use it in your manuscript.

## WHERE TO FIND OUT MORE

### BOOKS

*Self-Editing for Fiction Writers*, by Renni Browne and Dave King, is one of the most popular and useful guides to self-editing your fiction.

*Getting the Words Right*, by Theodore A. Rees Cheney, is a thorough guide on how to revise and rewrite any piece of writing.

### WEB SITES

Author Holly Lisle offers a very detailed and systematic approach for revising your manuscript at www.hollylisle.com/fm/Workshops/one-pass-revision.html.

### DVD

*So, Is It Done? Navigating the Revision Process*, hosted by Janet Burroway, is a not-to-be-missed multimedia presentation that steps you through the revision process. Many noted authors share their own revision secrets. Visit www.erpmedia.net to purchase a copy.

# 16

## WHAT ARE MY RIGHTS?

Beginning writers seem to be divided into two large groups: paranoids who are afraid someone will steal their work, and innocents who don't take the time to learn that they should hold on to as many rights to their work as they can. The questions and answers in this chapter will alert you to what's at stake and help you protect your writing.

The most important fact a writer should know about copyright is that copyright is effective as soon as a writer creates a work. The current law puts the burden on the publisher to notify the author in writing if she wants to acquire any rights other than one-time rights (that is, the right to publish the work one time). The law also contains termination provisions that allow an author to regain rights she assigned to others, after a specific period.

## COPYRIGHT BASICS

**Once my work is copyrighted, how long is it protected?**

For works copyrighted through the U.S. Copyright Office on or after January 1, 1978, copyright protection lasts for the rest of the author's life plus seventy years after her death. For works published prior to 1978, the term will vary depending on several factors; see the U.S. Copyright Office Web site (www.copyright.gov) for an explanation.

### What is public domain?

Any published or distributed material on which a copyright has expired is considered to be in the public domain—that is, available for use by any member of the general public without payment to, or permission from, the original author.

### When I sell various rights to my work, doesn't that affect my ownership of the copyright?

No. Various rights are all part of your copyright, but selling them in no way diminishes your ownership of the actual work. William Strong, in *The Copyright Book*, likens copyright to ownership of land. "If you own a parcel of land, you can sell mineral rights to *A*, water rights to *B*, and a right-of-way to *C*, and still be considered the owner of the underlying property," he writes. In the case of written work, you may sell paperback reprint rights to one company, film and television rights to another, and book club rights to still another without impairing your ownership of the original work.

### When an editor tightens up my article, correcting a weak ending and other flaws, is the resultant article still under my copyright?

Yes. Usually, an editor's changes in your manuscript will not be extensive enough to qualify as a new work derived from your own. However, if your work is going to be heavily revised, you should clarify with the editor that the article is still yours, not hers.

### If I transfer certain rights to my manuscript to another party, do I relinquish those rights forever, or can I get them back at some point in the future?

If a specific time period is not written into the rights you grant someone—for example, an option on your book by a motion picture producer might have a term of one year—then you still have the right to terminate the grant of those rights. Check current copyright law to find out specifics relevant to your situation.

### How do I copyright my articles and stories?

Under current copyright law, your work is protected by statutory copyright as soon as it is created in tangible form. It need not be published to be protected, and you do not have to display the copyright symbol on your manuscript.

Only if you think you might have to go to court and fight to prove your ownership of the work is it necessary to register the material with the U.S. Copyright Office. For the proper forms and more information, visit the office's Web site at www.copyright.gov.

**How necessary is the effort and expense of having a work registered at the copyright office before its publication?**

Since your work is copyrighted from the moment you create it, the existence or validity of your copyright will not be affected if you don't register the work. You can still bring a lawsuit against anyone who infringes upon your copyright without having a formal registration, though you may not be able to collect as much in damages and you may have a weaker case. In most cases, it's not worth the expense or bother to register your work; the only situation in which you do need to worry about registration is when writing scripts.

**Should I secure a copyright for my book manuscript before submitting it to trade houses?**

Frequently asked question

No, the publisher who buys the manuscript will copyright the book in your name. A clause in most contracts between publishers and authors sets up an agreement whereby the publisher takes out the copyright in the name of the author. The publisher merely handles the paperwork on behalf of the author, and the copyright is the author's property. If you glance through a sampling of current bestsellers, you'll find that the author's name, not the publisher's, usually follows the copyright symbol.

**A publisher has made me an offer that stipulates it will own copyright to my work—it's a work-for-hire situation. Should I take it?**

That's up to you. Normally, a writer should never give up her copyright to another party. To give up copyright means that you give up all legal rights to the work, meaning you cannot benefit from any use of the work after the initial publication. But if you're offered enough money for the work, and you wouldn't have interest in the material after its initial publication, it might be worth your time. You'll have to weigh the risks.

**I have copyrighted some pieces that I am trying to sell as columns to newspapers. If they are published in the papers, would I have any copyright problems putting the same material into book form?**

As long as you are selling only simultaneous serial rights to the newspaper columns you have copyrighted, book rights belong to you.

**Is there any situation in which I can lose copyright protection?**

No, not unless you grant your rights to someone else in writing.

**Does the copyright law give copyright protection to titles?**

No, it is not possible to copyright titles of any type.

## FOREIGN COPYRIGHTS

**How well does my U.S. copyright protect my work if it's distributed or published in a foreign country?**

It depends on which country. If the country belongs to the Universal Copyright Convention, the work will be protected in the same way that nation would protect the writings of any of its own citizens. The U.S. also belongs to the Buenos Aires Convention and the Berne Convention. See www.copyright.gov for a circular called "International Copyright Relations of the United States."

**If my work is published in Canada, will I need to register it there, too? How does Canadian copyright differ from U.S. copyright?**

Since Canada and the United States both belong to the Universal Copyright Convention, your Canadian-published work is protected just as if it were published in the United States.

**Is a word-for-word translation of any foreign-language book without the publisher's consent legal?**

If the foreign language book is copyrighted and copyright has not expired, it may *not* be translated without the consent of the copyright owner.

My brother and I worked together on his manuscripts. He asked me to help rewrite, edit, and type his work. When he passed away, all the manuscripts he had were packed into a box and given to me. I would like to submit these for publication using both our names. What are my legal rights? Will it be necessary to ask permission from his other heirs, and would I have to share any profits with them?

If these manuscripts were transferred to you by your brother's written will or some other valid form of transfer, then they are yours and you may get them published without asking permission of the other heirs. If there is any doubt about the legality of ownership, it would be best to consult an attorney.

**I'm having trouble getting paid by a magazine. Can I sue a publisher in another state?**

Many states have adopted a long-arm law that makes business transactions subject to the jurisdiction of courts in the state if some part of the transaction occurred there. Check with a lawyer to see if you can use this law to sue an out-of-state publisher. If you're unable to sue from your location, you will have to file suit in the district where the magazine is—usually a greater expense than it's worth.

**I work for a trade publication that owns a consumer magazine. I recently found my work for the trade magazine appearing in the consumer publication. I was not notified or paid extra. My fellow employees and I want to know if this practice is legal.**

Work produced by salaried and work-for-hire employees is usually the property of the employer. Therefore, the magazine probably has every right to reprint your work in its sister publication. You might wish to take the matter up with your employer, however, if you and your fellow employees feel that you deserve some compensation. Work-for-hire writing belongs to the company, but publishers have been known to make concessions when workers present a reasonable argument.

**If I sell a novel to a publisher, and a movie producer reads it and wants to buy the movie rights, does she buy from me or the publisher? Will the publisher be entitled to part of the money paid for the movie rights?**

As usual, it depends on what rights you sold to the publisher. If you sold the publisher the movie rights, then it will negotiate with the producer and you will receive a percentage of the proceeds. (This percentage should be stipulated in the  contract you signed with the publisher.) If you kept the rights, then you will be the negotiator and keep all proceeds.

**A recently published book contains verbatim, unattributed quotes from an article I wrote on the same subject for a magazine some time ago. What action, if any, should I take? Do I have the right to monetary compensation from the book's publisher for this unauthorized use of my work?**

How much material from your article was used? Would it be allowable under the fair use provision of the copyright act? If there is substantial quoting from your piece, the next question is: What rights did you sell to the magazine publisher? If you sold more than first serial rights to the piece, the magazine publisher could have given permission to the book's author to use portions of your work. If that is the case, then the offense is just one of nonattribution.

If you sold only first rights, and the quotations were extensive, you may have been the victim of copyright infringement, and you should have an attorney write to the book's publisher. The attorney should attach to the letter a copy of your article, and inform the publisher that you may sue for copyright infringement.

Whether you are able to collect monetary compensation from the book publisher will depend on whether you can prove you sustained actual damages as a result of the infringement, and/or whether the publisher was aware it was infringing your copyright.

**Can I use my published story as the basis for writing another piece to sell elsewhere?**

Unless you sold your right to create derivative works when the publisher bought the story, you can. The author of a work owns the right to adapt her work to another form or to create a derivative work. If you sold the first publisher all rights to the work, then you no longer have the right to use the piece. If you sold first rights only, then you can go ahead with your project.

**Can I use characters from my short stories in other works?**

Yes. The writer of an original story owns exclusive rights to her specifically created and named characters, so they may be used in future stories.

**I paid to have a collection of short pieces published by a print-on-demand publisher some time ago. Can I now submit them individually to magazine publishers? Can I submit the entire book to regular publishers?**

Unless you sold off your rights to the print-on-demand publisher (which is highly unlikely—most of them don't ask for any rights at all), the contents of your book are yours to use as you please.

**I sold my first article to a magazine that says it buys first North American rights as well as subsequent electronic publishing rights, so an archive can be maintained on the magazine's Web site. Nothing was signed, no contract was ever discussed. I did receive a fifty-dollar check for my story. I'm not sure what is meant by subsequent electronic rights. Is this magazine the only entity that can have my article on the Web? Can I try to sell this story to another magazine? Can I post this story on my own Web site as an example of my work?**

Electronic rights cover a broad range of electronic media, from online magazines and databases to CD-ROM magazine anthologies and interactive games. Presumably, in this situation, the magazine will post the article on its Web site shortly after it goes into print, and the article will remain in the archives for an unspecified amount of time. The magazine will not be the only entity that can post the article on the Web; it should just be the first. After the story runs in the magazine, you are free to sell your story elsewhere and/or post it on your Web site.

## WHERE TO FIND OUT MORE

### BOOKS

*The Copyright Handbook: How to Protect & Use Written Works*, by Stephen Fishman, is an excellent guide to the world of rights, including electronic rights, and is geared toward writers.

### WEB SITES

The U.S. Copyright Office (www.copyright.gov) is the best place to get answers to your questions about copyright law.

# 17

# WHAT ARE THE RIGHTS OF OTHERS?

When an author sues another for plagiarism, it usually makes the headlines. That's because it's so very rare. Most writers are scrupulous about getting permission and fairly attributing their sources when they borrow from another's copyrighted work. Here are some answers to questions about when, how much, and under what circumstances you can draw from other people's work.

## RULES OF QUOTING

Frequently
asked question

**In several articles I have written, I quoted briefly from books. How much can I quote without asking for special permission?**

There are no hard-and-fast rules on the fair use of a copyrighted work according to the Copyright Act. The act allows fair use for such purposes as criticism, teaching, scholarship, and research. The law says four factors should be considered in determining if a use is fair: the purpose and character of the use; the nature of the copyrighted work; the amount and substantiality of the portion used in relation to the entire quoted work; and the effect of the use on the potential market for or value of the quoted work. Court interpretations of the law provide little help in trying to state standards; most publishers (and their lawyers) have their own fair-use guidelines. Still, if you're picking up fewer than a hundred words from a full-length book, it's probably a fair use.

**Is it necessary to get permission to reprint personal letters?**

Thoughts and ideas in personal letters are the property of the sender, not the receiver, so you must get permission for their publication. Personal letters may seem to belong to the person to whom they are sent, but to publish the letters, it is imperative to seek the letter-writer's permission in all cases.

**What's the difference between a direct and an indirect quote?**

A direct quote is information presented in a source's exact words, enclosed in quotation marks. An indirect quote is information paraphrased by the writer. In other words, direct quotes present information verbatim, while indirect quotes present the *substance* of the information, rewritten to shorten it or make it more precise. When using indirect quotation, the writer must be careful that his paraphrase doesn't distort or misrepresent the original intent of the remarks. For example, if you were to quote a source directly, the form would be as follows:

> In answer to a question about U.S. monetary policy, the President said, "Well, you'd have to check with the chairman of the Federal Reserve System about that."

But an indirect quote would read:

> In answer to a question about U.S. monetary policy, the president referred reporters to the chairman of the Federal Reserve System.

**When quoting from another source, may I omit surplus words such as *the*, abbreviate, or engage in other editing without using distracting dots to indicate such minor deletions?**

The fact that a verbatim quote has been edited should, in all fairness, be indicated—primarily to show readers that you are not presenting the words exactly the way they were originally spoken or written. The use of the ellipsis (the three dots) is the accepted practice, and not usually considered distracting.

**If material is paraphrased from a published source (for example, a magazine or a book), is it enough to mention the source, or must written permission be obtained from the publisher of the original material?**

It depends on the extent of your use. If the material is presented in only a paragraph or two, you need only to refer to the source with the standard "According to [book author and title] ..." or "in the [month, year] issue of [magazine title], [author] states ...." If, however, what you are writing, in substance, deals extensively with material quoted or taken from the original source, you must obtain written permission.

## SEEKING PERMISSION

**If I quote extensively from a copyrighted source, should I get permission from the publisher and explain to him what material I'm using and how I'm using it?**

If you intend to quote at length from a copyrighted source, writing the publisher for permission is necessary; and, of course, when writing the publisher, you should specify exactly which words on which pages you're requesting permission to use. The context, length, and purpose of your material will determine any fee that might be required; publishers often have request forms online or an e-mail address you can write to with your permission inquiry.

Frequently
asked question

**Is it the responsibility of the author or the book publisher to obtain releases for the use of published material? How does a writer go about doing this?**

Although some book publishers obtain releases, most feel it's the job of the writer to do so. Permission requests are sent to the publisher (assuming the book is still in print), who either acts on behalf of the author or forwards the request to him for his action. If the book is no longer in print, then the rights have probably reverted back to the author, in which case you would contact the author either directly or through his agent.

If permissions fees are required, you should not pay them until the work is published, in case some items are cut in the editing process. When you receive letters of permission, you should forward copies to your publisher.

**How much do publishers usually charge to quote or reprint their copyrighted material?**

If the use of the material is incidental, obtaining permission usually does not entail a fee and is sometimes unnecessary. For instance, if a novelist introduces a chapter with a few lines from another book, or if a nonfiction writer quotes a paragraph from a book by an authority in the field, this would usually be considered fair use, for which permission is not required.

If a writer is editing an anthology of fiction or a collection of articles, however, he may be required to pay permissions fees to various copyright holders. These fees vary considerably. An anthology of poetry or plays could run over ten thousand dollars in permissions fees. Who is to accept responsibility for paying permissions fees must be settled before beginning work on a book, and is generally included in the book contract. Costs may be shared with the author up to an agreed-upon maximum or charged to the author completely. The author's share of the fees may be deducted from royalties.

For excerpts, fees vary widely—from as little as fifty dollars up to a thousand dollars, depending on the nature and extent of the use. A typical fee, though, is a couple hundred dollars.

**I completed an article on assignment for a magazine. When the magazine offered to buy it, a letter accompanying the author contract stated that I needed to obtain permission from the publisher of a book I quoted from. I contacted the book publisher and learned that a fee is required for using the quotes. How do I pass along this fee to the editor who is buying the article?**

Phone the editor. Discuss who pays such expenses *before* you sign the contract, if possible. If the contract has been returned already, send the editor a copy of the fee request and ask if he can reimburse you for this unanticipated expense. If he says no, you can still use the material. Rephrase it completely, not using direct quotes, and still give credit to the publisher—including the title and author of the book from which the information was taken. If the quotes are extensive and vital to your article, though, it's best to pay the permission fee if the editor refuses.

**In my book, I'd like to reprint an article that appeared previously in another magazine. How do I go about getting permission?**

In order to reprint the article, you will have to write to the editor of the publication in which it first appeared. If the magazine purchased all rights to the article, the editor may be able to grant you permission to reprint. If he bought only first rights, he will give you the address of the author or forward your letter requesting reprint permission. In most cases, you can expect to pay the author for the use of the material you are reprinting. If the editor purchased all rights, you may have to pay a reprint fee to the magazine, but this is negotiable.

**I would like to reprint a passage from a book that is no longer in print. In fact, even though the copyright is only ten years old, the publisher is no longer in business and the author is deceased. How do I go about getting permission to use the material?**

Even though the author is deceased, his heirs still own the copyright, which must run its course of seventy years under copyright law. You need their permission to use the material. If the author had a literary agent, you can try contacting him for permission as well.

**In compiling a cookbook, I am taking recipes from newspapers and magazines, as well as from pamphlets put out by companies that manufacture the various ingredients. What procedure should I follow to get permission to use this material?**

Generally, the list of ingredients in a recipe cannot be copyrighted, but the written directions can. For recipes that come from magazines and newspapers, the material is protected, and you should not reuse it without substantial modification. Successful cookbooks are generally compiled by excellent cooks who have tried intriguing recipes, adapted them to their own style of cooking, and in the process developed a new recipe. Ingredients are altered and the directions completely rewritten.

**Is it permissible to quote directly from a document issued by the U.S. government?**

Yes, materials published by the government are in the public domain. There are a few minor exceptions; for instance, you should be alert to copyrighted material inserted in an uncopyrighted public-domain government publication. In addition, some documents connected with the post office are protected. If you have any questions about whether a specific leaflet you want to use is copyrighted, the presence or absence of the copyright notice should be your guideline. Even though you are legally free to use materials from government publications, you should cite the source so that both your publisher and the reader will know where your information came from.

**Can I quote from the Bible without being concerned with copyright infringement?**

Yes, you can quote anything from the King James Version, which is in the public domain. However, most modern translations, such as the Living Bible and the New International Version, are under copyright and permission is needed. To quote from these later versions, treat them as you would any book: Request permission to use the material beyond fair use guidelines, and give a proper credit line. Some Bible publishers give guidelines on their Web sites on what they consider fair use. For instance, the New International Version allows quotation of up to one thousand verses without written permission. (Proper credit is still required.) Many religious magazine and book publishers have standard arrangements with the Bible copyright owners; check with the editor you hope to sell to before requesting permission on your own.

**I'm writing an article in which I quote from a university study. Is it permissible to quote or paraphrase the general findings of such a study?**

Quoting or paraphrasing the general findings of the study should pose no problem.

**For an article I'm writing, I want to use some statistics I found in a recent issue of _Reader's Digest_. If I quote from the article directly, must I obtain permission?**

You should not need written permission to use brief statistical material from _Reader's Digest_ or any other publication, as long as you cite the source of your information in the article. Whether you paraphrase or quote the source verbatim, you should always acknowledge the original source of the material. If you intend to use the article extensively when you write your article, then you must obtain written permission.

**I have written a poem using characters and themes from a novel that was published a few years ago. Do I need permission from the author or publisher of the original novel to do this?**

You may feel free to use the themes from the novel, since they can't be copyrighted. Characters, however, are a different matter. If a character—and especially a character's name—is associated with a particular work in the public mind, then the question arises of infringement of the author's right to adapt his own work to other forms. For example, Warner Bros., producers of the _Superman_ movies, sued ABC-TV, claiming that its _Greatest American Hero_ series infringed on the Superman copyright because the series featured a flying hero with a red cape and x-ray vision who used the same arms-extended flying position as the Superman character. In a similar case, a Los Angeles woman sued _E.T._ director Steven Spielberg for $750 million of the film's profits, claiming she originated the idea in a copyrighted one-act play. Although a Manhattan federal judge rejected the Warner Bros. claims, the studio appealed the decision. The _E.T._ case was eventually dismissed. But even if you successfully fought an allegation that you stole a character, the legal fees could be astronomical. It's always safer to write for permission before you begin a work based on characters from already-published sources.

**Can I quote personalities whose statements are included in daily newspaper columns? Where can I obtain permission to quote?**

Since news cannot be copyrighted, if you are using quotations that are in news stories about personalities, you would not have to request permission, assuming that the quotations were accurately recorded by reporters and not of a nature that the personality would subsequently sue for inaccuracy. Many newspaper features and columns, however, are covered by copyright, and you would not be able to use very long quotations from these without requesting permission from the newspaper or the syndicate.

**Is it okay for me to take a few hundred words from a previous book of mine and use them in a new one?**

The same fair use rules that apply to quoting someone else's work apply to quoting your own work. You may need to request permission from your first publisher. If you're on good terms with your editor, you're likely to be granted permission for short excerpts without any fuss, but keep in mind that few editors like authors who recycle their old material in a new book.

**In my story, it would help add realism to use the titles of a few currently popular songs, and some snatches of the lyrics. Would it be necessary to get permission or give credit for this use?**

Do not break this rule!

If you're going to quote directly from the lyrics, you will definitely need permission, even if it's just for one line. Songwriters are very protective of their rights—and permissions can be very expensive. Song titles, however, are not copyrightable and can be mentioned without any permission.

**How do I go about obtaining permission to use song lyrics in my novel?**

A good place to start is the CD booklet, if you have it, especially if the lyrics are printed inside. You'll usually see something like "Lyrics reprinted by kind permission of [name of music publisher or label]." There may be contact info right there in the booklet. The record label could also probably steer you in the right direction.

Also look for a note stating the musician's publishing affiliation. If this info is shown, odds are good the person is either an ASCAP- or BMI-affiliated songwriter. ASCAP, BMI, and SESAC are organizations that collect royalties for radio play, licensing for restaurant music services, TV, etc. You can search the online databases at www.bmi.com and www.ascap.com to get addresses and phone numbers for permissions requests. Another approach is to look up the musician's management company in the booklet.

**Can I use titles of television shows, books, and movies in a general way? How about brand names?**

Since titles are not copyrightable, you are free to refer to them in your writing. Brand names may also be used, as long as they are not used in a derogatory manner. Some companies, such as Coca-Cola and Xerox, object to their brand names being used generically—to refer to cola or photocopying in general, for example—since such use jeopardizes their trademark.

**I've seen poets use lines from famous poems in their own poetry without footnotes or other citation. What is the rule with this? When is it assumed that a line is so famous that it doesn't require citation?**

In poetry, a quote usually appears as an epigraph (a note or quotation that precedes the body of the new poem). Using lines quoted from someone else's poetry in your own poem without footnotes is okay as long as you follow a few guidelines. First of all, is the quoted poem in the public domain? If it is, you're safe to quote as much as you want (within reason—excess can be regarded as plagiarism), and you should credit the poet. If the poem is not in the public domain, current fair use standards dictate you can quote only one or two lines of the poem. (Advice seems to differ depending on who you ask; and, obviously, if the poem is only two lines long, you can't quote it in its entirety.) Again, you must credit the poet who wrote those lines. For longer quotes, you would need to get permission from the poet and/or the poet's publisher. In addition, there may be strict guidelines the poet or publisher requires you to follow in crediting the quoted poem (i.e., a full credit line at the end of the poem, maybe even a copyright date and publisher name).

Quoting from another's work can be a touchy situation, unless you're quoting from Shakespeare or similar classic poets whose work is in the public domain. To quote from a copyrighted poem and remain in safe territory, don't quote more than one line of the poem, and if you have any doubts at all, contact the poet or publisher and get permission to quote from the poem.

**How can I investigate whether a work has fallen into public domain?**

The Library of Congress has an online search for copyrighted works. It is fairly limited, though—it allows you to search only for registrations from

Frequently
asked question

1978 to the present. To look for earlier registrations, follow the directions given on the Copyright Office Web site (www.copyright.gov).

**I've based my book on extensive research of government information from government publications and files. Can I copyright my book when most of the information is in the public domain?**

While government material is not in itself copyrightable, your particular rewritten presentation of it is. However, any work that consists in any large part of verbatim government material must carry in the copyright notice a statement that identifies those parts of the work that are yours and those parts that are government-produced.

**Since ideas can't be copyrighted, is it necessary to obtain permission from the author of a short story before expanding the material to book length?**

You are not at liberty to base a book on another author's short story without the consent of that author, since he has the exclusive right of adaptation of his own work. If you're only using the theme (the point the author makes in the story, such as that perseverance pays off or crime does not) and not the actual characters and other aspects of the story, then you're only using the idea and you can proceed without permission.

**Are facts, such as those found in medical journals and reports, in the public domain? Scientific literature, the way I understand it, is in the public domain and can be used by other writers. Is this true?**

Most medical journals are copyrighted, so material in them would not be in the public domain. Facts as such cannot be copyrighted, however, so if there are well-established findings quoted in a number of medical journals that could therefore be called facts, you could work them into your articles without the original writers' or researchers' consent. You can't lift written copy verbatim, but the information—the facts—can be included in your writing.

**I've obtained a book of photographs taken and copyrighted in 1905. Can I use them as illustrations in my book without infringing on copyright?**

Under the new copyright law, any work registered for renewal of copyright or already in the renewal term before January 1, 1978, has had its copyright duration extended to a total of seventy-five years from the date of original copyright. Copyright protection for your photographs would have expired in December of 1980. They are now in the public domain and you are free to use them.

**I am writing a how-to book. Do I need permission to use names and addresses of sources of equipment and supplies necessary to execute the projects I explain in the book?**

No.

**I am writing a book that, though not an authoritative document, uses material from about twenty references. In all except one or two instances, I have taken no quotations from these sources. I don't wish to clutter up the book with a lot of reference symbols to indicate where I have drawn from sources. I would like to acknowledge all such unquoted references in an appendix. Can you advise me?**

Prepare a bibliography to accompany your manuscript and precede it with a statement such as, "The author acknowledges the following references used in preparation of this text." If your publisher prefers a different method, work that out with your publisher. Where you have quoted directly, you should note within the text the sources quoted.

**I haven't written nonfiction articles because I don't know where research ends and plagiarism begins. Where should I draw the line?**

If long passages are lifted verbatim, you must get permission from the copyright owner. Ideas can't be copyrighted, so after you've researched the facts, simply relate them in your own words. Make certain you use only facts from a work, rather than the author's conclusions or observations. Facts belong to everybody, but an author's conclusions and opinions are his alone.

## ANTHOLOGIES

**I want to compile an anthology of essays. Should I secure copyright releases before submitting it? Can I copyright the anthology?**

You shouldn't get copyright releases before submitting to a publisher, since a publisher may not want some selections, and may want others not included in the original manuscript. After the manuscript is accepted, you should write the requests for permission, citing chapter and page, preferably also including a copy of the passage. Any reprint fees are usually paid for by the publisher, but deducted from the anthologist's royalties.

Anthologies may be copyrighted in the name of the author/editor or the publisher, depending on the type of book and the terms of the contract. The use of essays in your anthology does not prevent their future use in some other anthology.

**Over the years, I've collected many articles on a particular topic that interests me. If they were compiled into an anthology, they would make very interesting reading. Putting together an anthology doesn't sound too difficult, but I don't know where to start. Any suggestions?**

Rather than jumping into the preparation of a full manuscript, send some queries first to find an interested publisher. With your query, include photocopies of the first pages of a few selections to be included. In your query, establish your authority in the subject area to be covered. You should know your subject well, or you'll have trouble compiling enough material for a book in a reasonable amount of time. You will have to work hard to convince an editor that your topic is important and warrants his risk in publication.

**I read a story in which the main character had many suppositions as to how his adventure would end. None was right. I want to write a short story using one of these suppositions for my ending, but my story would have to be very close to the original. Is this infringement?**

If you use the original author's character in a replay of his story, it would probably be considered copyright infringement. You wouldn't want another writer using your situations and characters, would you? Originality is your best bet.

## WHERE TO FIND OUT MORE

### BOOKS

*The Copyright Permission and Libel Handbook*, by Lloyd J. Jassin and Steven C. Schechter, is a helpful guide to avoiding infringement and lawsuits.

*Business and Legal Forms for Authors and Self-Publishers*, by Tad Crawford, is an excellent resource for all types of forms and contracts.

*Every Writer's Guide to Copyright and Publishing Law*, by Ellen M. Kozak, can give you a basic understanding of the laws that govern written work.

*Literary Law Guide for Authors: Copyright, Trademark, and Contracts in Plain Language*, by Tonya Marie Evans, is an easy-to-understand guide to legal issues that affect writers.

# 18

# CAN I USE OTHER PEOPLE'S NAMES AND STORIES?

While the previous chapter addressed issues surrounding using other people's written work (permissions, quoting, excerpting, etc.), you can also run into trouble simply writing about other people's lives. You are guilty of libel if you publish a false statement that is damaging to another living person's reputation. That false statement can be unintentional and still be ruled libelous in court, which is why the law requires writers to take every reasonable step to check for accuracy. While it is up to the plaintiff to prove the falsehood, it is up to you to prove that you made every reasonable effort to be accurate.

Few writers would knowingly publish falsehoods. Yet the potential pitfalls for writers are numerous. You can accurately print what you have been told and still commit libel—if the person giving you the information was wrong about her facts. Many writers get into trouble by failing to check minor facts, which is why you must double-check and triple-check information—even when you believe it is correct. The *Associated Press Stylebook and Libel Guide* is an excellent source of information on libel and how to protect yourself from committing libel or being accused of libel.

When writing about real people, you must also be concerned with invasion-of-privacy lawsuits, in which the plaintiff claims that even though the things you say about her can be proven true, they are "private and embarrassing facts not of legitimate public concern." The questions below address common situations that fiction or memoir writers might find themselves facing when writing about other people.

**A neighbor of mine is a disfigured recluse. I have built a story around such a woman. I slander her in no way, yet my husband feels I will have a lawsuit on my hands if the story gets published. I would appreciate any advice.**

It would be best to change as many of the obvious true-to-life facts as possible to avoid an invasion-of-privacy suit. Give your heroine a different age, size, hair coloring, nationality, etc. Add new mannerisms, idiosyncrasies, and other aspects of personality. Use a totally different setting if you can. After all, the only basic idea you need is that of a disfigured recluse. It is not necessary to make the type of disfigurement identical to that of your neighbor. Use your creative imagination to produce a completely new character based on the general idea but not the exact details of your neighbor's life. In fact, you might even experiment with the idea of making the leading character a man instead of a woman.

**How careful must a fiction writer be with names she contrives, but which could turn out to be names of living persons? For example, if I name the villain in a story Jack Bowlton, could a real Jack Bowlton sue me for defamation of character for characterizing him as a villain? Also, what about the old disclaimer, "Any similarity to persons, etc., is strictly coincidental"?**

Unless the real Jack Bowlton happened to be circumstantially similar in personality and actions to the fictional character you gave that name, there probably wouldn't be any cause for legal recourse. The old disclaimer doesn't appear much anymore because a person who can prove that a real person was used in a fictional account, and who can also prove defamation or invasion of privacy, may still have legal recourse in spite of the disclaimer.

**Could a person actually named William Faulkner, Ray Bradbury, or Ann Landers publish work under that famous name?**

No. Ann Landers, William Faulkner, and Ray Bradbury have already established the reputation of those names; anyone who tried to publish her work using these names would be guilty of infringing on the reputation those writers have already built. This holds true even if the writer's real name is the same as that of an already-published author. The second writer would have to take a pen name. (For more information on pen names, see chapter nineteen.)

**Do I need the permission of a corporation to publish an article or book about it?**

No, and if the company has been treated fairly, you should have no legal problems. However, if the company takes exceptions to any part of your work, you may have a lawsuit for libel on your hands. Even if what you write is true, the company might sue simply as a way of denying what you have written. Books about corporations written without their consent include *Disney War* and *Under the Influence: The Unauthorized Story of the Anheuser-Busch Dynasty*. Writers should exercise extreme caution when writing such material and make sure that all facts are verified.

**I am writing the life story of a remarkable woman I knew a couple of years ago, who has since died. I'm sure she would have given permission, but I'm not sure her husband would be so willing. Do I need permission to write about someone who isn't in the public eye?**

The husband may interpret your work as invading his privacy and institute a lawsuit. However, most state laws say heirs can't sue—only the live person who has been libeled or has had her privacy invaded can initiate legal action. You'll have to decide if it's worth the risk.

**Can I use the names of famous people in my fiction?**

Using the famous as characters in your fiction causes no problems as long as they are depicted in a favorable light. However, if your work makes negative allegations about the people involved, you could be asking for a lawsuit.

**Can I base my fictional characters on real people if I change their names?**

Even if you change their names, real people might think readers would recognize them, and therefore they might consider your work an invasion of their privacy. If these people believe they are shown in an unfavorable light, they might sue for libel. It's safer to make a composite character with traits and characteristics culled from several people. It's more creative to alter the events and characters of real life, since they are rarely suitable for use in fiction without some authorial manipulation or adaptation.

Frequently
asked question

**In a book of personal experiences, is it permissible to use real names and to relate real episodes without obtaining written permission from the persons mentioned? Or should characters and events be fictionalized?**

It's advisable to change the names of real persons and the locale of real events to avoid suits for invasion of privacy by the parties concerned. Even if your reference is complimentary, the individual may resent being placed in the public spotlight and go to court to prove her point.

**In writing a personal memoir that includes stories of family, do I have to obtain a release from other family members, or is there a way to present the characters without having such consent?**

The bottom line: Truth is a defense to any defamation charges that may be brought against you. However, you must also be concerned with an invasion-of-privacy suit, in which the person you wrote about can assert that even though the things you say can be proven true, they are "private and embarrassing facts not of legitimate public concern."

**I am doing research for a proposed biographical novel. The famous people on whom I am basing my novel lived in the early 1800s. I am not always able to get to an original letter or document written by the subject, so I am taking material from factual books by other authors in which they quote from these originals. Can you tell me the rules about biographical novels? Must I get permission from all the authors I have read in order to provide character dialogue? Must I get permission from the people who have the original letters, manuscripts, or documents, if I can find them? And how about a book that was written in this 1800 period by the famed person herself? May I use her material to build my character? Could living descendents of these famed people object?**

In a novel of this type, you could acknowledge, in an introduction or preface, the sources on which the factual material is based. Write to the book publishers, describing your project and asking their permission to use information in the letters they published. To be on the safe side, you might also write to the publisher of the book written by the famous character herself, requesting permission to make use of that material. As for the descendants, there is the delicate question of the right of privacy. Since each state has its own laws about this right, consult a lawyer who can advise you how much latitude you have under law.

**Can a writer legally use the name of a business firm in fiction if the story is not uncomplimentary of the business?**

Well-known companies do not look unfavorably on a little free advertising embedded in a nationally distributed piece of fiction, provided such usage is strictly for purposes of atmosphere and realism. Nothing even remotely illegal or distasteful should be connected with the company name. For example, if your story deals with a criminal who dupes a department store, you'd be on safer ground if you used a fictitious company name, to avoid the possible impression that the real store is not smart enough to escape being duped. As a rule: When in doubt, fictionalize.

**If I write a true story, but change the names, is it fiction or nonfiction?**

If the story is a factual account, with only the names changed, then it would be nonfiction.

**I would like to set my story in the city of Detroit. Do I have to use real names of streets and places, or can I mix fiction with fact?**

If you're going to use a real city as the setting of your story, you had better use names of real streets and places. It will give your story authenticity. Make sure all facts in your story are correct. Just because your story is fiction doesn't give you the right to present any factual inaccuracies. Fiction writers must spend time researching so that they can write with a sure knowledge of their subjects.

**My short story embraces a true event in a nineteenth-century man's life that is recorded in newspapers and books. Can I properly call it fiction?**

Yes, since you are creating the dialogue and much of the dramatic action, it can properly be called fiction.

**What is the difference between an authorized and an unauthorized biography?**

An authorized biography is written with the cooperation of the person it's about—or with the cooperation of her estate, if she's deceased. This means the writer has access to in-depth interviews with the subject and her family and friends, and to private records and correspondence. In some cases, the writer shares the byline, advance, and royalties with the subject. Authorized biographies are sometimes rejected by the critics for their lack of objectivity. An unauthorized biography, on the other hand, is written without the cooperation of the subject or her estate. Publication of these works is strongly based in current public interest, and these works cover such people as television personalities, rock stars, sports heroes, and political figures. Although some celebrities have claimed that unauthorized biographies violate their rights—that a biography is only legal if the celebrity herself has written or authorized it—the courts have not upheld these claims.

**In writing a biography about a deceased person, do you have to be careful about what you tell, or can you tell the truth?**

Most state laws prevent a person's heirs from suing for either libel or invasion of privacy. Usually these suits can only be brought by a living person who feels she has been defamed or that her privacy has been invaded. But if you also discuss living people when you are writing about a deceased person, be sure of your facts, since the truth (if you can prove it) is the best defense against libel. Truth is not a defense, however, against invasion of privacy, so if you have any qualms about possible suits from living persons on that score, you had best either get releases or eliminate those references.

**Through my experience as a freelancer, I have had contact with someone who would make a good biography subject. If I write the book, I think it will have national appeal. Any suggestions on how I can get started?**

Discuss the possibility of a biography with your subject before you approach any publishers. If that discussion goes well, write up a book proposal on the biography you wish to write, and include the reason the proposed subject would make a salable biography. If you fail to find an interested publisher, it may be because the publishers don't think your idea would sell well. You will either have to rethink it and change the slant, or abandon the idea. Once you *do* receive a positive response, you should read all material written about the person. Then interview the subject, family members, and close acquaintances. In planning the book, you will need to know about outstanding events and conflicts that your subject has encountered, so that you can show how she became the person she is now. Earlier biographies were usually done in strict chronological order, but now they often open with some dramatic episode attesting to the subject's character and/or fame, and then recapitulate the formative years. A sound knowledge of your subject and of the other people strongly influencing her is necessary to write a strong and viable biography. But avoid tedious detail and references to relatively unimportant people. Focus on highlights and the impact such events had on the subject's life.

## WHERE TO FIND OUT MORE

See the previous two chapters.

# 19

## SHOULD I USE A PEN NAME?

Writers use pen names for a variety of reasons—to keep their authorship a secret from their families and friends, to foil sexist editors, to establish audiences for different types of work. How do you select and use a pen name, but still receive mail and cash your checks? The following information will smooth the way for you.

**Suppose a writer dislikes publicity, and is very shy with persons outside the circle of his family and friends. What, in your opinion, would be the advantages and disadvantages of anonymity in such a case?**

If you had the publisher's (or agent's) complete agreement and cooperation in keeping your anonymity safe, you could possibly keep your real identity a secret, but at the risk of crippling your book sales. Most successful authors promote and market their own work both by assisting their publisher's efforts and by initiating their own guerrilla marketing campaign. (It's an unwise author who expects the publisher to do all the publicity legwork these days.) Also, think carefully about whether you would really value the lack of public acclaim. You would likely have to reject scores of interview requests, book signings, and other opportunities to meet and connect with your readership.

**What is the real value of using a pen name?**

Sometimes an author will use a pen name if he writes a different kind of book from what he has written before; for instance, mainstream novelist Evan Hunter wrote mysteries under the pseudonym Ed McBain. This practice kept an Evan Hunter fan from picking up a book radically different from what he expected from the author.

Prolific writers often have to adopt pen names, since some publishers ask for exclusive rights to the name of a successful author. In the words of novelist Dean Koontz, "He [the publisher] doesn't want *his* new Sam Hepplefinger novel to be in competition with some other publisher's new Sam Hepplefinger novel."

A college professor of mathematics who secretly authors cozy mysteries might not want the word to get around to his students and colleagues. Or a writer who simply dislikes his real name—it may be hard to pronounce or look unwieldy in print—may adopt a more suitable one. These are all good and valid reasons for using a pen name.

**I'd like complete anonymity, even from my publisher. Is this possible?**

If you had a cooperative agent who supported your anonymity, it's possible you could keep your identity secret from even your publisher. But if you were working with a publisher without the benefit of an agent, it would not be possible.

**My name is very ordinary, but I don't want to use a pen name. What would you suggest?**

Use your real name. Editors don't care. The subject matter and quality of the writing are what sell a manuscript to a publisher and a book to a reader. Names are incidental. (Look at Dan Brown.)

**I am a woman writer interested in writing for men's publications, such as *Outdoor Life* or *Field & Stream*. Will using a male pseudonym or my initials increase my chances of sales?**

Your writing should be judged on the basis of your authority on the subject, not your gender, but it is possible that some editors might have second thoughts about running a men's article written by a woman. Although discrimination against women has decreased, it still exists; a male editor *might* assume that a woman could not write a traditionally "male" article or that his readers would not accept it. If you have evidence that using a male pen name will help make a sale, use one.

The pen name situation would apply also when men are writing female-oriented material. A number of authors of romance novels, for example, are men using female pseudonyms.

### How do I go about choosing a pen name?

There are no guidelines for deciding on a pen name. It can be any combination of first and last names the writer finds attractive. Choosing a pen name is similar to naming a fictional character. The writer might wish to consider the name's appropriateness to the material carrying the byline. "Letitia Beauregarde," for example, would be more likely to write the saga of a southern family than a first-person account of a hunting trip in the Amazon jungles.

### I would like to adopt the pen name of George Orwell. Will I need permission from his heirs?

Yes, you will need permission, but it isn't likely that Mr. Orwell's heirs would allow you to cash in on his reputation. Try to make it on your own!

### How does the writer cash a check made out to his pen name—especially if he's well known in a small town?

When the manuscript is submitted under a pen name, the author usually includes his real name and address on the title page, so that the check will be made out to him and he can cash it without letting anyone know what the check is for. If the check is made out to the pen name, the author can simply endorse it with the pen name, then endorse it over to his real name and cash it that way. In any case, it's always best to notify both your bank and the local postmaster that you'll be using a pen name. Letting them know that you're doing business under your pseudonym will ensure that your mail will be delivered and that you'll be able to cash checks, should they be made out to your pen name. In some communities, a writer must file a d.b.a. (doing business as) registration when doing business under another name.

### If an article or book is written under my pen name, must I copyright it under that pen name, or can I use my real name in the copyright form to protect my rights to the work?

On the copyright registration form, you can list your pseudonym under Name of Author and your real name under Copyright Claimant, with a brief explanation of the name difference. This guarantees proof of your authorship of the work in the event your heirs need to establish that the work is yours. Publishers will generally file this form on your behalf.

# 20

## WHEN AND HOW
## DO I PROVIDE ART?

If you're lucky enough to be talented in both writing and art, then you might have ideas for articles and books that incorporate photographs or illustrations. Depending on the publisher or magazine, this could be a positive or a negative; some editors don't want to be bothered with your art ideas (especially if they're not convinced you can professionally execute them), while others will welcome them. Occasionally, you might be *required* to provide illustrations to accompany your written work, but there are no hard-and-fast rules on when or where. This chapter should help you understand when illustrations will be welcomed, required, or rejected.

### PROVIDING PHOTOGRAPHS

**Will including photographs with my article or book help sell it?**

It depends on the publication. Some prefer to assign the photography to professionals they know; others request or require that photographs come with the manuscript. (Consult the submission guidelines or *Writer's Market*.) If you must submit photos, and you're not confident in your abilities as a photographer, you may need to hire someone to take the pictures for you. Photographs must be sharp and clear, and you should give the editors a good variety to choose from. Study the publications to get an idea of the kinds of photographs they like to print with their articles.

Learning to take effective pictures is a matter of time and practice. Universities and colleges often offer courses in photography, as do continuing education programs in local school districts. You can also find information on the Internet. The salespersons at your local camera shop can provide advice and instruction after you've bought your equipment, and might also be able to direct you to the best places to learn how to use your camera.

**What equipment will I need to take my own photos?**

You don't need much to take effective pictures with today's digital cameras. You'll probably want a flash unit, a tripod, and an equipment bag. Depending on your taste and the equipment you choose, you should plan on investing between five hundred and a thousand dollars in your basic camera system. Eventually, you may wish to add wide-angle and telephoto lenses to increase the variety of your pictures. If you're unsure of your camera's ability to take quality photos that will reproduce well in a magazine or book, check with your editor for requirements, or ask to send a test photo. As a general guide, nearly every print publication needs photos at 300 dpi resolution at full size (the size at which they will be printed).

**I'm not a photographer, but I often need pictures for illustrations. Where can I find these images for free (or for a reasonable price)?**

Frequently asked question

There are a number of stock photo agencies you can turn to. Stock photo agencies have thousands of photographs in their files, which they license for a fee. You can find stock photo agencies at www.stockphoto.net, which lists several agencies and their specialties. Also check out iStockPhoto.com for incredibly low fees.

The most economical way to get a number of photos is to buy a royalty-free photo disc. You can buy a disc with a hundred photos on it, and you can use the photos as often as you like and in any way you like.

The only free photography you'll find will be in the public domain (meaning no one has a proprietary interest in the photos or holds a copyright on them). You can search the Internet by entering the following key words: *public domain photography*. The Library of Congress (www.loc.gov) also has images available in the public domain. However, not all public domain images are free—some may have fees associated with them.

**Who covers the fees involved in securing photographs—the writer or the editor?**

Generally speaking, magazines will secure and pay for the photos used in the articles they publish. The exception to this would be the photo/text package, in which the writer supplies both the text and the photos for the article and is usually paid a flat fee. In this case, if the writer does not take the photos herself, she must arrange a fair split of the proceeds with her photographer.

With book publishers, arrangements vary tremendously. When submitting your manuscript or proposal, mention whether you have the ability to provide professional-quality photography (or illustrations), if appropriate. It can definitely make your project more attractive.

**How many photos should I send with a magazine query?**

Remember: You're trying to sell your *idea* in a query, so photos aren't usually included. But if a couple of good photos buttress that sales effort, include them.

**I submitted an article and fifteen photographs to a magazine, and the article was printed with three of the pictures. However, I was not paid anything extra for the photographs. Is this a common practice?**

That magazine probably buys articles and photographs as a package, making one payment for the two items. Some editors buy pictures separately. Make sure you understand a particular editor's policy before you agree to sell her your work.

**I might have the chance to interview some celebrities this summer, but I cannot take the pictures. Should I contact a professional photographer before I query an editor, or should I get the writing assignment first? If the editor does not purchase the story and pictures separately, what percentage does the photographer usually get?**

Before you query the editor, explain your project to the photographer, and ask if she would be willing and available to furnish her services. If she agrees to the assignment, make sure you reach an agreement with her regarding payment. (As a professional, she will let *you* know her usual fees.) Then, in your query, you will have the added advantage of informing the editor you'll be able to furnish professional photos. It's up to you to make sure you're paid enough to cover your expenses as well as those of your photographer.

### How can I find a photographer to work with me on books and articles?

You could hire a professional photographer, but some charge hundreds (or thousands!) of dollars per day for their services, so unless you work out an agreement with an editor beforehand, hiring a photographer could be an unwise expenditure for you. The American Society of Media Photographers (ASMP) can recommend member photographers in your area if you or your editor want to hire an experienced professional. Visit www.asmp.org.

College art departments that teach photography might be able to recommend talented students; putting notices on the department bulletin board can also help. Local camera clubs and online classified ads can also help generate leads.

When selecting a photographer, examine her portfolio, checking subject matter, quality and style, and the relation of her work to the type of writing you do. After you've found your collaborator, the two of you will have to work together to find ways to enhance your writing with her pictures. Prints chosen for publication should be accompanied by a brief, signed statement in which the photographer grants permission for her work to be used in conjunction with your manuscript.

### What arrangements should I make to pay a photographer for her pictures I use to illustrate my article?

There are a number of ways to pay photographers. The writer and photographer can agree beforehand on a flat fee to cover the photographer's labor and the cost of prints. The writer can pay the photographer a percentage of the total article fee. If the photographer belongs to a professional organization, the writer may have to agree to a fixed price. In all of these cases, the actual amount of payment will depend on several factors, including the nature of the work, the amount of the photographer's time involved, and the quality and quantity of the photographs. The price should always be negotiated before work begins.

**What's the best way to send photographs with a manuscript so they aren't mangled by the postal system?**

Black-and-white prints should be placed between pieces of stiff cardboard and secured with a rubber band. (Paper clips can mar photos, so don't use them.) Mark your mailing envelope "PHOTOGRAPHS— DO NOT BEND." This will alert postal workers to what's inside the envelope, and your pictures should make it through without being damaged. Color photos should be submitted as slides, not prints. They're best submitted in the page-size plastic sleeves that hold twenty 35mm slides. If you number them, the caption material can be typed on a separate sheet of paper with numbers to match.

**I've written a nonfiction travel book. Should I send photographs with my proposal when I submit it?**

Yes, in your proposal, include your best photos printed on quality photo paper, and mention you have more available for review. Keep in mind that although some travel books, cookbooks, and art books are printed with color photographs, many nonfiction books are not. Using color illustrations greatly increases the cost of production, automatically leading to a higher cost for the consumer. So don't plan on including them unless color photos are indispensable to your book idea, or you know the publisher will be interested in them.

## ILLUSTRATIONS AND ART

Frequently asked question

**How do I arrange to get an illustrator for my children's book?**

You don't need an illustrator, as most editors prefer to receive manuscripts without illustrations. Publishers have their own preferences in illustrators, and sometimes keep illustrators on staff. An editor is usually good at visualizing artwork to accompany a story, and if her vision radically differs from the illustrations you send, she's likely to reject your manuscript/illustration package. The final decision as to who will illustrate a manuscript lies with the editor, who has a group of reliable illustrators for the books her company publishes.

**I'm preparing a travel article for which I will need maps as illustrations. Do I need permission to reproduce maps?**

Maps are copyrightable, so permission would be necessary to reproduce previously published, copyrighted maps. If you don't have the skills or resources to create your own maps, discuss options with your editor—travel publications probably have the resources to create maps.

## RELEASES AND PERMISSIONS

**I want to submit some photographs with my fishing article, but my two partners are in most of the shots. Do I need model releases from them? When is a model release necessary?**

Basically, a model release is a signed and witnessed statement from the subject of a photograph (the model) giving the photographer the right to use the photograph for sale or reproduction. A signed model release is usually necessary if the photograph in question—whether it be of a person, someone's pet, or a recognizable building or piece of property—is to be used for any commercial purpose (which usually means advertising or similar promotion).

To be on the safe side, you should obtain model releases for photos used for editorial purposes. That way you'll have the forms on file if your editor decides she needs them. (Note that if a photo does not reflect favorably on its subjects, especially if those subjects are juveniles, you could face legal problems whether or not a release form is signed.) You can easily obtain release forms at most photography stores, or you can get your own printed. A sample form appears in *Photographer's Market*.

**I've been asked to put together a book on a world champion track star who has a collection of photos that tells her story quite well. Some of the photos are snapshots of the track star, and some have been published before, and many (published and unpublished) are of nationally known personalities.**

**Do I need the permission of the numerous photographers or individuals appearing in the photos? What about previously published photos?**

Since the photographs are all of public figures, and you don't plan to use the photographs in any kind of advertising, you probably don't need model releases signed by the subjects in the pictures. However, your publisher may want you to obtain releases anyway, in case some of these photos appear in advertising or promotional materials for the book. Unpublished photographs belong to the photographer, so you'll have to obtain permission to use them. In the case of previously published photographs, who gives the permission depends on the rights the photographer sold to the original publisher. You'll have to write the publisher to find out the name of the photographer, and then obtain permission from the proper source.

**I bought two oil paintings done by a Native American a number of years ago and think they would make good illustrations for a book I'm authoring. Since I own the paintings, would a credit line be sufficient?**

No. Even though you own the paintings, reproduction rights still belong to the artist. You would have to contact the artist (or her heirs, if she's dead) to obtain permission to reproduce the paintings as illustrations in your book.

**I hope to write a book on teaching high school art. Such a book would include the works of famous artists and sculptors, past and present. How do authors go about using reproductions of these works?**

You'll have to request permission and photographs of the works from the museums where they're housed, assuming the museum owns the reproduction rights. If not, you'll have to ask either permission of the owner of the artwork, or the artist, if still living.

**A nonfiction book I'm writing would be greatly improved if I could use the charts and drawings from another book I found on the same subject. How can I do this?**

The usual procedure would be for your publisher to decide whether to write the original publisher for the art and reprint permission charges, or to write for permission to recreate art. For proposal purposes, you may simply include photocopies of the art you wish to obtain reprint permission on.

**What rights should I sell for photographs when they are submitted with a manuscript?**

Photographs are often bought in a package with the manuscript they accompany. Thus, editors will usually buy the same rights to the pictures that they buy to the manuscript. If they buy photographs independently, they will normally buy the same rights they buy for articles and stories printed in their publications. Ideally, you should sell only one-time rights to photographs, the same rights you would sell to an article, story, or poem.

**When an editor says "Rights remain with the photographer," what does she mean?**

This means the editor is only buying one-time rights.

## WHERE TO FIND OUT MORE

### BOOKS

*Photographer's Market*, an annual market guide by Writer's Digest Books, gives information on where and how to market your photographs.

*Artist's & Graphic Designer's Market*, another annual guide by Writer's Digest Books, gives helpful information for all types of illustrators and designers on how and where to market your work.

# 21

# SHOULD I COLLABORATE
# ON A PROJECT?

"I've always believed in writing without a collaborator," wrote Agatha Christie, "because where two people are writing the same book, each believes he gets all the worries and only half the royalties." Other writers believe that using a collaborator can lessen the work and increase the income for both partners. The following information can help you decide the best working method for you.

**A friend wants to collaborate with me on a writing project. Is this a good idea?**

Collaboration has obvious advantages. Two writers can pool their resources, contacts, and efforts. But two writers can also have differing opinions at any point in the development of an article, book, or story. One way to help ensure the success of a collaborative arrangement is to discuss each aspect of the partnership before work begins. Two writers should agree beforehand on exactly what contribution each will make to the project and what work each will do. In the case of a book collaboration, it would be a good idea to have this agreement in writing to protect all concerned—including the heirs, should one partner die before the other.

The secrets of successful collaboration are congeniality, respect for the other writer's abilities and opinions, and a willingness to compromise. Collaboration means dividing any fees you receive; but if you've carefully considered the projects you do, and plan accordingly, collaboration can decrease the number of hours each author invests, and ultimately increase sales.

**I'm writing a book for which I'd like to find a writing partner—someone with experience in the field I've chosen. How do I find a collaborator?**

In the age of the Internet, finding a collaborator can be as easy as posting a note on a writers message board. But that might not get you the kind of collaborator you can trust or rely on. First, try networking through the people you do know and trust, and spread the word about who you're looking for. Gather leads at writing workshops and conferences, writing groups, and writing classes. You can also review recent magazines and newspapers—especially local or regional publications—that are likely to publish work by potential collaborators.

The more writers you meet, no matter their field, the better the chance you'll find a writer who'd like to work with you.

**I have been offered the opportunity to collaborate on some stories. A friend of mine went on safari to Africa and took some excellent photographs of his hunting trips. He wants me to write up his experiences, and he will furnish the photos. If the stories are sold, what percentage do I pay him?**

There is no set rule for collaboration fees between writers and photographers. You have to decide how much each person contributed to the sale (in your case, both the writing *and* the selling) and make your share of the check reflect that.

**I've become friendly with a professional who would like to collaborate with me on magazine articles in his field of expertise. There is also the possibility of doing a book. Would his contribution of expertise and the status of his title help make a sale?**

In certain markets, it would be a necessity for you to collaborate with a professional. For example, if you were writing about the problems of executive stress, a joint byline with a clinical psychologist specializing in that area could increase your chances of a sale to a magazine like *Psychology Today*. Teaming up with a practicing attorney for a book on avoiding lawsuits might make a book more attractive to a publisher than one written by a layman alone. However, it isn't wise to expend a lot of time and energy on a book until you get some expression of interest from a publisher based on a provocative, practical book proposal, the value of which will also be bolstered by your co-author's credentials as an expert in the field.

**A writer I know has recently abandoned a book project (for which he had obtained a book contract) due to unforeseen circumstances. He has already amassed and organized a great deal of research material; all that remains to be done is the actual writing, which he has asked me to do. How should we handle the division of money for this project?**

Assuming that the first writer is not expecting you to act as a ghostwriter, the book's editor should be notified first (send samples of your writing), to find out if he is willing to accept your participation as co-author and to change the original contract to include you. As to the separate working agreement between you and the first writer, you should agree to no less than 50 percent of the advance and royalties for the work, including any subsidiary rights for film or other media. Paying a flat fee to the original author so that you can take over the entire project is another possibility. All such transactions must be in writing.

**A friend has offered to relate to me the very unusual story of his life, for use in a novel. The entire writing project will be mine, and it will be my responsibility to market the work. I feel my friend is entitled to some percentage of any profit from the novel. What is the usual percentage in such cases?**

In cases of this type, as well as in biographies, the subject whose life is being used is not usually given any payment except the satisfaction of seeing his life story in print. If you feel a personal obligation, simply offer a flat sum (whatever is agreeable to both parties) for use of this material—dependent, of course, on its sale to a publisher.

## GHOSTWRITING AND WRITING FOR HIRE

Frequently
asked question

**A person with an interesting background has asked me to write his life story. Do I sign a contract with him, and what should the financial arrangements be?**

In any situation where a writer is working with someone else before a publisher is lined up, the writer should not begin work on the project until there is an agreement on paper, spelling out exactly how much the writer will be earning while he's doing the writing, and how he'll be credited and paid on publication. The agreement should be as detailed as possible, covering not only the book itself, but any further money the book might earn, including subsidiary rights such as serialization, paperback and foreign reprints, and dramatic, film, radio, and television adaptations. It's advisable to have a lawyer draw up the agreement, which should also cover the exact amount of work each party is to contribute.

The big question is always how much you should charge. If the book is published, ask for at least 50 percent of the royalties (or advance); even 75 percent is reasonable if you're doing all the writing. It might be wise to query a few publishers to see if there is any interest in the book idea before you—and the subject—invest time and money in the project. If the subject intends to self-publish, then make sure you are adequately paid for your time up front; you should not expect any compensation from book sales.

**If I agree to ghostwrite a book for a celebrity, do I get a cover credit? How about a percentage of the royalties? Are ghostwriters looked down on by other writers?**

Unless the work is specifically intended to be an as-told-to book, ghostwriters generally don't get a byline, and rarely receive any sort of public acknowledgment, even if they are established professionals. But because a ghostwriter must subdue his own voice, write entirely in the style of another person, and satisfy both subject and editor, he is recognized and respected in the publishing community.

While public acclaim is rare for ghostwriters, there are considerable monetary rewards. Ghostwriters usually receive a flat fee, rather than a percentage of the royalties. What that fee will be depends on the book publisher, the celebrity, the reputation of the ghostwriter, and the book's salability, but it could be $25,000 or more.

**I've recently been asked to collaborate on a book with a man who is interested in self-publishing his autobiography. He has already completed a first draft of the manuscript and wants me to finish the book. How much pay should I request for a job like this?**

If you are being asked to do a rewrite of the completed manuscript, the amount of pay you receive should depend on how much work is to be done on the book before it can be submitted to the printer. If the draft needs minor rearranging and rewriting, you probably should charge an hourly rate or a set fee per page. If, on the other hand, you'll be doing a complete rewrite and will receive no author's credit on the finished book, ghostwriting rates might apply, depending on the length and difficulty of the project and the resources of the person hiring you.

**What is an as-told-to book or article? What types of subjects lend themselves to this kind of writing?**

An as-told-to work is a first-person narrative in which the actual writing is done by someone other than the person allegedly telling the story—in other words, the work is ghostwritten. The resulting book or article may have a joint byline, giving the author credit by saying the work is written "as told to Frank Jones" or "with Joe Smith." In some works, credit is given only on the acknowledgment page.

The as-told-to format is most often used in three kinds of material: a story of a dramatic personal experience, an authority's opinion on a matter of public interest, or the commentary or autobiographical narrative of a celebrity. The writer develops the concept for the work, sells the subject and the publisher on the idea, and works out the financial arrangements with both. These arrangements vary. For articles, the writer usually gets the check, while the subject gets the publicity; other times they split all monies fifty-fifty. If a book is being written, the author negotiates the division of advance money and royalties depending on the relative contributions of the two parties to the book's salability. Sometimes the author enlists the help of an agent or lawyer to do this. Professional writers often prefer to cover their work on a book up front, by negotiating to receive 75 percent of the advance and a lesser percentage of the royalties, in case the book doesn't sell as well as expected. When the manuscript is completed, the subject gives the writer permission to publish the material by signing a release form.

**What are the opportunities for writer-artist collaboration on magazine articles or stories?**

There are very few opportunities for this type of collaboration. Acceptability of a manuscript with accompanying artwork is limited because an editor has to like both the writing and the artwork. Most editors prefer to assign illustrations to artists whose work they know.

# 22

# WHAT BUSINESS KNOW-HOW DO I NEED?

Each year, thousands of writers fail in their dream of becoming freelancers. Sadly, many fail not because they couldn't write well enough, but because they never mastered the business side of the profession. While just as important to success, the business side of freelancing is a lot less appealing. So it's easy to shove business matters into the bottom drawer, where they slowly kindle into a blaze of uncollected bills and overdue taxes. If you take the right approach, however, the details of a business need not consume much of your time and effort. A few hours a week keeping your business matters well organized and up-to-date is all it really takes.

This chapter focuses on what you need to know to keep the business side of freelancing from overwhelming you—so that your success as a writer is unfettered by the mundane details of business and taxes. This advice is not meant to substitute for the advice of a qualified accountant. If you have any questions about how to handle writing income and expenses, speak to an accountant; it's also worthwhile to have a qualified accountant handle your business tax returns.

**I'm just starting out as a freelancer. How do I handle my bookkeeping?**

Consider setting up a separate checking account for your writing business; keeping writing-related income and expenses separate will make it easier for you to keep track of them. Avoid paying cash for writing expenses; if you must, establish a petty cash fund, putting money in the fund each month and keeping receipts for cash outlays.

You'll need to keep a filing system for all your receipts so you can verify expenses at the end of the month. A budget sheet for each month can help you keep track of any problems arising in your writing business—what expenses are exceeding expectations, which markets aren't buying as much as you had planned, etc. A file for submissions helps you keep tabs on your marketing track record: what you submitted where, how long ago, what you were paid, etc.

Make sure you have documentation for each business transaction, such as a canceled check or a cash receipt. You should write the business purpose on the receipt or check.

These simple procedures will get you started. As your writing business gets more successful, you'll probably want to consider a more detailed system. Many computer software companies make programs that help keep track of finances; Quicken is most well-known in this area.

### How much do I have to earn before claiming the income on my tax return?

Important information

Any money you make from writing is reportable income and must be claimed on your tax return. The trick is deciding whether you're going to claim the earnings as part of a hobby or a business.

If you plan to claim your writing as a business, you'll have to fill out the long form 1040 and Schedule C for business profit or loss. (If you plan to deduct car or equipment expenses, you'll have another, even more complex form to fill out.)

If you make little or no money from your writing, then you'll want to claim your income as hobby income (that is, "other income") on your 1040. The drawback to doing this is that your ability to take deductions is much more limited. (The IRS has different standards for hobby deductions than for business deductions.)

How do you decide between hobby and business? If you aim to make a profit from your writing (and you do make a profit), you should be operating as a business. If you're not concerned with profit or earnings, then treat your earnings as hobby income.

**I've been writing for years, but I don't make a lot of sales. Can I still take business deductions for writing-related expenses?**

If you've been pursuing a writing career for years without much success, the IRS may challenge your deductions on the basis that you did not have any profit motive in writing, and therefore you were writing only as a hobby, not as a business. In that case, you would only be able to deduct expenses up to the amount of income you made from writing. If the IRS regarded your writing as a business, you could deduct any business expenses, even if they exceeded any profit from writing. Remember that tax laws change every year, and these changes might affect your status. Keep informed.

**At what point can I be considered a business rather than a hobby writer?**

You should make a profit in three of five consecutive years. If you don't meet that milestone, you may be able to qualify even if you haven't made a profit but still have a professional business. When the IRS is determining whether you qualify as a business, they will look at your profit motive, or the effort you're making to conduct a professional business and earn money. Keeping detailed records is important when claiming deductions and qualifying as a business.

**What types of things are deductible?**

Writing supplies, including paper, carbons, pens, ribbons, and mailing and copying costs, are deductible. Typewriters, word processors, and other equipment can be depreciated. Courses and conferences can also be deducted, as long as they enhance or refresh writing skills; you can also deduct transportation, lodging, and meal expenses when traveling for business purposes. You can deduct auto expenses; you'll need a mileage log to substantiate them. The log must show the date of each trip, the beginning and ending mileage, and the business purpose. Dues to writers organizations are also deductible.

The IRS applies the "ordinary" and "necessary" rules in judging the validity of a business expense. This means the expenses should be ordinary for your profession and necessary for carrying out your business.

The IRS strongly recommends that you keep expense records for as long as the period of limitations for audits. In most cases, that's three years from the date the return was filed or two years from when the tax was paid, whichever is later. Keep income records for six years from the date you reported it to the IRS on your tax forms; the IRS has six years to go after unreported income.

**I don't have an office outside my home, but I write in my home and have sold a few freelance articles. Is there any way I can deduct my home work space on my tax return?**

A home office can be deducted, but only up to the amount of your writing income, and only if it is a room or distinct portion of a room set aside for writing alone, and is used on a regular basis. For example, if you rent a five-room apartment (not counting the bathroom), and use one room only for research and writing, you can deduct one-fifth of your rent, heat and electric bills. If you own a seven-room house, and have a writing room that represents one-seventh of the total space, your deductions can include one-seventh of your total interest on your mortgage, real estate taxes, repairs to the house, utilities, home insurance premiums, and depreciation on the room. In either case, any long-distance phone calls and similar home expenses directly related to your writing are deductible. If you have a second phone in your home office used just for your business, then, of course, the entire cost of that phone is deductible.

In the late 1980s and early 1990s the government severely tightened the restrictions on home-office deductions. It's crucial that you check the appropriate IRS publications or consult a tax expert annually for new regulations.

**If I take a vacation and pick up information on that trip that I later use in my writing, can I deduct the trip as a business expenditure?**

If the trip is a mixture of business and pleasure, then the author must keep accurate records of how much time she spent on business during the trip, and deduct only that percentage of the costs. For example, if you took a trip to California for three weeks, and spent a week of that time researching an article about the movie business (while the remaining two weeks were spent visiting relatives), you could deduct only one-third of your expenses for travel and lodging. If the entire trip was spent on business, then all such expenses could be deducted, but you must be able to produce receipts and records to that effect. You must also be able to prove to the IRS that you're a business writer, not a hobby writer.

**I write for outdoor, travel, recreation, and other such magazines. Can I deduct any costs related to my recreational vehicle or boat as business expenses?**

The amount you can deduct on these vehicles depends on what percentage of their use is related to your writing. If you spend one-fourth of your time on each in the pursuit of freelancing, then that amount of the maintenance and repair costs for each could be deducted. However, the IRS would probably assume that you use the vehicles for your own pleasure and recreation too, so it's doubtful you could deduct these expenses in full. Keep a log of your travels with these vehicles, along with receipts and documentation that they were being used for business.

**The magazines for which I've worked have paid me the fee and expense money in one check. Since business expenses aren't real earnings, how do I treat this on my tax forms?**

Since publishers don't have a convenient method for separating business expenses from payment for manuscripts, they usually send one check to cover both. You can, however, deduct your expenses on your IRS tax form. Even though reimbursed expenses are shown as gross income on your tax form, they would be deducted before figuring the net income on which your tax is paid.

**How can a full-time freelancer provide for retirement?**

The best way for a writer to provide for retirement is to start an Individual Retirement Account (also called an Individual Retirement Arrangement), or IRA. The maximum amount per year you can invest in an IRA varies. Consult the IRS Web site (ww.irs.gov) for more information.

**It seems like I constantly have cash flow problems, and payments never arrive on time. How can I minimize the stress this causes?**

The best way to avoid cash-flow problems is to continually work on developing new clients. That means sending out queries and/or contacting potential clients even when you're busy. Try to set aside a couple of days each month for such marketing.

Additionally, never rely too much on any one source of income. Developing a few key accounts, preferably large and reliable enough to cover your overhead and living expenses, is important. But don't become complacent. Nothing lasts forever, so don't let any single account become more than a third of your business.

Dealing with the choppy seas of cash flow requires discipline. Using your budget, establish a maximum amount that you will spend in any month. Keeping your earnings in a business account separate from your personal savings or checking account is one good way to keep from spending it at all.

You should also meticulously track what your clients owe you. Record who owes you money, how much, and when it's due. As best as possible, arrange payment on your terms. You may be able to get some money up front for copywriting, or even expense money from magazines.

Fast action is key to good cash flow. To maximize your income:

- Incorporate billing into your weekly schedule.
- Record your phone or other expenses when the bill comes due.
- Bill as soon as payment is due.
- Don't let a new, unproven account run up huge tabs. In most cases, you won't know how good publishers' or clients' payment practices are until they owe you money.

## LEGAL ISSUES

### Should I incorporate?

Generally, when professionals form corporations, only the assets of the corporation (as opposed to the assets of the individual) are liable for seizure by creditors or potential litigants. Libel is one of the largest litigation traps a writer faces. But because libel may be considered a personal statement, a court could still make your personal assets part of a settlement, even if you are incorporated.

Whether to incorporate is a complex question best handled by an accountant or lawyer who knows your situation. Should you opt for incorporation, the state office that oversees corporations, such as the secretary of state, will send you information detailing the steps you need to take and the practices you must adopt as a corporation.

### What should I look for in a lawyer?

To find a lawyer versed in publishing and copyright law, contact the local lawyer referral service of your state or city bar association. Be sure the lawyer knows something about laws that pertain to publishing; a lawyer inexperienced with publishing customs and procedures can create a lot of confusion and unnecessary fuss.

### Where can I get legal assistance?

Volunteer Lawyers for the Arts (www.vlany.org) is a national organization of lawyers offering free legal services to creative artists, including writers. Eligibility for the service is based on the writer's income, with the writer sometimes paying court costs even if representation is free. Also helpful is the National Writers Union at www.nwu.org.

### Are there any special provisions an author should make when drawing up a will?

When a writer dies, her literary works remain for someone to look after. In the will, the writer may specify who is to inherit the copyrights to her works and who is to receive any royalties after her death. She may also appoint a person to make artistic decisions about her work after her death, such as whether and under what circumstances unpublished works may be published posthumously.

## WHERE TO FIND OUT MORE

## BOOKS

Many IRS publications and help guides are available online and at public libraries. Be aware that the IRS's publications will only detail how the IRS interprets the law; they may not explain all the deductions for which you qualify.

*Writer's Pocket Tax Guide,* by Darlene A. Cypser, is an invaluable resource for the freelance writer; you can find it at www.foolscap-quill.com.

*The Writer's Legal Guide: An Authors Guild Desk Reference,* by Tad Crawford and Kay Murray, provides a nice overview of the business side of publishing.

*The Writer's Legal Companion,* by Brad Bunnin and Peter Beren, has a small section on taxes, but the rest of the information (on negotiating contracts, protecting your rights, managing permissions, etc.) is sure to come in handy.

# 23

# HOW DO I WRITE AND SELL SHORT FICTION?

The competition for publishing short fiction—especially in popular magazines and journals—is fierce, and the days when a fiction writer could earn a living writing short stories are long gone. Only a select few magazines—such as the *New Yorker*, *Harper's*, and *Esquire*—publish literary short fiction. To get an acceptance letter from one of these publications, you'll need to be writing at the level of John Updike and Alice Munro (and even then it's tough).

On the other hand, there are hundreds, if not thousands, of small-circulation literary journals and magazines (and online zines) that actively publish new writers and will give your work a fair chance. This chapter gives you an overview of what it takes to write successful and publishable short fiction.

## CRAFT AND TECHNIQUE

**I like to write short stories, but people say the things I write are not exactly stories. How can I find out what a short story is?**

A traditional short story (with a beginning, a middle, and an end) features a character who meets with conflict either within himself, with another character, or with some other force outside of himself. The conflict and its resolution should change the character. It is this change, for better or worse, that makes a story.

Consider, for example, a story about two young boys on a Saturday afternoon fishing trip. If the author tells us about the nice time they had looking for the right spot along the bank to cast their lines, and the large number of fish they caught before they trotted happily home, would it be a story? Not unless one of the boys, who always thought of himself as a coward, had to muster up his courage to save the other boy after he fell into the rushing river. Here, a character is in conflict with what he sees as his own limitations, and he learns that he can go beyond them—the series of incidents has become a story.

Look closely at what you've written. Does your story contain character conflict, change, and growth, or are you just relating a series of events that involve one or more characters? That may be the difference between what you've written and what a story is.

### What is the difference between crisis and climax in a traditional short story?

The crisis in a short story arises from conflict that leads to a turning point. After a series of obstacles, the major character experiences a dark moment in which he sees no way to solve the problem. Then, there is a moment of revelation as the character figures out everything. The climax normally follows the crisis and represents the most intense point in the story line. The story should end shortly thereafter.

### What is a story theme? Is it any different from a story problem?

Writers disagree on the exact definitions, but here's one explanation: A theme is the message an author imparts to his readers through the plot and characters in his story. The writer starts with an idea, and as his story develops, it is influenced by his own philosophy or observation of the human condition. This is his theme. A story problem is the vehicle by which an author presents his theme. For instance, the problem facing Dorothy in *The Wizard of Oz* is getting home to Kansas. Through her trials and adventures in the Land of Oz, she realizes her folly in wanting to run away from home in the first place, and finally decides "there's no place like home," which is the overall theme of the story.

**I'm having trouble coming up with fresh ideas for my fiction. What are some ways I can jog my imagination?**

First of all, you should read widely—not just novels and short stories, but magazines and newspapers. Something in a factual article might spark an idea. If something makes you think "I wonder what kind of person would do something like that," chances are you could use it as a starting point for your next story. Sometimes meeting an interesting person, recalling an event that happened to you at work, or remembering a daydream (or nightmare) can be a catalyst.

Another way to come up with new ideas is to listen to what people say—on the street, in a restaurant, etc.—and jot in your notebook any interesting pieces of dialogue. Remember: A good writer is also a good listener.

Your own life experiences can also provide the foundation for a short story or novel, but you must be careful to avoid becoming trapped by the facts. Remember that you're telling a story and that what was really said or what really happened will have to be modified (or ignored altogether) in the interest of creating readable dialogue and an entertaining plot.

Many writers have found that events in history and the classics of literature can be retold in modern surroundings—Othello as chairman of a corporation, or a Napoleon figure as president of the U.S., are only two of the many possible twists on old stories.

Above all, remember inspiration doesn't always strike like a flash of lightning. Ideas tend to ripen slowly, starting from a single impression or bit of information. The more opportunities you give your imagination, the greater the chance ideas will come to you.

**I have a story in mind involving several character types, but I'm having trouble coming up with a strong plot. What can I do about this?**

Most fiction is based on what the characters do. Interesting, believable characters create the atmosphere and conflict necessary for a successful short story or novel. Every story must have a basic conflict. By carefully examining your characters—their backgrounds, likes, dislikes, beliefs—you can get ideas about how to set up conflict. Ask yourself questions: What does the main character want? What obstacles might interfere with his goals? How do the characters relate to one another? Once you've set up the basic conflict, you can begin to outline the action of the story. If you're still having problems developing your story's plot, you may want to read 20 *Master Plots*, by Ronald B. Tobias, which discusses twenty plots that recur in all fiction.

### How does a writer get his point across in a story without repeating it?

The change that occurs in the major character as a result of his experiences should make your point. In the course of the story, the major character must experience a moment of revelation or make a decision and, just as in real life, he changes as a result of these experiences. It is through these revelations and decisions that the writer sends his message, not through overtly stating it.

### What is the difference between a plant and a false plant in a story?

A plant is something (a person, place, object, or fact) that the writer "plants" early in a story so when it is used later, it won't seem unrealistic or like too much of a coincidence. For example, imagine you're reading a short story in which a cowboy's horse has just died; the character is sun-parched and dying of thirst himself as he traverses the desert of the American Southwest, but is saved when he suddenly comes to an old deserted homestead that has a spring close by. Wouldn't you be bewildered? Where did that house and spring come from? A good writer will find a way to plant them earlier in his story, thus getting rid of the contrived coincidence.

The false plant is something deliberately placed by the author that ultimately has no connection with the conclusion or resolution of the conflict in the story. Introducing innocent suspects with viable motives in a mystery is a common use of this device. False plants must always be adequately explained somewhere in the story. If the writer of that cowboy short story mentioned an old homestead with a spring close by and *didn't* put it to some use later in the story, he would have placed what is called a dangling plant. These can be annoying to the reader and should be avoided.

### How can I effectively create a character in the limited space of a short story?

Try to determine what is so unique about him that warrants a story. Find a single fact that sets him apart and gives him a recognizable trait. Then portray him in *one* sentence. Though difficult to write, one-line character descriptions can be extremely incisive.

Character traits should not be thrown at the reader, but rather should be woven gradually into the story. A writer should let dialogue, actions, and reactions be the defining features of a particular character.

**I have often wondered whether a man can write effectively about a woman, and vice versa. What is the practice among successful writers?**

There is significant proof in literature that a writer can successfully portray a member of the opposite sex. Look at what Flaubert did with Madame Bovary, what Margaret Mitchell did with Rhett Butler, and what Tennessee Williams did with Blanche DuBois, to name just a few. The ease with which a male writer can slip into the consciousness of a female character and vice versa depends ultimately on the individual writer and how much insight he has into the workings of human nature, regardless of gender.

**In dissecting a short story, how does a writer go about isolating a scene? To me, the scenes seem somewhat continuous. I fail to see any sharp dividing line in a taut story.**

Whenever the action moves to a different setting, that's automatically a new scene. If, for example, a story opens in a young couple's kitchen, then moves to an incident in the husband's office, these two different settings constitute two different scenes. But suppose the story is a short-short in which all the action takes place in the kitchen. In that case, look for a division in time. A story may begin with the husband and wife in the kitchen at breakfast time, then jump to five o'clock, when the wife is preparing dinner. This is a device used often. For example: "Jim stomped out during breakfast without finishing his coffee. As Ellen prepared dinner, she thought of the silly argument they had had early that day."

**When writing a short story, are you supposed to italicize everything that is spoken or thought?**

Use quotation marks for dialogue spoken by story characters. Styles vary for denoting a character's thoughts: Some use quotation marks, some put a character's thoughts in italics, some merely set them off with a comma and capitalize the first letter, and some make no special designation at all if it's clear that the thoughts are the narrating viewpoint character's.

## FLASHBACK QUESTION

**I don't understand most modern poetry. Is there some book which has taken these kinds of poems apart, analyzed them and discussed what the poet is saying?**

Yes, *The Poet and the Poem* by Judson Jerome has chapters on this subject along with discussions of other matters of interest to poets attempting to become "professional" poets. What Jerome means by "professional" poet as opposed to an "amateur" or "trade" poet is described in his column in the November 1968 issue of *Writer's Digest*.

**An editor told me I should strive to present a single viewpoint in my short story. Why should I? How do I decide whether third person or first person is better?**

In a short story, strong reader identification with one of the characters is very important and is easily disrupted when the author employs a multiple viewpoint. Suspense and continuity are often lost in the transition from one viewpoint to another. For these reasons, short stories told from more than one viewpoint are rarely successful. The choice between first and third person should be made with the plot and characters in mind. Using first person can be subjective, and first-person point of view lends itself well to strong emotion and fast reader identification. Third person, on the other hand, is useful if your plot and characters demand an objective treatment.

**One of the editors who rejected my story told me he liked the basic idea very much but the whole story was much too complicated. How can I simplify it?**

If you have too much going on in your story, it may be because you've tried to incorporate too many characters or incidents into it. You have to decide who the story is about and focus your narrative on that character and his problem. All other characters should be a part of the story you build around the major character. You may have to reduce arbitrarily the number of characters (to three or four at the most) and restructure your plot from there. The result should be greater simplicity and unity.

**I submitted my story to an editor, and he returned it, saying it was too slow-paced. What is he talking about?**

If your story is too slow-paced, you are giving too little attention to action and dialogue that moves the story toward the problem and its resolution. Editors often complain that stories written by beginners don't even start until page five of the manuscript. If the reader must watch the main character wake up, light a cigarette, make coffee, and start breakfast before he learns what the problem in the story is, the story is too slow-paced. Since word space is so limited in short stories, the opening scene (as well as every other scene) should be short on exposition and quick to provide action and dialogue that engages the reader and is pertinent to the story's end.

**The transitions in my stories never seem to work. How can I handle them without being abrupt or taking too much time?**

Scene transitions involve changes in time, place, and emotion; the key to smooth transition is to link the old with the new. In the last paragraph of a scene, preferably the last sentence, indicate the present place and time period, and if possible, imply the new ones. Then the first sentence in the new scene can establish the time lapse and change of place. Note these points in the following example: "She hoped the Crandalls wouldn't like her antiques. *But that must wait until tomorrow*, she reminded herself, and tried to get some sleep. The next morning, worry about the Crandalls completely left her mind when...."

**How do I detect rambling in my story? A teacher told me I was rambling at some places where I thought description was necessary.**

Examine the passages your teacher marked and evaluate them for their relevance to the story. Be able to define the purpose of each episode and descriptive passage. If you can't determine a function for each part, either discard it or rewrite it. If you determine that the information really is necessary, your teacher's assessment that it rambles is a sign that it should be incorporated into the story more subtly. For instance, can your spelled-out characterization be compressed into the character's actions or his dialogue? Every passage must perform three or four functions at the same time—advance the plot, add to the characterizations, introduce background information, and so on. Being able to write this concisely takes practice, but in the long run, your stories will be better.

## When an editor says my story has loose ends, what does he mean?

It means the story has unresolved complications, lingering questions, or problematic inconsistencies. You may need to add or omit incidents, or merely add a phrase that refers to an earlier part of the story. Your story needs to be unified in time and action, and the course of events must be logical. For instance, don't introduce some line of plot action for which the reader expects some meaning in the story and then arbitrarily drop it. It only confuses and annoys the reader.

## Looking at the short story I've written, I can see that the conclusion is weak and unconvincing. How can I fix it?

Endings can be the most difficult element of short story writing, since an ineffectual one (or the wrong one) will make the story dissatisfying and unpublishable. Is your ending too obvious? Is the outcome exactly what a reader would expect from your characters and plot? Your problem may be that you failed to plan for your ending before you started writing the story or, conversely, that you overplanned and stifled the real story. If you were hoping something would come to you as the story progressed, and nothing did, your ending undoubtedly seems irrelevant or illogical.

At this point, you have a few options. Your solution could involve going back to the beginning of the story and doing some replotting. Make your major character's decision a difficult one rather than an obvious one. Or use the conflict structure to misdirect your reader, leading him to expect a different ending than what you finally give him. Changes like these must be incorporated into the whole story, for if you merely tack on an ending, it will remain inappropriate and weak because it is not justified by the rest of the story. Ask yourself what you're trying to communicate to the reader through your story. Revisiting your themes might shed some light on the proper conclusion. If you still can't create a convincing and emotionally powerful ending, then it's possible you may need to set the story aside and begin work on something else. Sometimes distance from the material and fresh eyes are all you need to realize what's missing or to gain new insight into where your story should go.

**I'm taking a course in short story writing and my teacher keeps noting "overstatement" in my stories. But he's never given me a solid definition of the problem.**

Your teacher may be referring to what others call overwriting or purple prose. Redundancies, an excess of adjectives and adverbs in descriptive passages, or an overplay of emotion can all be considered overstatement. Passages that seem contrived or that just don't fit the tenor of the story may be overwritten. While overstatement is most easily spotted by someone other than the writer, you should develop the skill of recognizing and correcting this flaw, which would obviously hinder publication.

## DECIPHERING STORY TYPES

**Fiction requirements of many magazines specify "no contrived stories." What do they mean by these terms?**

By *contrived*, editors usually mean plots in which the action is constructed in an artificial, implausible way. For example, if a character purposely sets fire to a barn to kill the man inside, that's a credible, well-motivated act. But if a fire happens to break out in the barn for no reason other than the obvious one of helping the author dispose of the man inside, that's contrived.

**Many guidelines state "no vignettes or slice-of-life pieces." What does that mean?**

A slice-of-life story or vignette is usually one that depends less on plot for its interest than on mood and atmosphere and the detail with which the setting (and its effects on the characters) is described. It is a seemingly unselective presentation of life as it is—a brief, illuminating look at a realistic rather than a constructed situation, revealed to the reader without comment or interpretation by the author.

**How long is a short-short story compared to a short story?**

The average short-short story is from 500 to 1,500 words long, and the short story runs from 2,000 to 7,000 words. Individual publishers may have varying requirements, which would be listed in *Novel & Short Story Writer's Market*.

**Besides the obvious one of length, are there differences between short stories and short-short stories?**

Plot in a short story is limited to a small chain of events. In a short-short, it is confined to a single power-packed incident that gives the story its thematic value. There is no room for extensive character development, and the writer doesn't try to do more than focus intensely on one truth of life that may or may not be new to the reader. Good subjects for short-shorts include changes in parent-child or husband-wife relationships, a child's awakening to some facet of life, or an individual's reevaluation of his role in society.

**It's hard to draw the line between short stories and novels, since there are also novellas. Just what are the differences in length, subject matter, and form in all of these types of fiction?**

Although there are no set rules of length, the short story usually runs 2,000 to 7,000 words. Long stories, which are more difficult to sell, generally run 8,000 to 15,000 words. Novellas will range anywhere from 20,000 to 50,000 words. Herman Melville's *Billy Budd* and Ernest Hemingway's *The Old Man and the Sea* are examples of this genre. Novels are the longest type of fiction. The novel's structure is similar to that of a short story in that it presents a series of conflicts and temporary obstacles leading to a climax in which the major conflict is resolved or accepted as unsolvable. The difference lies in the fact that the novelist has more time and word space to develop his plot, subplots, and characters, and can more easily change the viewpoint of the narrator.

## WHEN TRUTH MEETS FICTION

**Why aren't true-life experiences the best model for planning a story? How could I possibly improve on the way it really happened?**

True-life experiences often make a good skeleton for a short story, but they usually need to be dramatized before they will interest others. If the basic action of your story needs a lot of exposition, which it invariably does, you may need to invent action and dialogue to get it across more effectively. Readers will be bored by a straight narrative explanation. If your characters are based upon people you are acquainted with, chances are you don't know them as well as a writer of fiction must know his characters. In order to provide them with sufficient motivation, you may have to provide traits that make them unique and worthy of the reader's sympathies. Plot may need changes in time span and in order of events so that it effectively moves the story along.

## MARKETING YOUR STORIES

### Should I send a query for my short stories?

Because of the nature of short fiction, editors rarely expect to be queried about it. Most editors prefer to receive the complete manuscript.

### There are very few magazines that contain stories. Magazines print mostly articles. Who buys stories today?

While a few major magazines still have active fiction markets, the majority of markets for short stories aren't on the newsstand. You should look to literary magazines and journals, which are listed in *Novel & Short Story Writer's Market*.

### How do literary magazines differ from general publications?

Literary magazines or journals are publications with limited circulation—generally of five thousand or less—that offer writers a vehicle of expression not found in commercial magazines. They aim for an audience of writers, editors, and students and teachers of literature. Their contributors are usually writers striving for literary excellence. T.S. Eliot, Flannery O'Connor, and John Gardner all received their early attention by having their work published in literary magazines.

Literary magazines are often sponsored by universities or nonprofit organizations and do not rely on general public support; hence, their editors don't have to compromise the ideals of their publications toward a popular or commercial taste. A literary magazine can be centered on a specific theme or can be eclectic—open to work on any idea. Pay is usually low or nonexistent; contributing authors are often paid with copies or subscriptions to the magazine.

**Do book publishers put out collections of short novels and stories that haven't previously been published?**

Yes, but rarely. In the case of an unknown writer, the publisher is usually reluctant to start off with a short-story collection; novels are greatly favored. Many university presses and small presses do hold competitions for short-story collections; first prize is almost always publication of the collection.

**My local bookstore has a very limited supply of magazines, and I can't afford to send away and pay for a lot of sample copies. How can I find out what kinds of stories magazine editors consider good so I can read and learn from them?**

There are several anthologies published annually that will give you a good overview. *The O. Henry Prize Stories* (with earlier editions published under the title *Prize Stories: The O. Henry Awards*) and *The Best American Short Stories* reprint stories that have appeared in magazines like the *New Yorker*, *Redbook*, and leading literary magazines. *The Pushcart Prize: Best of the Small Presses* reprints stories from some of the smaller magazines that you wouldn't find in most libraries. Each anthology prints a list of the magazines from which they selected stories. You can also check magazines' Web sites, which often offer sample editions or representative stories in their electronic archives.

## WHERE TO FIND OUT MORE

### BOOKS

*Novel & Short Story Writer's Market* lists more than a thousand places to publish your stories, and includes interviews and articles on the craft and business of fiction writing.

*The Art of the Short Story: 52 Great Authors, Their Best Short Fiction, and Their Insights on Writing*, edited by Dana Gioia and R.S. Gwynn, is a massive anthology and an excellent resource for learning the craft.

*Writing in General and the Short Story in Particular*, by former *Esquire* fiction editor L. Rust Hills, is one of the best instructional guides to the craft; the author cuts right to the chase and tells you exactly what to do and what *not* to do.

### WEB SITES

Flogging the Quill (http://floggingthequill.typepad.com) is guaranteed to improve the art and craft of your storytelling.

The Writer's Resource Center (www.poewar.com) offers hundreds of articles on the craft of fiction, as well as poetry and freelancing.

Writesville (www.writesville.com) is run by an aspiring fiction writer who shares what he's learned so far.

# How do i publish
# my poetry?

Robert Graves once remarked, "There's no money in poetry, but then there's no poetry in money either." And so writers continue their pursuit of the perfect poem even though the rewards often are only psychological.

## THE MARKET FOR POETRY

**I've written poems over the years, and everyone tells me the same thing—that I have a gift and a way with words. How do I get started publishing my poems?**

Your best bet is to pick up the latest version of *Poet's Market*. It lists current publishers and what they're looking for, as well as tips for submitting your work. Also look for *The Directory of Poetry Publishers*, which lists thousands of publishing opportunities for poets of all skill levels. *Poets & Writers*, a bimonthly publication, is filled with markets, contest announcements, and calls for poetry manuscripts. The Internet can provide information on poetry markets as well; use search terms such as *poetry markets* and *publishing poetry*.

**I have been published in three books from the poetry.com site. But I was wondering how I would go about getting my poems sold or getting them all published as a book?**

It's important to remember that there aren't a lot of poetry book publishers, and those publishers want poets with proven track records. That's why the

Frequently
asked question

best way to start is by submitting your poems to literary magazines and building up a strong publishing history. Also keep in mind that anthologies like the one you mention often aren't considered viable publishing credits. Your work needs to appear in a variety of magazines that publish good examples of the kind of poetry you write. *Poet's Market* lists magazines and publishers you can check out, as well as contests.

Only when you've published about fifteen poems in different magazines is it time to think about collecting them in a single volume. You may have a better chance of publishing a chapbook, which is a soft-cover booklet of about twenty-four pages. There are many more chapbook publishers than book publishers when it comes to poetry.

**Is poetry.com a legitimate place to publish poetry? I'm not too sure if my work is good or if they are just selling books, memberships, and awards to me.**

At the very least, the site's claims are truthful (they do what they say they'll do), but poetry.com is widely known for accepting nearly every poem submitted.

**I don't see much poetry published in magazines these days. Does anyone buy poetry?**

Few editors buy poetry in the sense that they pay cash for it. However, there's much poetry being published if you know where to look. In print, literary journals and magazines produced by colleges and universities or by small presses or individuals publish poetry, as do a few major publications like the *Atlantic* and the *New Yorker*. (In fact, literary journals devote a large percentage of their pages to poetry.) The Internet is another source of poetry publication, offering many online journals as well as special sites where poets can post their work and comment on each other's poems.

Most literary magazines offer contributors a copy or two of the issue in which their work appears. Magazines like the *New Yorker*, and some of the more prestigious literary journals, do pay cash, but competition makes acceptance of your work very difficult. Often, online publications offer no payment at all, except for publishing credit and the value of a poet's work being available to a worldwide readership.

**I want my work to be read, so why should I publish my poetry in an obscure literary magazine? Shouldn't I aim for bigger markets?**

Literary publications only seem obscure when compared to the mass-circulation publications that fill the racks at the supermarkets and bookstores. True lovers of poetry know where to find literary magazines, and they turn to them for the best poetry being written today. Serious poets do place their work in these magazines—so much so that submitting work to the best of the literary journals is highly competitive. However, don't assume the smaller magazines, even those that are truly obscure, are beneath your consideration. The editors of these journals are dedicated to the art of poetry and are delighted to give exposure to promising poets; plus, the journals themselves are often visually interesting and artistic. Publication in literary magazines can offer exposure to a knowledgeable and appreciative audience, and make an attractive showcase for your work.

**I have a book manuscript of over three hundred poems, and I'd like to see it published and available in bookstores. How can I make this happen?**

Frequently asked question

First, three hundred poems is a lot for a first volume of poetry. It's nearly unheard of for a book-length manuscript of unpublished poetry to be accepted (unless you're a celebrity). Most poets start out by submitting their poems to magazines. Doing so helps them build a publishing history and enables them to show a book editor that their work has been accepted and appreciated in its own right.

Second, your dreams are precious to you, but you need to bring them in line with the realities of the publishing world. Few major publishers accept or consider poetry manuscripts, and those that do focus on poets with major reputations. Even university presses and small presses known for publishing poetry can be tough for beginners to break in to (although some may sponsor competitions to publish a first book of poetry).

As for bookstore placement, you won't find much shelf space dedicated to poetry (at least relative to fiction and nonfiction), and that space is dominated by offerings from the bigger publishers and the poets you probably read in school. Books of poetry rarely make it to the best-seller lists because the reading audience for poetry is small and specialized.

Serious poets don't expect to get rich and famous. They work hard at their craft, relish communicating with readers, and celebrate their triumphs. (For some poets, breaking in to a prestigious literary journal may be the highlight of their careers.) If you're hoping for more from your writing, particularly in terms of money and notoriety, seek out a different form of writing.

## SUBMITTING POETRY

### What are typical submission guidelines for poetry?

Guidelines usually indicate what kind of poetry the editor or publisher is looking for, how many poems to submit, the length of the poem, whether to submit by regular mail or e-mail, payment, response times, and similar information. In addition, especially where contests are involved, the magazine or publisher may outline exactly how the manuscript should be prepared (for instance, whether to include a cover sheet, or whether the poet's name should appear on the manuscript pages). Submission guidelines may appear in the magazine or on a Web site, or may be available for a self-addressed stamped envelope (SASE).

### I want to submit some poems to a magazine. How should I prepare my manuscript?

Set your word-processor margins to one inch. At the top of the sheet, type your name, address, phone number, e-mail address, and line count in the right corner. Drop down about six lines and type the title of your poem, either centered on the page or flush with the left margin. (Titles may be initial-capped or in all capital letters.) Drop down two more lines, and begin your poem flush with the left margin; never center the lines of your poem in the middle of the page.

Most editors prefer poems to be single spaced, with double-spacing between stanzas. Type only one poem per page, even if your poem is very short. For poems longer than one page, type your name in the upper left corner of subsequent pages; on the next line, type the poem title, the page number, and either "continue stanza" or "begin new stanza," depending on how your poem breaks between the pages.

**How do I prepare my poems if I want to submit them by e-mail?**

First, make sure the publication accepts e-mail submissions. Check guidelines, market listings, or the magazine's Web site to see how the editor wants electronic submissions formatted. Many editors forbid attachments, and they may automatically delete any e-mail that arrives with an attachment. For those editors, paste your poems into the body of the e-mail. For editors who do not mind attachments, format your document the same as you would if you were submitting it by regular mail. If you're including a cover letter, you can insert it at the beginning of your e-mail, whether you're pasting poems into the body of your message or attaching a document.

Take note of any special requirements an editor may have regarding e-mail submissions, such as whether to paste only one poem at a time in a message, whether an attachment should be in Word or another format, and what to put in the subject line. (Editors use the subject line to screen for spam and to direct the submission to the appropriate departmental editor; they can be very picky about what appears there.)

A growing number of magazine Web sites provide online contact forms for electronic queries as well as submissions. Depending on the form, you can paste your poem(s) into a field or load your manuscript from your hard drive. Click a button and your work is submitted.

**How do I figure the number of lines in my poem? Do I count the title and the spaces between stanzas? Do I also include a word count for my poem?**

The standard method is to count only lines of text in a poem and to not include the title or the spaces between stanzas. Sometimes magazine guidelines state to include spaces between stanzas, but this doesn't happen often. However, if magazine or contest guidelines mention it specifically, be sure to include spaces in your line count. You don't need to provide a word count for your poem unless guidelines ask for it.

**How many poems should I submit to a magazine at one time?**

It's best to follow a magazine's guidelines, but an average number is three to five poems per submission. More than five poems overloads the editor, but less than three doesn't really give the editor a sense of your abilities or a wide enough selection of poems from which to choose.

**Do I need to include a cover letter with the poems I submit to a magazine?**

There was a time when a cover letter wasn't expected with a poetry submission. However, many modern editors appreciate the personal touch of a cover letter. Such a letter shouldn't be long—it's simply a polite introduction of yourself and your work. List the poems you're submitting, and briefly mention something about yourself (publishing credits are fine if you keep them short). It's also nice to comment on the magazine in some way so the editor knows you're familiar with the publication. Editors often indicate their preferences regarding cover letters in submission guidelines and market listings.

**Is it OK to submit my poetry to more than one magazine or journal at the same time?**

For some editors, simultaneous submissions are fine; for others, they're taboo. Check submission guidelines or market listings. If you submit the same poems to more than one publication at a time, keep careful records to avoid confusion. If a poem is accepted by one publication, you *must* notify the other editors that the poem is no longer available for consideration. Failure to do so is unprofessional and discourteous and can be harmful to future poet/editor relationships.

**When is a poem considered "previously published"? If I post one of my poems on a Web site, is that the same as publishing it? Is the poem considered published if I print it in a wedding program that's distributed to a limited number of people?**

If your poem has appeared in print for public viewing—in a magazine or journal, anthology, postcard, or broadside—it's considered published. (A broadside is like a poster with a poem on it.) Your work is also considered published if it appears in a collection such as a chapbook, even if you self-publish the chapbook and distribute it only to friends and family.

In theory, publishing also includes printing your poem in a program for a private ceremony or event, such as a wedding, funeral, or anniversary. However, some editors may not be as strict about this type of publishing. If you want to submit a poem you've published in this way to a magazine, let the editor know in your cover letter so she can decide up front whether the previous publication matters. To be safe, don't submit a poem you've printed in a program or similar publication to a contest when the guidelines stipulate you must send an unpublished entry.

Opinions differ as to whether posting a poem on a Web site constitutes publishing it. For instance, some experts say if you post your poem to a forum where others can offer criticism, it doesn't count as publication, especially if the forum requires membership to participate. On the other hand, if you post your poem specifically to be read and enjoyed by an online audience (even on your own Web site), or if you have a poem accepted by an online journal, you should consider the poem published.

**My poem won a prize in a competition. I received a cash award, but the poem wasn't published in any way. Is the poem still considered unpublished?**

Yes, as long as your poem doesn't appear in print, it remains unpublished. It wouldn't hurt to mention the award in your cover letter if you submit the poem to a magazine, just to let the editor know the poem has already won some acknowledgment and might be worth extra attention.

**When editors say they'll consider traditional forms of poetry, what do they mean?**

They mean they'll consider poetry other than contemporary free verse, including poetry that rhymes or adheres to a fixed form. Traditional fixed forms include sonnets, villanelles, terza rima, Japanese haiku, ghazals, and American cinquain. The term *traditional* may mean different things to different editors, so it's best to study a particular publication before submitting work.

**In market listings, many editors say they don't want greeting card poetry. What does this mean?**

When editors speak of greeting card poetry, they're referring to poetry that has more in common with greeting card verse than serious poetry. Some of the characteristics of greeting card poetry include cliché topics, high sentimentality, sing-song rhythms, and predictable rhyme words and patterns.

## BOOKS AND CHAPBOOKS

**What's the difference between a book and a chapbook of poetry?**

A book of poetry is usually more than fifty pages long and may be hardbound or softbound. Most modern poetry books are slim volumes of seventy-five to one hundred pages, although collected works of better-known poets may be much longer.

A chapbook consists of approximately twenty-four to fifty pages (shorter lengths are most common). It's usually 5″ x 8″ (digest size), saddle-stapled, with a soft cover—although chapbooks can have any dimension and style of binding. (Some are even published within literary magazines.) Chapbooks are often most successful when the poems have a theme or are connected in some way to create an overall effect, rather than being a batch of disjointed poems gathered for the sake of collecting them in one place. Poets usually publish chapbooks of their work before pursuing book publication.

**Are book and chapbook manuscripts formatted the same way as manuscripts sent to magazines?**

Some of the same guidelines apply, including making sure your name and the title of your manuscript are at the top of each page, and typing only one poem to a page. You would also want to number your pages successively, include a credits page that lists where poems were originally published, and provide a title page and table of contents. Unlike fiction and prose manuscripts, poetry book or chapbook manuscripts usually aren't double spaced.

However, different publishers may have different guidelines. This is especially true in book/chapbook contests, where submission guidelines may state that a poet's name shouldn't appear anywhere in the manuscript, that a cover letter should be provided, or that the pages should be clipped or bound a certain way. Never submit a manuscript to a publisher or competition without carefully reading the guidelines.

**I'm putting together a list of publishing credits for my chapbook manuscript. A couple of my poems appeared in anthologies. Does this kind of publication count in the same way magazine publication does?**

Yes, a list of publishing credits should indicate where every poem to be included in the chapbook previously appeared in print. For an anthology, list the title of the collection, the publisher, the copyright date, the title of your poem, and even the page on which your poem appeared, so the publisher has all the background information. And don't forget to make sure you have the right to reprint your poem in your own chapbook. Some anthologies, especially those that acquire all rights, may require written permission to reprint the poem. Sometimes poets wait until a chapbook or book manuscript has been accepted for publication before pursuing reprint rights. However, it never hurts to plan ahead and make sure everything is in place legally before you submit your manuscript.

**I've had several poems accepted by literary magazines. Now I want to include those poems in a collection and submit it to publishers. Do I have to consult the magazine editors before I reprint my poems? What if an editor says I can't use my poetry?**

First, check to see what kind of rights the magazines acquired when they published your poems. Many literary journals acquire first rights, meaning you own those poems again once the magazine has published them.

Often, a magazine will simply say the copyright reverts to the poet upon publication of the poem. In such cases, you don't have to get permission to reprint your poems. Some editors may request you contact them for permission as a courtesy, or stipulate that in reprinting a poem you must give proper credit to the magazine. If you have any doubts, write to the editor and request written permission to reprint the poetry in your collection.

If any of the magazines acquired all rights to your poetry, you face a different situation. The purchase of all rights means the magazine controls the poems and may use them as it wishes, including producing the poems as postcards or reprinting them in their own anthologies, without notifying you. If you wish to use these poems in your collection, you *must* contact the magazine's editor and get formal permission in writing. If an editor refuses to grant you permission, you may have to negotiate for reprint rights, perhaps paying a reprint fee. You may even face the possibility of cutting that poem from your collection if an agreement can't be reached.

**I have many thoughts and emotions I'd like to express in poetry. I've kept a journal for many years, but I can't seem to get from prose writing to poetry writing. Any suggestions?**

If you've never studied the techniques of writing poetry, consider taking a class, or at least read some books on the subject to help you understand the differences between poetry and prose. Try *The Art and Craft of Poetry*, by Michael J. Bugeja; *The Poet's Companion*, by Kim Addonizio; or *Writing Metrical Poetry*, by William Baer. Your librarian or bookseller can also make good suggestions.

You also should be reading lots of poetry to improve your ear and help you distinguish between the characteristics of poetry and prose. Read classic as well as modern poets to develop a rounded appreciation of what poetry is (and isn't).

### What's the difference between free verse and blank verse?

Blank verse is unrhymed iambic pentameter—that is, five sets of two syllables (an unstressed syllable followed by a stressed syllable) per line, and the lines do not rhyme. Free verse is free of meter—nothing is counted or measured (such as accents or syllables). It has no predetermined pattern or fixed form, and lines can be of any length.

### I get very confused by poetic forms—the different types of sonnets, what a villanelle is, and so on. Should I memorize them?

You could memorize the forms that interest you the most; if you frequently write in a certain form, such as sonnets, you may automatically learn them. Memorizing *all* poetic forms would be daunting, though.

There are many helpful books that define as well as explore poetic forms. These include *The Poetry Dictionary*, by John Drury, and *Writing Metrical Poetry*. Keep such resources handy for when you forget the difference between a Shakespearean and Petrarchan sonnet, or the word order in a sestina.

**When I show my family and friends my poetry, which is all free verse, they tell me, "That's not poetry! It doesn't have any rhythm. It doesn't rhyme." What can I tell them?**

You can try to explain that there are no rules about poetry having rhythm or rhyme. Tell them how modern free verse has rich roots going back to the nineteenth century and Walt Whitman, whose poetry was influenced by the long lines of Biblical verse. Help them understand free verse is not simply prose broken into lines; it encompasses many poetic elements, such as imagery, diction, alliteration, and enjambment.

### What is light verse? What are some markets for it?

Light verse is poetry written to amuse and entertain, rather than to impart any deep literary message. Although it may comment wryly on a serious topic, light verse evokes a laugh, or at least a chuckle. It often rhymes and may employ a playful rhythm pattern. Usually light verse does not find a home in serious poetry magazines. Check conventional and commercial publications to see if they have a need for light verse to use as filler material. Sometimes there are categories for light verse in contests sponsored by state poetry societies or in the annual competition of the National Federation of State Poetry Societies (www.nfsps.com).

### I think some of my poems would make good song lyrics, but I can't write music. How can I get some of my poems put to music?

It's important to understand that poetry and song lyrics are two completely different things. Song lyrics are meant to be sung rather than read on the page or recited as poetry. Song lyrics usually make use of repetition in a way poems don't (e.g., returning again and again to a particular hook phrase in the chorus or refrain). Also, the syllable structures (or meter) and rhyme schemes in song lyrics usually repeat in exactly the same way from verse to verse.

To create lyrics from your poems and have them set to music, your best approach would be to collaborate with a musician. If you're not in contact with someone who can write publishable music, seek musicians in your area and approach one of them about collaborating. Make sure you're aware of a particular songwriter's talent with melody before you get in touch. Also beware of song sharks, unscrupulous people who advertise that they'll set your lyrics to music, for a fee. Many of them are interested only in profit for themselves and will accept lyrics that have no chance of earning any money for the writer. Don't pay anyone to set your words to music. It's better to collaborate with a songwriter/musician and allow a reputable publisher to decide whether your work is good.

**What are some reasons poems don't get accepted by editors?**

Some are related to the quality of the poem itself, others to things like editorial bias, the volume and quality of competing submissions, and other issues.

Never send a poem unless you're confident it's your best work. Review it with a critical eye. Is your poem fresh and original, reflecting imaginative insight and language even when treating a worn-out subject? Have you let it "cool off" before revising it and sending it out (i.e., have you left the poem alone for a few days or even weeks, then reread it for awkward wording, weak lines, and other flaws)? Have you read your poem out loud (if only to yourself) so you can judge how it sounds? Have others read your poem and provided feedback? Are you reading lots of other poets' work so you can sharpen your ear and fine-tune your own poetry?

Even if your poem is well written and highly polished, there are many reasons why it may be rejected. It may not be right for the journal (a quality that's hard for editors to explain sometimes). It may be too similar to another the magazine has accepted recently. Maybe the editor just doesn't like your style (editors are human and have their preferences, too). Or the editor may love your poem but has to pick and choose from an abundance of good poetry.

Consider the quality of your poetry first. Once you're certain you're submitting your best work, take rejections in stride and try to be patient. Eventually your poem and the right editor will find each other.

**I always get printed rejection slips or form letters when my poems are returned, never any feedback. Does that mean my work isn't any good?**

Generally, printed notices mean the editors don't have time to comment personally on the poetry they reject. Form rejection slips or letters may seem cold, but editors turn to them out of necessity. Between reading through piles of submissions and struggling to meet deadlines, editors are swamped. Take the form rejection as it's intended—as a simple "no thanks, not for us"—and send your poems out to the next publication. There are many reasons besides poor quality for rejecting work. As long as you're confident your poems are as good as they can be, keep them circulating to editors.

## RIGHTS AND PERMISSIONS

**I've had a poem accepted by an online literary journal. The editor says the journal retains archival rights to my poem when it's published. What does this mean?**

Archival rights are the rights to make your poem available online indefinitely. Ask the editor if the archival rights are nonexclusive; if they are nonexclusive, the journal does not claim to be the only online publication that can publish and archive your poem.

Most online literary journals (and many print publications with associated Web sites) archive work electronically—as content of a current or past issue, as a sample of that content, or as Web-exclusive content that doesn't appear in a print edition. There are other kinds of rights an online publication may acquire when accepting your poems. These include first electronic rights (you would be free to reprint your poetry in any medium after it first appears in the online publication); one-time electronic rights (which doesn't specify a time limit for usage but does allow you to submit your poetry to other markets); nonexclusive electronic rights (such rights may be requested indefinitely, but you're able to republish your work electronically at any time); and exclusive electronic rights for a specified amount of time (you grant a publisher exclusive use of your work for a specific period, usually three to six months, after which the publisher has the nonexclusive right to archive your poetry indefinitely). Always be sure what rights you're granting to an online publisher before agreeing to have your work printed.

**Our weekly newspaper started a poetry column and invited contributions. I've contributed several poems and enjoyed seeing them in print. A friend tells me I've lost all rights to the poems I've published in the newspaper.**

**Would I be able to sell them to a magazine? I hate to lose these poems, as someday I might want to put them in a book.**

Check with the editor who accepted the poems. If the newspaper itself is not copyrighted, you still own rights to your work under the general copyright law. If the newspaper does acquire rights, find out what kind. Only in the case of the newspaper acquiring all rights would you lose ownership of your poems. Even then, you may be able to negotiate for permission to include them in a collection of your work.

If you own the rights to the poems, you may only submit them to magazines that consider previously published work. Inform the editor of the magazine where and when the poems first appeared.

**A few years ago, I had a volume of poetry published at my own expense. Fortunately, the books sold well. Now I would like to submit some of these poems to magazines, but I've hesitated to do so as I'm not sure if this is permissible.**

As long as the poems appeared only in the book you self-published, you own the rights and are free to submit the poems to magazines. However, keep in mind many editors may not be interested in previously published poems, especially those that have appeared in a book that has been available for some time. Target only magazines that say in their market listings or guidelines that they consider previously published work, and be clear in your cover letter that certain poems already appeared in your self-published volume.

**I've written and sold a poem based on an idea I'm not sure was original. Is such borrowing considered unethical?**

Ideas can't be copyrighted, so basing your poem on another's idea isn't unethical. As long as the idea is expressed in your own words and voice and you present a fresh take on the idea, it's neither stealing nor copying.

**If my poetry is published in other formats—such as greeting cards, calendars, or broadsides—do I retain my copyright?**

It depends on who is using the work and what kind of legal agreement you enter into. Personal expressions publishers (i.e., greeting card publishers) and calendar publishers often buy all rights to a work they purchase for product use. That means you give up any ownership of that piece of writing; and in this case, you probably wouldn't be able to get permission to reuse it—the company may want to use it again on a future card or calendar, and it has purchased the right to do so. If a small press publishes a broadside or postcard using your work, it will probably acquire first rights or one-time rights, meaning that once the broadside or other product has been published, rights to the poem revert to you. You can then include the poem in a future collection of your work (provided you confirm any permissions requirements and provide publishing credit in your manuscript).

There are operations that will print your poem on T-shirts, coffee mugs, plaques, and other merchandise for a price; you can also work with a printer yourself to create such items. In such circumstances, you're basically paying someone to print the poem *for* you. You're not selling your work to the operation or printer for their own business use, so you retain all rights to the poem.

## WHERE TO FIND OUT MORE

### BOOKS

*Creating Poetry*, by John Drury, and *The Art & Craft of Poetry*, by Michael J. Bugeja, are accessible guides to writing poetry that provide a strong foundation in the craft.

*Writing Metrical Poetry*, by William Baer, is an introductory course to writing formal poetry (as opposed to free verse).

*The Poetry Dictionary*, by John Drury, explains poetry terminology.

*The Practice of Poetry: Writing Exercises From Poets Who Teach*, by Robin Behn and Chase Twichell, is a popular collection of ninety writing exercises for poets.

*Poemcrazy: Freeing Your Life With Words*, by Susan G. Wooldridge, is an inspirational guide to writing poetry.

*The Poetry Home Repair Manual: Practical Advice for Beginning Poets*, by Ted Kooser, provides practical, accessible guidance for poets of all skill levels.

*In the Palm of Your Hand: The Poet's Portable Workshop*, by Steve Kowit, helps readers hone their writing skills through lessons and exercises.

## WEB SITES

The Academy of American Poets site (www.poets.org) offers poet profiles, poems, essays, podcasts and audio clips, resources, the National Poetry Map, and much more.

The Web site of the Haiku Society of America (www.has-haiku.org) includes membership information, contest announcements, and submission guidelines for their journal, *Frogpond*.

The National Federation of State Poetry Societies (www.nfsps.org) is the umbrella organization for affiliated state poetry organizations. Their Web site includes NFSPS contest guidelines, contact information and links for state societies, and an online edition of their quarterly newsletter, "Strophes."

The Poetry Foundation Web site (www.poetryfoundation.org) offers a unique search function, Poetry Tool; a daily round-up of poetry-related news; a wide range of features and book reviews; *Poetry* magazine's online content; and much more.

The *Poet's Market* site (www.poetsmarket.com) offers free e-newsletter sign-up and other features.

The Poetry Society of America site (www.poetrysociety.org) includes membership information, PSA contest guidelines, links, and features from their journal, *Crossroads*.

# How do i break in to children's writing?

In his National Book Award speech, Isaac Bashevis Singer gave a number of reasons why he began to write for children, and one of them was "Children read books, not reviews. They don't give a hoot about critics." If a book is boring, children won't read it just because an adult says they ought to. If a book is interesting and enjoyable, they can't wait to tell their friends. Beginners who want to write for young readers must know what children are like today, and not write only from their own childhood memories. When you successfully capture their emotions and dreams, you'll find young readers eager for stories, articles, and books.

## GETTING STARTED

**I've written stories for adults for many years and would like to try writing for children. Can you give me some general advice concerning the differences between writing for children and writing for adults?**

When it comes to the basics of producing a good story, there isn't much difference between writing for children and adults. You must work in the same way to create believable characters with plausible motivations, and strong plot is still important in stories for all age groups. Conflict and emotion must be integrated into the story. The difference is that all of these things must be accomplished with simplicity and with subject matter geared to young readers. Children's books are also more age-specific within the genre. Books popular with seven-year-olds, such as Barbara Park's Junie B. Jones series, will not be very entertaining to twelve-year-olds, who would be more interested in Cecily von Ziegasar's Gossip Girl books.

You must be well aware of the problems and attitudes of children, so you can incorporate them realistically into your stories. The complexities of characterization increase with the age of the reader, to the point that stories written for teenagers differ from adult stories only in the age of the characters and the kinds of situations the characters face. Try to put yourself on the level of your readers so you don't inadvertently talk down to or patronize them. The best way to get a feeling for how stories for children are written is to read lots and lots of them.

### What are the most common age groups for which children's publishers produce books?

Generally, children's fiction and nonfiction fall into one of these five categories:

- board books for pre-readers
- picture books for preschool to age eight
- easy readers for emerging readers ages five to eight
- middle-grade books for ages nine to eleven
- young adult (YA) books for ages twelve and up

Important information

### What are the differences between a picture book, a picture story book, and a chapter book?

A picture book is a book for meant for younger children (pre-readers or beginning readers). It features pictures on every page and tells the story through both the text and the pictures. A picture book can include anywhere from zero words to five hundred or a thousand words, but shorter is generally better. They are almost always thirty-two pages long, including copyright page, title page, etc., which means they include about twenty-eight pages of text and art).

A picture book can have many forms. Concept picture books promote an understanding of the children's world; these books include ABC books and books about giving up a blanket or getting a new baby sister. Concept books can also be novelty books; for example, one might be printed in the shape of a truck or duck, or contain some other gimmick, like pop-ups or tabs to pull. A picture book can be fiction or nonfiction. It can be contemporary or historical. It can be sweet or sentimental or educational or funny. It can be written in prose or verse. Almost anything goes.

A story book is also for younger children. A story book may be longer than a picture book (perhaps double the word count, forty-eight pages), but doesn't have to be. A story book may be a retelling of a folktale or fairy tale, a fantasy story, or a contemporary story, but it will always be fiction. A story book may not be as dependent on illustrations as a picture book. It has a plot with a main character, and generally that character encounters a problem, works out the complications, and finds a solution.

A chapter book is for young readers who have moved up from picture books and easy readers, but are not quite ready for novels. These books may include illustrations, but the story is told solely through the text. Chapter books are generally forty to eighty pages in length, and can run anywhere from 1,500 to 10,000 words, depending on the publisher. They're intended for young readers who can sustain interest through a longer plot, and they may be the first books kids pick out for themselves at the library.

**I'm working on a middle-grade novel and I'm worried it's too long. What's the appropriate length for middle-grade and young adult novels?**

There are no set-in-stone rules when it comes to the length of middle-grade and young adult novels. It varies from publisher to publisher and project to project. Middle-grade novels can range from 10,000 to 30,000 words, and young adult novels can range from 25,000 to 50,000. Recently, though, the Harry Potter series and Christopher Paolini's Inheritance trilogy have offered page counts exceeding what anyone thought middle-grade readers could handle. And YA novels-in-verse, which have grown in popularity in recent years, offer familiar page counts but spare text.

The Society of Children's Book Writers and Illustrators (SCBWI) does offer length guidelines in terms of the appropriate number of manuscript pages for various genres (meaning the number of pages a writer would submit to a publisher). For fiction, they suggest middle-grade works be anywhere from 40 to 150 manuscript pages and YA from 175 to 200 pages.

Consult listings in the current edition of *Children's Writer's & Illustrator's Market* for information on both fiction and nonfiction word counts for various publishers. Also consult submission guidelines for individual publishers that interest you. Spending some time in a children's bookstore looking at mid-grade and YA titles from a number of publishers is a good exercise as well.

It's unlikely your work will be automatically rejected if your submission exceeds a publisher's guidelines by few thousand words. However, if they generally publish mid-grade books that are around 25,000 words and you send them 65,000, you'll likely get a quick rejection. Try your best to stay in the ballpark, but also do what's appropriate for your story.

### What kinds of subject matter are most popular in novels for young readers?

The interest areas of young readers are limitless. They enjoy contemporary, fantasy, mystery, and historical novels and more—trends in subject matter for children's books often reflect trends in adult publishing. Realistic treatment of current themes—including conflict with siblings or peers, dating and relationships, and struggles with school or family situations—interests both middle-grade and YA readers. Contemporary YA novels often delve into edgier material, including sexual situations and drug use. Books written for middle-grade and YA readers are often geared either for boys or girls, and the protagonist is generally several years older than the reader. It is best to keep adult involvement in children's novels to a minimum, allowing the protagonists to solve their problems without adult intervention.

### I am interested in writing children's stories for elementary school children. Where can I obtain a suitable word list for these stories?

Publishers of trade books for leisure reading by children do not use formal vocabulary lists. Don't hesitate to use a big word in a children's story if you think it's the best word—as long as young readers can ascertain the meaning through the context of the story. After all, books are great tools for increasing young readers' vocabularies.

Publishers of textbooks for the primary grades often have formal restrictions on vocabulary. Consult individual educational publishers for vocabulary requirements. You might also refer to *The Children's Writer's Word Book*, by Alijandra Mogilner, which includes a dictionary of words and the grade levels for which they are appropriate.

## CRAFT AND TECHNIQUE

**I've always wanted to write for children, and I've got some ideas for stories. I thought I'd start out writing picture books, since they're nice and short. Can you offer some tips for writing them?**

Don't let the length of picture books fool you—writing them is difficult. You have very few words—not to mention a limited vocabulary—in which to tell your story. You've also got to keep in mind that a good part of a picture book story is told in the *pictures*. Some picture books have no words at all. Picture books top off at about 1,000 words, but for editors and readers, shorter is better.

The text of picture books is generally only twenty-eight pages. (There are thirty-two total pages, a few of which are taken up by endpapers, the title page, copyright page, etc.) Creating a book dummy is often a helpful exercise for picture book writers. Breaking up your text into twenty-eight pages can help you identify many problems in your manuscript. Ask yourself a few questions as you go through your mock-up: Is there an illustratable action on each spread? Is there a beginning, a middle, and an end? Are you writing out details that could be expressed through the illustrations? Is the text too long? Read and study as many picture books as you can get your hands on to help in your learning process.

**I see a lot of rhyming picture books in the stores, but I've heard editors at conferences discourage submitting rhyming text. What gives?**

Indeed there are a number of rhyming picture books on the market. They are fun to read aloud and kids enjoy them. And new writers seem to gravitate toward rhyming stories. Rhyme is difficult to write, however. As one editor put it, you're either Seuss, or you're *so* not Seuss. Anyone can write a rhyming text—only a select few authors can write a *great* rhyming text. And nothing will get your picture book manuscript rejected quicker than bad rhyme. If you write in rhyme, be sure to read your work aloud (better yet, have someone new to the manuscript read it to you) to observe places where the rhyme or rhythm is awkward or forced. Rhyme should feel good coming off your tongue; it should flow. Again—read. Pick up rhyming books by master rhymers like Mary Ann Hoberman, Sarah Weeks, and Lisa Wheeler.

**I've tried to write biographical pieces for children's magazines, but I can't seem to get the total picture of the subject's life into a short article that children would understand. Any suggestions?**

One of the hardest things about writing biographies for children is deciding what to leave out. This is especially true when the writer is confined to the length of a magazine article. When researching your subject, pick out one important event and focus the entire article on it. You might concentrate on some childhood experience, if you are lucky enough to find information on it. Then your ending can state what this child grew up to do that made him famous. Lacking any good information on your subject's childhood, it's still a good idea to open the article with a reference to his early years in order to let young readers know that these famous people were children once, too. Then focus the article on an incident important in your subject's adulthood—probably the one that made him famous—but keep it simple. Force yourself to delete anything extraneous, remembering that children don't have the conceptual framework to remember historical details.

And it's okay, when working with the basic facts, to create conversations and incidents that will best dramatize them. However, don't devise anything that would not be in keeping with the character of the subject or times.

**I've been trying to sell a children's fantasy with no luck at all. What could be wrong with my book?**

Fantasy for young readers has enjoyed a resurgence in popularity thanks to authors like J.K. Rowling, Christopher Paolini, and Phillip Pullman. But fantasy is difficult to write because it demands that you make the unbelievable believable. If you are just starting out as a children's writer, you may need practice writing here-and-now stories before you attempt to write fantasy. A solid understanding of the techniques for establishing plot, character, setting, and viewpoint are necessary, because a fantasy story must be as logical as any other story. It must give the illusion of reality.

It may be that the kind of fantasy you're writing just isn't in vogue in the current marketplace. The market for stories like the classical fairy tales of Hans Christian Andersen and the Brothers Grimm is nearly nonexistent today; also, few fantasies today feature inanimate objects, like in classics such as *The Little Engine That Could*.

---

## FLASHBACK QUESTION

If my story were acceptable in every other way, do you think that a publisher of teenage books would reject it because it has: (1) a fight between two teenage members of a high school football team; (2) a college-ager who is restricted to a wheelchair because of a football injury; (3) football action that gets rough, i.e. an elbow thrown at the face, nothing worse; (4) another character getting his arm broken in practice? I need to know if these could be objectionable.

It is highly doubtful that any of these elements alone could be responsible for the rejection of your book manuscript.

---

**It seems like a lot of what makes up adult mystery novels, such as crime, violence, and suspense, just doesn't belong in children's mysteries. What elements can be included?**

You are right in assuming children's mystery editors shy away from descriptive violence—especially murder. Most juvenile mysteries contain elements of humor along with the hair-raising suspense that makes the story effective. Tight plotting and a fantastic climax are important, as is a main character that is actively involved in solving the problem of the story. To learn of current subject matter and techniques used in writing children's mysteries, read and analyze books from that section of your bookstore (for the most current topics and techniques) or public library.

## GETTING YOUR STORIES PUBLISHED

**I'm interested in writing children's books, but I don't know how to prepare the manuscripts. How do I format them?**

Children's books are typed in the same standard manuscript format that applies to short stories and novels for the adult market.

See chaper five for more on formatting manuscripts.

See chapters
four and five for
more information

**I've written a few short stories for children and would like to get them published. The problem is, I don't know how or where to sell them. What would you advise?**

Markets for your work can be found in *Children's Writer's & Illustrator's Market*. Children's magazines are geared to specific age levels and publish both fiction and nonfiction. Get some sample copies of magazines you think might be prospects for your stories and read a few issues before you submit your manuscripts to the editors. Also, be sure to visit their Web sites—most children's magazines have Web sites offering sample stories and tables of contents, writers guidelines, theme lists, and more.

Do not break
this rule!

**Should I include illustrations with my picture book manuscript when I submit it to publishers?**

No, the publisher will choose the illustrator. Writers do not need to find an illustrator or offer illustration suggestions. If your story will be unclear without illustrations—you have included pages where the story is told entirely by the picture, for instance—include illustration notes within your text.

**I'm collaborating on a picture book with an illustrator. How should we go about submitting our material once we've gotten our project together?**

Partnering with an illustrator is not recommended, particularly for first-time authors. As stated above, publishers prefer to match up authors and illustrators for picture book projects. It's very difficult to get manuscript-illustration packages by collaborators accepted by publishers. (Professional illustrators who also write do better in this arena.) If an editor does not like part of the package, the whole package will likely be rejected. It's best to submit your manuscript on its own.

**I've written some stories aimed to help physically disabled children deal with their problems. Do you think I could get them published?**

There are a few publishers that specialize in books aimed at special needs children, and it's becoming more common for general trade publishers to offer books including children with special needs and disabilities. Consult the entries under "special needs" in the subject index of the latest edition of *Children's Writer's & Illustrator's Market*.

**A friend sold all rights to his children's book to a small publisher and only received a flat fee for the book. Is that common practice?**

No, but whether a publisher pays an advance and royalties or buys outright varies with each company. Terms are presented in a contract that a writer can accept or decline.

**I have an idea for a series of children's books. How would I sell this series to a publisher?**

It can be difficult, particularly for newer authors, to sell a fiction series to a publisher right out of the gate. You might try querying publishers about the first book in your series and mention that you have ideas for subsequent books with the same characters. Once you sell the first book and it shows good sales numbers, publishers will be open to capitalizing on that and may be willing to continue with sequels. You might also consider contacting a book packager. These companies often produce series for trade publishers. Book packagers are marked with a special icon in *Children's Writer's & Illustrator's Market*.

**I think my twelve-year-old niece has the potential to become a very good fiction writer. Her imagination seems boundless, and she has a knack for developing good stories. Is there any way she could get some of her stories published?**

Some children's publications have sections for stories, poems, articles, and drawings by children. There are a number of other magazines, such as *Stone Soup*, that are written entirely by children. Other magazines, such as *Seventeen* and *Cicada*, accept material written by teenagers. Consult the section on markets for young writers and illustrators in *Children's Writer's & Illustrator's Market*; also take a look at *The Young Writer's Guide to Getting Published*, by Kathy Henderson, and *A Teen's Guide to Getting Published*, by Jessica Dunn and Danielle Dunn.

**Do I need an agent to get my children's book published?**

No, you don't. There are a number of children's publishers who accept unsolicited manuscripts and query letters from children's writers, so whether to pursue an agent is up to you. Working with an agent, however, can help

See chapter six for more on agents.

get your work to editors much more quickly than going through the slush pile. And an agent may get you a better contract than you could get on your own. But if you're a creative type who is also comfortable marketing your work and negotiating contracts, you can pursue publication on your own. For listing of agents who handle children's material, see *Children's Writer's & Illustrator's Market* and *Guide to Literary Agents*. There is also a list of agents available to members of the Society of Children's Book Writers & Illustrators (www.scbwi.org).

## WHERE TO FIND OUT MORE

### BOOKS

*You Can Write Children's Books* and *You Can Write Children's Books Workbook*, by Tracey Dils, are excellent guides for beginners writing for children.

*Children's Writer's Word Book*, by Alijandra Mogilner, is a comprehensive reference on what words are appropriate throughout the grade levels, and also what topics and issues are taught in each grade.

### WEB SITES

The home page of the Children's Book Council is www.cbcbooks.org.

Write4Kids (www.write4kids.com) offers one of the biggest online collections of free how-to information for children's writers.

The plentiful resources of the Colossal Directory of Children's Publishers can be found at www.signaleader.com.

Kid Magazine Writers maintains an online magazine for children's writers at www.kidmagwriters.com.

The Purple Crayon, a resource site run for children's writers by a children's book editor, is at www.underdown.org.

SmartWriters (www.smartwriters.com) is dedicated to providing professional information to children's writers.

# 26

# HOW DO I MARKET MY SCRIPTS?

Some of the pitfalls of scriptwriting were pinpointed by Hubert Selby Jr. in a *New York Times* article: "A couple of years ago a network was going to do a series on the Ten Commandments," he recalled, "and I wrote one of the two-hour segments. The entire project was ultimately cancelled, probably because it was too radical. But the thing that really amused me was the fact that the network only took five of the Commandments with an option on the other five. That, my friend, is television."

While many other types of work can be successfully marketed directly by the writer, scripts usually require the intermediary of an agent to make it to the producer. In fact, breaking in to Hollywood almost always requires that you know someone who knows someone; trying to make it as an outsider will likely lead to frustration and failure. This chapter is provided as a resource for writers who might have a passing interest in what scriptwriting entails or how it works, but it doesn't even begin to scratch the surface of the movie and TV industry; you'll need to seek other resources for a real beginner's education; preferably, you should take a course.

## SCRIPT MECHANICS

### What's the proper way to type a movie or TV script?

It's too complex to describe here; you should look for a sample script and a reference a book on scriptwriting. If you plan to spend any amount of time scriptwriting, you should invest in scriptwriting software, such as Final Draft, Movie Magic Screenwriter, or Dramatica Pro.

**I am writing a screenplay for the movie industry and need to learn more about the camera shots.**

Your best bet would be to study some actual movie scripts to get a feel for how this is done. Look online for Web sites that sell scripts or let you view them for free—Simply Scripts (www.simplyscripts.com) is a good place to start. Alternatively, several publishers produce books that contain the complete scripts of both classic and contemporary movies.

Usually, it's not desirable to include production technicalities (such as camera angles) in a script you're selling on speculation. Those details will be added by the production staff after the script is purchased.

## BREAKING IN TO SCRIPTWRITING

**Is it crucial for scriptwriters to find an agent?**

It is not crucial to obtain the services of an agent; you can always try sending query letters directly to producers and ask them if you can submit your script. But you're likely to have an easier time if you find an agent, especially if you live outside the Hollywood community and have little opportunity to make connections with the people who would be interested in your work.

**Under what conditions will television producers look at a script submitted directly by the writer rather than through an agent?**

If you submit your script with a signed release form, and indicate that it is registered with Writers Guild of America (WGA), you might be able to get a producer to look at it. The release form makes it clear that you understand your idea may not be new to the producer, and the company is under no obligation to you if, although your script is rejected, a similar idea appears later on television. To avoid having the script returned unopened, be sure to type "Release Form Enclosed" on the outside of the envelope.

### How can a writer register a script?

The Writers Guild of America (www.wga.org) can register your script for a fee. Registering simply verifies that you were the author of that particular script on that particular date. The registration comes in handy if a similar story is produced later and you wish to challenge the other author, the producer, or the agent.

### I would like to propose a series concept to a television network. How do I go about doing that while protecting my idea?

First, unless you are famous or are willing to pay millions of dollars for the production of a new series, no one in Hollywood will consider working with a first-time screenwriter on a new series concept. This is why almost every television writer breaks in to the business by writing and selling a spec script (an original script for a current show).

Additionally, the only way to be taken seriously as a first-time script-writer is to write a complete script—not an outline, synopsis, or a page of ideas. Network executives, producers, and directors receive countless query letters and phone calls from amateurs who think they can sell their ideas. Unfortunately, this is not how it works in Hollywood. Ideas, no matter how wonderful they sound to you, are a dime a dozen. If you give the same idea to a dozen writers, you'll get a dozen completely different scripts. What matters in this business is the execution of that idea—the specific character traits, dialogue, and plot turns that make a script into a movie or TV show. Here's an example: "A sports team made up of players without a shred of athletic talent struggles to overcome far superior opponents. Through perseverance and blind luck, the team transforms from an underdog to a contender." Is this the idea behind *The Bad News Bears*, *Major League*, or *Necessary Roughness*? The answer: all three.

What's worse is that there are nine thousand professional screenwrit-ers and tens of thousands of aspiring writers throwing out ideas every year. With those kinds of numbers, similarity of ideas is inevitable. In the busi-ness, it's called simultaneous creation. We all watch the same TV shows, movies, news broadcasts, and plays. We all read the same books, magazines, and newspapers. When multiple people are exposed to the same stimuli, they develop very similar ideas. Your friends and family might think you have an original idea, but there are tens of thousands of other creative souls out there, and at least one of them has had the same idea.

This also explains why you cannot copyright ideas. Copyright does *not* protect ideas or concepts. New scriptwriters worry about having their ideas stolen all the time. Since you cannot copyright your idea and can only copyright the way in which you tell the story, I highly recommend writing a complete script before you hand over an idea. Your script is your key to the front door of Hollywood.

**What is the difference between a synopsis and a treatment?**

A synopsis is a short, concise summary of the story. A treatment is a scene-by-scene explanation, indicating specific action, motivation, possible special effects, etc. It provides a fuller interpretation of the script's potential. Established writers can sell a script on the basis of a treatment, but beginners must have a complete script if they wish to make that important first sale.

**I've cruised around the various Web sites that advertise "coverage" for as low as forty-nine dollars to ninety-nine dollars or more. What is coverage? How does it aid in selling my screenplay?**

When you submit a script to a producer, the producer or a professional script reader will write coverage. Coverage is a one- or two-page synopsis of your script, detailing what does and doesn't work. This gives a producer or studio executive a quick sense of the screenplay without having to read it. Coverage is usually broken down into five categories—premise/concept, characterization, dialogue, story/structure, and set/production values.

A screenwriter might want to pay someone to write coverage for her script so she has a second opinion about what does and doesn't work in the script before she submits it to a producer. If you submit a bad script to a producer and the producer writes negative coverage, your name is placed "in the system" and you may never be able to submit another script to that producer.

Generally, coverage is very critical. Producers and professional readers are looking to separate the good from the bad, and no one wants to risk her career on a bad script.

**Is it possible to make a decent living writing scripts that don't necessarily become movies?**

Yes, it is possible, but few writers make a stable living doing such work. The only people who really make money on scripts that don't get produced are staff writers for television series and the lucky scriptwriters who are hired to develop novels, stories, and other material into scripts for producers.

If you live in or around Hollywood and can impress a producer with your writing skills, a producer may hire you to write a script based on material she purchases elsewhere; this is called a development deal. For example, if a producer purchases the rights to a best-selling book, the producer will hire a scriptwriter to develop that book into a script. In most cases, the scriptwriter will be paid for her services regardless of whether the script is produced.

Development deals usually pay from $30,000 to $500,000, depending on the experience of the writer. That said, the majority of development deals are given to scriptwriters close to Hollywood. So if you don't live in Southern California, make plans to move there.

An overall deal is one in which a scriptwriter is paid (usually in the low millions) to work exclusively with a single entity (a studio, a network, a producer, or a production company). Unfortunately, very few scriptwriters are able to land overalls.

**Is there a way I can submit story ideas to movie producers and directors without writing the entire script?**

The only way to be taken seriously as a first-time television or screenplay writer is to write a complete script. There are plenty of scam artists out there who will try to sell you on the myth of "sell an idea, make a million bucks," but the only person getting rich off that myth is the scam artist.

**For years I have dreamed about adapting my favorite novel into a screenplay for film. When do I require the original author's permission? How does one go about acquiring such permission? Does the original author have any rights to the screenplay?**

Frequently asked question

Many amateur scriptwriters have dreams of adapting their favorite book (or even their own book) into a feature film. Unfortunately, few will ever be able to write an adaptation because of the way the film industry does business.

First, understand that even *before* a book is published, either the author's agent or the book's publisher will send the manuscript to production companies and studios all over the country. The initial goal is to make as much money as possible from the sale of the film rights. So, chances are, if a book has been even remotely successful, the film adaptation rights have already been sold.

Now, assuming the rights haven't already been sold, there are several things you need to consider. First, you have to find out who holds the rights. The author may have retained film rights, or the author may have turned them over to the publisher. Is the book or story in the public domain? The reason so many classical stories and novels are adapted into feature films is that the stories are in the public domain—anyone can adapt them to film or television.

If the story/book is not in the public domain, call the publisher and ask for the name of the writer's agent or attorney, whoever handles rights. After you have this information, call or write the person, explaining that you are interested in developing the work into a screenplay. That person will then tell you whether the work is already under option or otherwise unavailable for adaptation. If you're lucky, the representative will tell you that the work is available and you can begin negotiations.

If the book is new, the price will be high. If the book has been around for many years and has been rejected by multiple production companies and studios, the price will drop. Keep in mind, however, that you will probably have trouble selling the script if the book has already been rejected by many producers. If the book has been around for a while and no one has purchased rights, you may be able to convince the representative to give you a two-year option for free. This means that you have the rights to adapt the book for two years. If you are successful and sell the script, the representative will take a percentage of the sale price. If at the end of two years you are unable to make a sale, the rights revert to the original owner(s).

Once you have obtained option rights to the work, you can begin querying agents and producers. That said, you will have a much greater chance of success if you have a completed script ready for the agent or producer to review after she accepts your query.

Adaptations can be successful, but because of the rights involved, most scriptwriters have a greater chance of success with a completely original screenplay. Still, if you feel passionate about the story and are willing to put up with the possible legal headaches, adaptations can be great fun.

## WHERE TO FIND OUT MORE

### BOOKS

*Story*, by Robert McKee, is one of the best-selling instruction books on the craft of screenwriting, and is also helpful to fiction writers.

*Making a Good Script Great*, by Linda Seger, helps the beginning script-writer with characterization and script structure.

*The Writer's Journey: Mythic Structure for Writers*, by Chris Vogler, details the archetypes that are used over and over again in successful Hollywood movies.

*The Screenwriter's Bible*, by David Trottier, is an excellent starting point, especially if you don't know the terminology of Hollywood or how to format a script.

### WEB SITES

Alex Epstein publishes a detailed FAQ for beginning screenwriters at www.teako170.com/faq.html.

Screenwriters Web (http://breakingin.net) contains advice on how to market your script.

Done Deal Professional (www.donedealpro.com) allows you to find out, for a fee, who's buying what scripts. Offers some valuable free content as well.

The Artful Writer (http://artfulwriter.com) is a blog for professional screenwriters. Amateurs can learn a lot here.

The Hollywood Creative Directory (www.hcdonline.com) is an essential print and online directory for anyone looking to sell a script or find an agent.

# 27

## HOW DO I SELL MY SONGS?

The specialized field of songwriting has specific requirements that must be followed for success. Here are some starting guidelines; for more information on the topic, a good place to start is *Songwriter's Market*.

## BREAKING IN TO SONGWRITING

**How can I learn to write songs? Is it easy to break in to that area of songwriting?**

Just as in any other type of writing, songwriting success comes with concentrated study of the existing market and commercial songwriting technique. You must have a solid understanding of the writing principles behind hit songs. Because co-writing and collaboration is so widespread in the songwriting industry, you must also know how to get along with people and build a network of contacts.

**If I write poetry, will I be able to write song lyrics?**

Songwriting and poetry are quite different, although they both make use of rhyme and rhyme schemes. Song lyrics make use of repetition in a way that poetry doesn't, specifically through the use of hook phrases (usually the title of the song). Songwriters build songs around these hook phrases, placing the hooks in key positions—in choruses or at the beginning and end of verses. Song lyrics are also meant to be sung, not read on a page, and the pattern of syllable rhythms (matched to a musical melody) repeats with little variation from verse to verse or from chorus to chorus.

### I just write lyrics. Is it okay to submit my lyrics to a music publisher?

Lyrics by themselves are not accepted. You must have both lyrics and music together as one complete composition when you approach the music industry. If you only write lyrics, you'll need to find a musical collaborator who can set your lyrical ideas to music (melody and harmony). Songwriters organizations, music schools, online message boards, and music store bulletin boards are good places to look for musical collaborators.

### Is it helpful to join a songwriters organization?

Membership in songwriters organizations can be a great help to networking and learning the craft of songwriting. Many songwriters organizations will send information on memberships, workshops, and the services they offer to both beginning and established songwriters. Helpful national organizations include the Nashville Songwriters Association International (www.nashvillesongwriters.com) and the Songwriters Guild of America (www.songwritersguild.com).

## SONG MARKETING

### What's the best way to sell my songs?

Never sell your songs outright. Instead, you should maintain an interest in the copyright. A song that goes on to be a standard (with perennial radio play and multiple recorded versions by various recording artists) will generate royalties for many years beyond its initial release. If you sold your song outright for a one-time flat fee, you might miss out on years of income. Be forewarned—no ethical music company would make such an offer.

### If I don't sell my songs outright, how do I make money?

Songwriters make money by getting their songs recorded and released on albums and played over radio, on television, in restaurants, etc. Whenever you hear a song in a restaurant or on the radio, or see a song on an album in the record store, the songwriter is being paid for the use of that song.

(Note that the songwriting royalty is a completely different and separate royalty from the recording artist's royalty on the retail sale price.)

### How does the songwriter get paid?

Songwriters join a performing rights organization (PRO), and these organizations track and collect performance royalties for their members from radio stations, television stations, restaurants, and so on, and then pass these royalties on to their members. The three main PROs are the American Society of Composers, Authors, and Publishers (ASCAP); Broadcast Music Incorporated (BMI); and the Society of European Stage Authors & Composers (SESAC), which, despite the name, does represent American songwriters.

When a record company presses and distributes recorded versions of songs (on CDs, vinyl albums, cassettes, etc.), the record company then owes what is called a mechanical royalty for each copy made. An organization called the Harry Fox Agency (HFA) collects these fees and passes them on to the music publisher, who then pays the songwriter. If a songwriter has a song on an album that sells millions of copies, these royalties can be enormous, especially if other recording artists go on to record cover versions on their albums and generate more royalties.

### Do I need to find a music publisher to make money?

It's a good first step if you have no connections of your own. A good music publisher can help you find recording artists to cover your song, place your song in commercials and television shows, etc. Music publishers can also take care of a lot of the paperwork involved in administering the song. In return for their connections and services, they generally take part (usually 50 percent) of the royalties generated from the sale of the song.

### Do co-writers and musical collaborators receive royalties?

Yes, and you will have to decide how to split the royalties by percentages. If you co-write a song, and a music publisher accepts the song, the publisher will take 50 percent (100 percent of what is termed the publisher's share) while the songwriters split the other 50 percent (100 percent of the songwriter's share) between themselves however they see fit. This division into the publisher's share and the songwriter's share is standard in music publishing.

### Do I need to record a demo?

Yes. The main way people will hear your song is from a demonstration recording, or demo. You will rarely be asked to perform a song in person, and a recording can be mailed and go places you can't physically go. You should always strive to make the best possible recording, with the lyrics and vocal melody clear, in tune, and placed up front. All other instruments should be cleanly recorded and in tune. Simple vocal-and-guitar or vocal-and-piano demos are usually acceptable, but if your song is meant to be an up-tempo rocker, a full band demo is a better idea. Demo studios often advertise in the back of songwriting magazines, and some will record two to three songs for just a few hundred dollars. Don't pay big bucks for master-quality recordings. Songwriting demos are meant to be simple and represent generic styles so recording artists and producers can create their own interpretation.

### I just finished writing a song I know would be perfect for one of my favorite popular singers. How do I bring my song to his attention?

You can first try approaching the artist's record producer, since he has the most say in the artist's choice of material. Locating him may take some detective work. If you can't contact him directly, find out all you can about your artist's record company, publishing company, and manager, and submit demos to them. Names can be found on album covers and record labels; check *Songwriter's Market* for addresses and phone numbers. Be forewarned, though, your song must be good—you'll be directly competing with the singer (if he writes his own songs) and the record producer (as songwriter).

### I've written a couple of songs I'm sure would be acceptable to a couple of the radio stations in my area. How can I get my songs played on the air?

As a rule, big radio stations have tight formats and usually play only major-label music backed with hundreds of thousands of dollars in promotion money. Also, corporate program directors, not the disc jockeys, control the playlists. If you have a few thousand dollars to spend on a small promotion campaign, it might be possible to get your music on specialty shows or college radio, which are a bit more open. Disc jockeys at local community stations often get to program their own shows, however, and if you know one of them and he likes your song, he might agree to play it. Internet radio is also very open to unknown bands and songwriters, but the audience for Internet radio, as of this writing, is still small.

## AVOIDING SCAMS

**I often read about song sharks and scam artists. How do I avoid getting ripped off? Are there any specific things should I should look for and avoid?**

Avoiding the scam artists requires a combination of knowledge and mindset. The more you know about how the legitimate music industry works, the better your chances at avoiding scams. It's up to you to resist the efforts of unscrupulous characters who appeal to dreams of easy success or stardom and who attempt to undermine your ability to think rationally.

In general, any request for money up front is a bad sign. Song sharks will take any and all songs, regardless of quality. Because they get money upfront, they have no incentive to do the real work of making a song successful. Other "services" you should avoid include those that involve any sort of submission fees (review fees, service fees, filing fees, etc.), or any up-front fee to have your song published. Shun any company that requires money to pair you with a collaborator, and never pay to have your lyrics or poems set to music.

It's also a good idea to avoid: "pay-to-play" compilation deals; songpluggers who offer to "shop" your song for a fee; paying any music publisher an up-front fee to record demos of your song; record companies that ask you to pay them or an associated company to make a demo.

Always make sure to carefully read all contracts before signing them, and, if you're unsure of any element within a contract, have an entertainment attorney look it over. Also, if you have any doubts about claims made by an individual or a company, make sure you verify those claims.

**I perform my own songs, and I want to release an album. Do I need a music publisher?**

If you don't already have a music publisher, then you will have to be the publisher. This is always an acceptable option, and you will make more money, but you will have to do the related paperwork yourself and then also affiliate with the PROs as a publisher to get the publisher's share of that income. If you want to pursue further avenues as a writer, a publisher could ultimately help you make more money. Another option is to contract with a music publisher to handle the paperwork; they take a smaller piece (often around 15 percent) of the publisher's share in exchange.

If you are your own publisher and land a recording contract, you'll earn the retail sales royalty plus the publishing income, and the record company will also owe you mechanical royalties. You should also affiliate with ASCAP, BMI, or SESAC to get performance royalties (which the record company is not involved in securing). Also, most big record companies have affiliated sister publishing companies and will often offer to sign you to a parallel publishing contract—it's up to you whether to take this option.

## WHERE TO FIND OUT MORE

### BOOKS

*The Craft and Business of Songwriting*, third edition, by John Braheny, is a friendly and thorough guide to both writing songs and selling them.

*The Craft of Lyric Writing*, by Sheila Davis, is a classic guide to writing lyrics.

*This Business of Music*, by M. William Krasilovsky, Sidney Shemel, and John M. Gross, is the industry textbook, published since 1964.

*All You Need to Know About the Music Business*, by Donald S. Passman, is another popular guide to the business.

## WEB SITES

The online site for the Nashville Songwriters Association International is www.nashvillesongwriters.com.

The Just Plain Folks music organization (www.jpfolks.com) helps song-writers network and get educated.

GetSigned (www.getsigned.com) offers advice from industry experts.

# 28

## How do i write
## for newspapers?

Newspaper readers, often the first audience for many freelance writers, want news and human-interest material directly related to their local community, and they want it accurate and easy to read. Filling those needs are the first lessons in writing for this market. Writers who have developed the techniques for newspaper reporting and writing have laid important groundwork toward future work in any type of writing.

### OPPORTUNITIES FOR BEGINNERS

**I understand that a stringer is one who relates local news to a newspaper—a correspondent of sorts. Is obtaining a job like this a good way to break in to newspaper writing? How does one become a stringer?**

Yes, if you are interested in obtaining a staff reporter's job, it could be a plus for you to be a stringer, because you will get practice in being on top of the news, digging for facts, and writing as a journalist, and your editor will know your abilities. If your town does not already have a stringer corresponding with a particular newspaper, you may be able to get the job by noting eight or ten local news stories that the paper missed over the last month, then writing up three of them and submitting them with a cover letter to the editor of the local paper or to the state editor of the nearest large city daily. If an editor needs stringers, she will be most impressed by those who show the enterprise to approach her. Freelance writers pursuing other writing interests will also find that being a stringer keeps them out in the real world, in touch with ideas, and up-to-date on information of value to the creative mind. Stringers are usually paid by the column inch, though some earn a flat monthly fee.

**What's the difference between hard news and feature stories? When it comes to freelancing, is one easier to write and sell than the other?**

Economics, business, politics, education, crime—these are all hard news beats. Even smaller daily papers usually have staff members dedicated to covering these topics. Features are the softer stories—the human-interest pieces about the county fair, a local science fair champion, or a church's summer Bible school program. If you're trying to break in with your local paper, human-interest pieces are ideal for proving your worth as a reporter. Remember though, even a human-interest piece needs a hook. If you want to write a piece about the county fair, do more than ask attendees if they're having fun. Examine the upcoming day's schedule of events and look for something that sounds interesting or different. Go prepared to make the piece special.

**Are there any freelance opportunities as a stringer with wire services like AP (Associated Press) and UPI (United Press International)?**

Not really—most of the wire service stringers are full-time news reporters with daily papers. Once in a great while, the state bureau chiefs for wire services will contract for certain columns or features from freelancers. Visit the Web site of the AP or UPI wire services (www.ap.org and www.upi.com) to look for contact information.

**I am interested in writing editorials. Is there a market for them?**

Unfortunately, there isn't much of a market for editorials, since most newspapers have their own staff writers who prepare the editorial page. Newspapers do, however, welcome op-ed pieces. (*Op-ed* is short for "opposite editorial," which is the page where such pieces generally appear.)

## CRAFT AND TECHNIQUE

**How is newspaper writing different from other kinds of writing?**

Since newspaper writing has to fit a specific space on a page, writers will often find their stories have been cut. The most important parts of a newspaper story are in the first few paragraphs, so the ending is what is deleted if space is limited. Newspaper editors also tend to cut adjectives, imagery, and other nonessential additions to a sentence when space restrictions force tighter editing. Magazine article writers and book authors have greater freedom to write more imaginatively and still include all the facts.

**What style guidelines do newspapers follow?**

Experienced journalists use *The Associated Press Stylebook and Briefing on Media Law*. This style bible is updated regularly and includes guidelines on capitalization, abbreviation, spelling, numerals, and usage, as well as information on legal issues such as libel and the right of privacy. Having a working knowledge of AP style may just give you the professional edge you need to beat out competing freelancers for an assignment.

**I've submitted several factual articles to my local newspaper, but all of them have been rejected. Having read the paper for years, I know the kinds of things they publish. Could it be my writing? If so, what kinds of things should I consider when writing features for a newspaper?**

It's possible that the newspaper doesn't accept freelance material, or perhaps your stories were badly timed. The paper might have already covered the story or assigned it to a staff reporter. Or, it just might be that the editor wants more than just the facts in the features she prints. Newspapers use features to intersperse life and emotion in the factual news, to interpret the news, and to inform readers on subjects that are not news in the sense that they do not rise out of current climactic events.

Feature writing style is not a slave to the strict formula required for straight news articles and can be as varied as styles of fiction. A good basic structure for the feature article starts with an attention-getting lead that sets the mood and theme of the article, then continues with a narrative body sprinkled with anecdotes and direct quotes, and a quick conclusion.

Features are human-interest stories, so a good article will cover something or someone unusual or worthy of note. Often, it's the slant that makes the subject unusual. For instance, a dry listing of facts about the opening of a museum of Indian artifacts will hold readers' interest a lot more easily if it is slanted toward the crazy adventure one of the curators had while she was searching for artifacts for one of the displays. Your editor may be looking for articles that are short, to the point, and lively.

**How important is an article's timeliness when it comes to writing for newspapers?**

In the age of the Internet and twenty-four-hour cable news networks, timeliness is extremely important, especially for breaking news events. That said, even news few would consider "breaking" still needs to be fresh. Don't expect anyone to want to read your school board piece if it takes you three days to write it. It will be old news by then. However, if you do a human-interest piece on a local humanitarian and the piece isn't time sensitive, the timeliness factor is less crucial.

**How accurate do I need to be when it comes to cold hard facts? Do most newspapers have fact-checkers who will verify my work?**

Major newspapers have fact-checkers, while local daily newspapers do not. Regardless, it is *your* responsibility as a professional writer to verify your own facts. Double-check your work. Do not make assumptions. If you're not sure about something in your story, if you only *think* you know the latest figures or how to spell a name, then you need to do more work. You need to make sure. Failing to ensure the accuracy of your own work will only hinder your long-term career objectives.

**For a given article, how many people do I need to quote?**

In order to provide your readers with centered, accurate, and unbiased coverage, it's best to quote at least three people, but you should *talk* to as many people as possible. For instance, if you're covering a features event like a holiday festival or a rally, talk to organizers, attendees, speakers, etc. Ask them different questions and get a full picture of the event and its significance. When it's time to write your story, you'll be able to look through your notes and pick and choose the very best quotes. If you only bother to talk to three people, then your choices are going to be pretty limited—every quote will have to be strong.

**It seems like a lot of journalists on TV give their opinions all the time. Do I need to keep my personal opinions on a topic out of my newspaper articles?**

There's a difference between TV news personalities who loudly vocalize their opinions on their own shows and those who set forth an issue and question guests without inserting their personal agendas, and it's important to understand the difference. Unless you are writing an editorial or a letter to the editor, your opinions have no place in your articles. None. Your job as a journalist is to provide readers with the facts and allow them to form their own opinions. Slanting your story to favor one side—the side you personally support—over another is simply not professional.

**I think I got manipulated by a source. How can I keep this from happening again?**

Sources, especially those speaking on behalf of corporations and government bodies, definitely have their own agendas. Even individuals speaking for themselves can have an agenda. Remember that some—or all—of their comments may be self-serving. If someone is giving you information—praising the speed at which a project is progressing, for instance—ask yourself why. Is the person involved in the project? Does an article with a favorable slant benefit this person? Is there another side to the story that you should consider, or another source you should consult in order to produce a balanced piece? Look at each story from every angle. And, as the saying goes, consider the source.

## RIGHTS AND PAYMENT

**Is it ethical for me to submit a freelance feature article to more than one newspaper at a time?**

Yes, as long as they are in noncompeting circulation areas.

**What rights are usually bought by a newspaper?**

A newspaper or magazine buys only one-time publishing rights unless otherwise indicated in writing to the author. Thus, if a copyrighted newspaper prints an article of yours, you are free to use it again.

**If another newspaper lifts my article and prints it, are they obligated to pay me for it?**

Yes, you should write or call and ask for payment.

**I'm a novice freelancer and submitted a piece to a newspaper for consideration. The editor really liked it, made me an offer that I accepted, and indicated she'd publish the piece in a week or two. That was over a month ago. As a new writer, I want to be totally flexible, but at the same time I want to make sure my best interests are covered. Should I have drawn up a contract?**

It's not unusual for editors to run pieces weeks or months after acceptance, especially if the topic isn't time sensitive. If the editor indicated the piece would run in a week or two, however, and it hasn't, there's no harm in contacting her again and checking in. She should be able to tell you when (tentatively) it will run.

As for payment, the editor should have followed up a verbal agreement with a contract to confirm it. If not, you should prod the editor until you have something in writing. If you're really unhappy with the situation and feel it's in your best interest to cut ties, call the editor and politely remove your piece from consideration. You may burn a bridge by doing it, but if you feel that you and your work have been mistreated, then you likely won't want to work with that paper again, anyway.

## SYNDICATING YOUR WORK

Frequently
asked question

**I want to syndicate a column. How much material will I need to present to newspaper editors? The idea only? A sample? A month's or year's worth?**

It depends on whether you're suggesting a daily or weekly column. If a daily, then it would be best to have a month's columns ready to show; for a weekly column, have two months' supply written. In both cases, have ideas written for another three to six months' columns.

**Can you give me a basic definition of a syndicate? Exactly what is the difference between self-syndication and national syndication? What are the advantages of each?**

A syndicate is a business that will simultaneously sell a piece of writing to many different publications. A writer can sell her column or feature to one hundred or more daily or weekly newspapers through a syndicate. Self-syndication involves a writer herself marketing her work to many newspapers. The major advantage of self-syndication is that the writer can collect full payment directly from the publications to which she sells her work, whereas she only gets 40 to 60 percent of the gross receipts when operating through a syndicate. However, the self-syndicator must do all of her own promoting and selling, which costs time and money. Syndicates, on the other hand, provide this service for the writer.

**Where can I find a list of newspaper markets for my column?**

The worldwide *Editor & Publisher International Year Book* lists daily, weekly, and international papers, along with feature agencies. Visit their Web site (www.editorandpublisher.com) to find out more.

**How much can I expect to be paid for my self-syndicated weekly column?**

Pay rate is for the most part what the paper is willing to pay and what your column is worth to the editors. You may only get fifty dollars (or less!) from a small paper, but larger dailies may pay hundreds of dollars per column. Of course, well-known columnists will make much more than that for their columns. In some cases, especially if you're trying to break into suburban and small-town papers, you might want to offer the column on a trial basis, free of charge. If the column receives good reader response, then you can ask for payment after a few columns have been printed.

**How do I market my column to a national syndicate?**

To find out what competition might already exist for your idea, check the directory of syndicate services published by *Editor & Publisher*. It lists by title, author, and subject matter all of the syndicated columns, features, and cartoon strips currently published. It also tells which syndicate currently distributes them, and gives the name and address of the editorial director of the syndicate. If your syndicated column idea, for example, was a tips for consumers idea, you could see which syndicates already have similar continuing features. After you find a syndicate that best suits your needs, query the editorial director. Enclose at least six sample columns.

## WHERE TO FIND OUT MORE

### BOOKS

*Newsthinking: The Secret of Making Your Facts Fall Into Place*, by Bob Baker, is an excellent textbook for beginning journalists.

*The Art and Craft of Feature Writing*, by William E. Blundell, is a step-by-step guide for reporting and writing.

*Reporting and Writing: Basics for the 21st Century*, by Christopher Scanlan, helps writers with little background in journalism build a foundation in newswriting.

*Associated Press Stylebook and Briefing on Media Law*, from the Associated Press, is a must-have if you spend any amount of time writing for newspapers.

*Associated Press Reporting Handbook*, by Jerry Schwartz, provides expert advice on how to report on stories locally, nationally, and internationally.

### WEB SITES

Poynteronline (www.poynter.org) contains, as its tagline reads, "everything you need to be a better journalist"; bookmark it. Jim Romanesko's blog on the Poynter site is one of the most popular in the media business.

Journalism Resources (http://bailiwick.lib.uiowa.edu/journalism) provides links to major journalism organizations.

JournalismJobs (www.journalismjobs.com) is a good place to scout for freelance work or a permanent position.

# 29

# SHOULD I SELF-PUBLISH MY BOOK?

Writers who get frustrated by the endless process of submission and rejection often look to self-publishing for satisfaction. Why waste countless months or years trying to please this or that picky editor—who will tear apart your work until it's unrecognizable—when you can easily get your book in print for a modest sum?

Self-publishing or print-on-demand publishing may afford you the chance to hold your book in your hands, but it will not get your book into stores or lead to many sales unless you're willing to put significant and persistent effort into marketing and promotion. Most self-published authors find that selling their book (or finding distribution) is just as hard—if not harder than—finding a traditional publisher or an agent.

To the credit of many who self-publish, they can be fiercely passionate about their work, and much happier and satisfied going it alone. But those who truly succeed (or profit) often devote years of their life, if not their entire lives, to marketing and promoting their work, and often set up small, independent presses of their own. In other words, they begin a publishing business.

Most people who self-publish simply want an easy, straightforward way to get their book into the world. Some people are disappointed by the results; others are happy with their decision. It all depends on your expectations. This chapter helps establish what expectations you should have as a self-publisher and whether it's the right path for you.

## What is self-publishing?

If an author submits his book and it is published by Random House, Penguin, or another commercial publisher, then the editing, design, sales, promotion, production, and other facets of publishing are handled by them. If you self-publish your book, you in essence become your own Random House or Doubleday, and all the steps in publishing and marketing a book become your responsibility. You pay for the manufacturing, production, distribution, and marketing of your book, but you also keep all the profits. Each step involves considerable effort and expense with no guarantee of a positive return on your investment.

However, most self-publishers today do not have to make the sizable investment they would have even ten years ago. The advent of print-on-demand technology, which allows books to be produced one at a time, has revolutionized the face of self-publishing by eliminating the need for an expensive traditional press run. Now just about anyone has the time and money to self-publish his book, either on his own or through a subsidy or print-on-demand publisher.

## What are subsidy publishers?

Subsidy publishers, sometimes called vanity presses, charge you to publish your book, and will issue your book only if you pay for the printing or production costs. That's the difference between subsidy and commercial publishers. Commercial publishers are willing to take a chance on the books they publish, and profit from book sales alone, whereas subsidy publishers make most of their profits from the author.

Subsidy publishers will warehouse your book, fulfill and ship orders, and send you a royalty check based on your book's sales, just like a traditional publisher. And just like a traditional publisher, they share in the sales profits, since they're the ones paying for the cost of sales. However, subsidy publishers provide minimal sales and promotional effort. They usually agree to distribute copies of the book to reviewers and reprint rights buyers at other publishing companies, but these people usually ignore subsidy publishers' books. Consequently, publicity and sales prospects are not very encouraging.

## DRAWBACKS TO SELF-PUBLISHING

The major drawbacks to self-publishing include (but are not limited to):

1. You have to build credibility on your own, without a publisher backing you up. Since anyone can pay money to self-publish, you have to prove that yours is a quality product.
2. You'll have to convince a distributor to sell your book into bookstore chains or other retail outlets. This can be as difficult as getting traditionally published. If you subsidy publish, your subsidy publisher is your distributor, but little or no power to get your book into stores.
3. You must be media savvy—or hire someone who is—to get meaningful publicity. You won't have the marketing and promotion expertise (or dollars) of a major publisher to give your book a big push at publication.
4. Many publications will not review self-published books or pay them any attention. The publishing industry tends to perceive self-publishing as a last resort and a sign of impatience.

**What are print-on-demand publishers?**

Print-on-demand (POD) publishers, such as Xlibris, iUniverse, and AuthorHouse, are the same as subsidy publishers, except they use print-on-demand technology. They rarely use traditional print runs, and your book is not printed or produced until it is ordered. Their upfront fees usually include the cost of getting your book set up in their system; any design, production, or editing work they do to prepare your book for publication; and other add-on services such as editing, marketing, promotion, advertising, etc. It's very affordable for most people to publish through a POD service, since the production cost plummets when you don't have to pay upfront for a traditional print run.

Some POD publishers claim they're not subsidy presses, but rather a new form of technology that empowers authors. But their model is exactly the same as the "old" subsidy presses: For a fee, they'll publish your book and make it available for sale. Your book is not stocked in the bookstores, though it may be available on Amazon's site. In contrast, a traditional publisher employs sales reps who call on the bookstore buyers to make sure all of their books get placement in stores; this does not happen with any POD or subsidy presses, who do not have sales reps who call on the bookstores.

Sometimes you can get your POD book stocked in a handful of bookstores if you approach them on your own, and some POD companies have relationships with bookstores that are willing to take selected titles. But this is not the norm. Bookstores have a bias against most POD publishers, since there's little or no quality control as far as the material they publish, the books rarely have the same quality look and feel as the traditional houses' titles, and few POD companies offer books on a returnable basis, which all bookstores expect.

Frequently
asked question

**I hear that self-publishing and POD publishing carry a stigma. Is this true? Are there ways to publish one's own works without the stigma?**

There is a stigma associated with self-publishing, and with POD-published books especially. When a subsidy or POD publisher accepts your work, they're not accepting it based on literary merit, marketability, or salability. They're accepting it and publishing it because you're paying them—and so anything goes, good or bad. Subsidy and POD publishers defend themselves by claiming that many books published by the traditional presses are poorly edited or are of poor overall quality. You can decide for yourself if this is a valid argument, but like it or not, the traditional presses still make the judgment calls and act as quality filters for the large majority of the reading public; either you have their stamp of approval or you don't.

One caveat: For those who self-publish in the "traditional" manner—the people who take great pains to ensure their manuscript is properly edited and proofread; the people who hire designers and layout artists to create their book's cover and interior; the people who carefully choose their book's production quality and specifications—their resulting product is often indistinguishable from the work of a traditional press. In fact, you can find many examples of stunning work that a traditional publisher wouldn't have been able to pull off. However, such a product does not come easily, nor does it come through a POD or subsidy publisher.

Today's "traditional" self-publishers sometimes frown upon the mass of writers rushing to POD services and online publishers that promise immediate publishing gratification on the cheap. They say many POD books and e-books aren't edited or designed well, and as a result, it casts a shadow on those self-publishers who produce quality books that rival or surpass traditional publishers' offerings.

However, a traditional printing is not right for every book, and you may not have the time, energy, or expertise to act as your own publisher, distributor, and warehouser. Many writers need the help of a fee-based publishing service, and sometimes POD is the only viable option. Just be sure you know what to expect from it.

### What kinds of projects are right for print-on-demand or subsidy publishing?

Family histories, memoirs, cookbooks, poetry—anything with limited market value—are ideal candidates for POD publishing. POD can also be useful if you want to market and promote a very niche book on your Web site or via e-mail, and if you have excellent and direct connections to your target audience. (If you're in this type of situation, check out Lulu.com; it's completely free if you're happy with just an electronic version of your book. You pay when you want or need POD service.)

In general, you should seriously consider POD publishing only if:

- you know your book has limited potential in the marketplace (or holds little interest for mainstream publishers)
- you only want to have the book published for family and friends
- you want a few copies for personal promotional/marketing purposes
- you know how to sell and market the book on your own, direct-to-consumer, and don't want to bother with the fuss of a traditional press run
- you want to get your out-of-print titles back into print

POD will disappoint writers with dreams of best-seller status who haven't had any luck breaking in to the traditional publishers. POD rarely leads to bookstore placement, best-seller lists, or media attention. In fact, most POD books sell a few dozen copies at most.

**What are the biggest mistakes people make when using subsidy or POD services?**

The biggest and most common mistake is not hiring a professional editor to review your work line by line. Mainstream publishers use an in-house editor, a copyeditor, a proofreader, and an indexer for each work they publish. If your book is full of errors, it will immediately lose credibility with readers. Don't rely on the subsidy or POD service to do the editing—they're not there to edit your work, and they pay little attention to its quality.

The second biggest pitfall for many self-published books is a poorly designed cover. Your book will not be taken seriously if it does not look professional and appropriate for your genre. Many authors make the mistake of designing their own covers, or using artwork provided by family and friends who are not professional artists or designers. The cover of your book is often the number one sales tool, especially when it's sold primarily online. You want to make a positive impact and avoid an amateurish book cover. So make an investment in a professional designer, and get a cover that looks like it's from a traditional publishing house. It will lead to better sales because it will make a better first impression. (Note: Even if your POD or subsidy publisher provides a cover design as part of its services, sometimes what it produces isn't much better than what you could do yourself. Again, look to a professional who will do it right.)

**I've heard that it's a good idea to self-publish your book first through a POD company, then shop it around to editors, agents, and readers as a kind of test-run—that it shows you're willing to invest in your work. Is that true?**

It can be useful to have a few POD copies of your book if you want to test-market it with your audience and peers. In general, this kind of test marketing works best when combined with a strong nonfiction book concept and a strong marketing platform. It's probably not a good idea if you're a novelist hoping to interest an agent or editor—you won't score any points if you use it as a pitching or querying tool.

**Should I be worried about the publishing contract my POD company gave me to sign? What should I look for?**

You should grant limited rights for print publication for a limited period. You want to be able to cut ties with the POD publisher upon written notice, or have a defined time limit on its ability to print and sell the work. You should not give the POD company any of your subsidiary rights. Visit the Writer Beware site, listed at the end of this chapter, for more information on what to look for in POD contracts.

## IF YOU'RE SELF-PUBLISHED

**I have recently self-published my book. How can I get it stocked in bookstores?**

You need to find a distributor. A distributor is essentially a middleman company that sells your book into major accounts such as Barnes & Noble. Getting a distributor can be just as difficult as securing a publisher—you have to convince them there's an audience for your book and that it's a quality work. A couple of the well-known distributors are Publishers Group West and Consortium. Distributors will ask you for a substantial discount (as much as 60 percent off retail price), then they will sell at discount to their accounts (usually at 50–60 percent off).

If you don't have a distributor, you are not likely to get your book into stores nationwide, though you may have some luck getting your local or regional bookstores to stock a few copies.

**If I have a book published, have it copyrighted, and advertise and sell a few copies, will I later be able to offer it to a larger publisher, or do you think this would ruin my chances of selling it to a larger firm?**

If you couldn't interest a larger publisher in your book before self-publishing it, you're not likely to find a buyer later unless you rack up significant sales on your own—usually several thousand copies for a novel, more for nonfiction. There are cases where a publisher will take on a successful self-published book, but the success stories make up a miniscule percentage of all the self-published books out there.

**If I have a self-published book that I'd like an agent to consider representing and selling to the traditional publishers, should I send him a copy of the book?**

It depends on how proud you are of your self-published book and how successful it is. If you produced a remarkable book that sold well, you may want to send the book to the agent, especially if it's an attractive nonfiction book. (Query first, or follow the agent's guidelines.) If your book did not do well, or if it looks unprofessional, start all over again; pretend you never self-published the work. Most people who find themselves in this situation have self-published novels or children's books that sold a handful of copies; in such cases it's better to start fresh unless you have an unusual story to tell about the self-published book (e.g., John Grisham read it and commented on how much he liked it).

## E-BOOKS

### What are e-books? Who publishes them?

E-books are electronic books that you download and read on your computer screen or on a handheld device. In the late 1990s, major publishers established divisions devoted entirely to e-books, but once the technology bubble burst, those divisions quickly evaporated. Nowadays, e-books are still released by the traditional publishers, but almost always in conjunction with print and audio editions.

For the most part, e-books have failed to capture the public's imagination. One problem is that the e-book industry has yet to develop a dominant format or reading device, not to mention that the reading devices themselves are clunky, expensive, and unattractive. Until the publishing industry finds its own iPod, mainstream publishers will focus on other ways to sell and distribute books.

Yet there is a market for e-books, even if it is still a small one. Sales of e-books increase every year, and more educational institutions are using them worldwide. Small publishers and self-publishers have been quick to embrace the technology and have found dedicated readers, especially in the niche romance genres. One look at Ellora's Cave (www.elloras cave.com) will quickly illustrate there's an enthusiastic audience, even if not visible, for e-books.

### Should I consider an e-book publisher for my work?

If you think an e-book publisher is a good fit for what you've written, and you like a particular e-publisher's offerings and services, it might be worth it. Many reputable e-book publishers exist, though you shouldn't expect an advance or future riches by publishing through one. EPICon (www.epicauthors.com), an organization for e-book authors, is a good resource for learning the basics of e-publishing and to find reputable e-publishers. It hosts an annual conference that's the best education any writer could have on the electronic publishing world.

Before you sign with an e-publisher, make sure you carefully read the contract. You don't want to give away every possible right, and it should be clear how often royalties will be paid. The EPICon site lists several red flags you should look for when reviewing an e-book contract.

### What are the drawbacks to e-publishing?

The big and obvious drawback is that you may not have a print book to show people, and your book will probably not be stocked in brick-and-mortar bookstores. Distribution is often limited to the e-publisher's Web site, Amazon, and a few other sites. Some e-book publishers do offer print-on-demand services (or even traditional press runs) and can sell print editions of your book, but you're still unlikely to get any bookstore play. Also, many people in the publishing industry don't consider e-books published through e-publishers to be legitimate publishing credits; for them, electronic publication is barely a step above self-publishing, though you will find some e-book publishers more respected than others.

## WHERE TO FIND OUT MORE

### BOOKS

*The Complete Guide to Self-Publishing*, by Tom and Marilyn Ross, is a comprehensive guide to publishing your work, your way.

*The Self-Publishing Manual* (www.parapublishing.com), by Dan Poynter, is the best-known self-publishing guide on the market, authored by the acknowledged guru in the field.

## WEB SITES

Writer Beware (www.sfwa.org), hosted by the Science Fiction and Fantasy Writers of America, has excellent information on POD publishing, as well as scam alerts on publishers and agents.

POD-dy Mouth (girlondemand.blogspot.com) is one person's quest to find worthwhile print-on-demand books. Excellent reading if you're thinking about print-on-demand publishing.

The Small Publishers Association of North America (www.spannet.org) is a nonprofit association of small publishers and self-publishers. Another good place to start to learn more about self-publishing and what it means to start a small press of your own.

Lulu (www.lulu.com) offers outstanding self-publishing services—not to be missed.

EPICon (www.epicauthors) is an organization for electronically published authors.

Fictionwise (www.fictionwise.com) is one of the most popular online e-book stores.

eReader.com is another superstore for e-books.

# APPENDIX 1

This appendix not only extends the information given in the previous twenty-nine chapters, it also gives you a sampling of content available from other Writer's Digest Books.

- **Fiction genre descriptions** (including mystery and romance subgenres). This list does not cover every possible genre and subgenre, but it does provide you with a starting point. Also keep in mind that there are differing opinions on genre definitions, and there is no "official" definition for most genres. The descriptions found here came from *Writer's Encyclopedia*.
- **Word-count guidelines.** This is a rough guide for word counts in fiction and nonfiction genres, published annually in *Writer's Market*.
- **Sample query letters** (including magazine, nonfiction book, and novel queries) and **formatting your manuscript**. Most of the instruction here comes from *Formatting and Submitting Your Manuscript*, 2nd Edition, which is a visual guide to querying, submitting, and formatting your work in nearly every genre.
- **Publishers and their imprints.** A bird's-eye view of the biggest publishers and their imprints. Featured annually in *Writer's Market*.
- **How much should I charge?** An annual feature in *Writer's Market* that helps you understand what your work is worth. By Lynn Wasnak.
- **Helpful Web sites.** A selection of the best sites for writers.

# FICTION GENRE DESCRIPTIONS

**Action-adventure.** Action is the key element (overshadowing characters) and involves a quest or military-style mission set in exotic or forbidding locales such as jungles, deserts, or mountains. The conflict typically involves spies, mercenaries, terrorists, smugglers, pirates, or other dark and shadowy figures. Usually for a male audience.

**Biographical novel.** A life story documented in history and transformed into fiction through the insight and imagination of the writer. This type of novel melds the elements of biographical research and historical truth into the framework of a novel, complete with dialogue, drama, and mood. A biographical novel resembles historical fiction, save for one aspect: Characters in a historical novel may be fabricated and then placed into an authentic setting; characters in a biographical novel have actually lived.

**Gothic.** This type of category fiction dates back to the late eighteenth and early nineteenth centuries. Contemporary gothic novels are characterized by atmospheric, historical settings and feature young, beautiful women who win the favor of handsome, brooding heroes—simultaneously dealing successfully with some life-threatening menace, either natural or supernatural. Gothics rely on mystery, peril, romantic relationships, and a sense of foreboding for their strong, emotional effect on the reader. A classic early gothic novel is Emily Brontë's *Wuthering Heights*.

**Historical Fiction.** A fictional story set in a recognizable period of history. As well as telling the stories of ordinary people's lives, historical fiction may involve political or social events of the time.

**Horror.** Howard Phillips (H.P.) Lovecraft, a master of the horror tale in the twentieth century, distinguished horror literature from fiction based entirely on physical fear and the merely gruesome. "The true weird tale has something more than secret murder, bloody bones, or a sheeted form clanking chains according to rule. A certain atmosphere of breathless and unexplainable dread of outer, unknown forces must be present; there must be a hint, expressed with a seriousness and portentousness becoming its subject, of that most terrible concept of the human brain—a malign and particular suspension or defeat of the fixed laws of Nature which are our only safeguards against the assaults of chaos and the daemons of unplumbed space." It is that atmosphere—the creation of a particular sensation or emotional level—that, according to Lovecraft, is the most important element in the creation of horror literature. Contemporary writers enjoying considerable success in horror fiction include Stephen King and Dean Koontz.

**Mystery.** A form of narration in which one or more elements remain unknown or unexplained until the end of the story. The modern mystery story contains elements of the serious novel: a convincing account of a character's struggle with various physical and psychological obstacles in an effort to achieve his goal, good characterization, and sound motivation.

**Popular fiction.** Generally, a synonym for category or genre fiction; i.e., fiction intended to appeal to audiences for certain kinds of novels. Popular, or category, fiction is defined as such primarily for the convenience of publishers, editors, reviewers and booksellers who must identify novels of different areas of interest for potential readers.

**Psychological.** A narrative that emphasizes the mental and emotional aspects of its characters, focusing on motivations and mental activities rather than on exterior events. The psychological novelist is less concerned about relating what happened than about exploring why it happened.

**Roman à clef.** The French term for "novel with a key." This type of novel incorporates real people and events into the story under the guise of fiction. Robert Penn Warren's *All the King's Men*, in which the character Willie Stark represents Huey Long, is a novel in this genre.

**Romance.** The romance novel is a type of category fiction in which the love relationship between a man and a woman pervades the plot. The story is often told from the viewpoint of the heroine, who meets a man (the hero), falls in love with him, encounters a conflict that hinders their relationship, then resolves the conflict. Romance is the overriding element in this kind of story: The couple's relationship determines the plot and tone of the book, and the characters and plot both must be well-developed and realistic: Contrived situations and flat characters are unacceptable. Throughout a romance novel, the reader senses the sexual and emotional attraction between the heroine and hero.

**Science fiction and fantasy.** Science fiction can be defined as literature involving elements of science and technology as a basis for conflict, or as the setting for a story. The science and technology are generally extrapolations of existing scientific fact, and most (though not all) science fiction stories take place in the future. There are other definitions of science fiction, and much disagreement in academic circles as to just what constitutes science fiction and what constitutes fantasy. This is because in some cases the line between science fiction and fantasy is virtually nonexistent. Despite the controversy, it is generally accepted that, to be science fiction, a story must have elements of science. Fantasy, on the other hand, rarely utilizes science, relying instead on magic and mythological and neo-mythological beings.

Contemporary science fiction, while maintaining its focus on science and technology, is more concerned with the effects of science and technology on people. Since science is such an important factor is writing science fiction, accuracy with reference to science fact is important. Most of the science in science fiction is hypothesized from known facts, so, in addition to being firmly based in fact, the extrapolations must be consistent. Science fiction writers make their own rules for future settings, but the field requires consistency.

**Techno-thriller.** This genre utilizes many of the same elements as the thriller, with one major difference. In techno-thrillers, technology becomes a major character, such as in Tom Clancy's *The Hunt for Red October.*

**Thriller.** A novel intended to arouse feelings of excitement or suspense. Works in this genre are highly sensational, usually focusing on illegal activities, international espionage, sex, and violence. A thriller is often a detective story in which the forces of good are pitted against the forces of evil in a kill-or-be-killed situation.

## MYSTERY SUBGENRES

**Classic mystery (whodunit).** A crime (almost always a murder or series of murders) is solved. The detective is the viewpoint character; the reader never knows any more or less about the crime than the detective, and all the clues to solving the crime are available to the reader.

**Amateur detective.** As the name implies, the detective is not a professional detective (private or otherwise), but is almost always a professional something. This professional association routinely involves the protagonist in criminal cases (in a support capacity), gives her a special advantage in a specific case, or provides the contacts and skills necessary to solve a particular crime. (Examples: Jonathan Kellerman, Patricia Cornwell)

**Cozy.** A special class of the amateur detective category that frequently features a female protagonist (Agatha Christie's Miss Marple stories are the classic example). There is less on-stage violence than in other categories, and the plot is often wrapped up in a final scene where the detective identifies the murderer and explains how the crime was solved. In contemporary stories, the protagonist can be anyone from a chronically curious housewife to a mystery-buff clergyman to a college professor, but she is usually quirky, even eccentric. (Examples: Susan Isaacs, Lillian Jackson Braun)

**Private detective.** When described as hard-boiled, this category takes a tough stance. Violence is more prominent, characters are darker, the detective—while almost always licensed by the state—operates on the fringes of the law, and there is often open resentment between the detective and law enforcement. More "enlightened" male detectives and a crop of contemporary females have brought about new trends in this category. (For female P.I.s—Sue Grafton, Sara Paretsky; for male P.I.s—John D. MacDonald, Lawrence Sanders, Robert B. Parker)

**Police procedurals.** The most realistic category, these stories require the most meticulous research. A police procedural may have more than one protagonist, since cops rarely work alone. Conflict between partners, or between the detective and her superiors is a common theme. But cops are portrayed positively as a group, even though there may be a couple of bad or ineffective law enforcement characters for contrast and conflict. Jurisdictional disputes are still popular sources of conflict as well. (Example: Ridley Pearson)

**Historical.** May be any category or subcategory of mystery, but with an emphasis on setting, the details of which must be diligently researched. But beyond the historical details (which must never overshadow the story), the plot develops along the lines of its contemporary counterpart. (Examples: Candace Robb, Caleb Carr, Anne Perry)

**Suspense/thriller.** Where a classic mystery is always a whodunit, a suspense/thriller novel may deal more with the intricacies of the crime, what motivated it, and how the villain (whose identity may be revealed to the reader early on) is caught and brought to justice. Novels in this category frequently employ multiple points of view and have a broader scope than a more traditional murder mystery. The crime may not even involve murder—it may be a threat to global economy or regional ecology; it may be technology run amok or abused at the hands of an unscrupulous scientist; it may involve innocent citizens victimized for personal or corporate gain. Its perpetrators are kidnappers, stalkers, serial killers, rapists, pedophiles, computer hackers, or just about anyone with an evil intention and the means to carry it out. The protagonist may be a private detective or law enforcement official, but is just as likely to be a doctor, lawyer, military officer, or other individual in a unique position to identify the villain and bring her to justice. (Examples: James Patterson, Michael Connelly)

**Espionage.** The international spy novel is less popular since the end of the Cold War, but stories can still revolve around political intrigue in unstable regions. (Examples: John LeCarré, Ken Follett)

**Medical thriller.** The plot can involve a legitimate medical threat (such as the outbreak of a virulent plague) or the illegal or immoral use of medical technology. In the former scenario, the protagonist is likely to be the doctor (or team) who identifies the virus and procures the antidote; in the latter, she could be a patient (or the relative of a victim) who uncovers the plot and brings down the villain. (Examples: Robin Cook, Michael Crichton)

**Courtroom drama.** The action takes place primarily in the courtroom; the protagonist is generally a defense attorney out to prove the innocence of her client by finding the real culprit. (Examples: Scott Turow, John Grisham)

**Woman in jeopardy.** A murder or other crime may be committed, but the focus is on the woman (and/or her children) currently at risk, her struggle to understand the nature of the danger, and her eventual victory over her tormentor. The protagonist makes up for her lack of physical prowess with intellect or special skills, and solves the problem on her own or with the help of her family (but she runs the show). Closely related to this category is the romantic suspense. But, while the heroine in a romantic suspense is certainly a woman in jeopardy, the mystery or suspense element is subordinate to the romance. (Example: Mary Higgins Clark)

## ROMANCE SUBGENRES

This list is just a brief gloss of the many categories of romance. Before querying a publisher with your romance, make sure you understand their categories and imprints. (A good place to start researching romance categories is eHarlequin.com.)

**Historical.** Can cover just about any historical (or even prehistorical) period. Setting in the historical is especially significant, and details must be thoroughly researched and accurately presented. Some specific historical romance categories include the following:

> **Gothic.** Historical with a strong element of suspense and a feeling of supernatural events, although these events frequently have a natural explanation. Setting plays an important role in establishing a dark, moody, suspenseful atmosphere. (Example: Victoria Holt)

> **Historical fantasy.** Traditional fantasy elements of magic and magical beings, frequently set in a medieval society. (Examples: Jayne Ann Krentz, Kathleen Morgan)

> **Early America.** Usually Revolution to Civil War, set in New England or the South, or frontier stories set in the American West.

> **Native American.** One or both of the characters are Native Americans; the conflict between cultures is a popular theme.

> **Regency.** Set in England during the Regency period, from 1811–1820.

**Category or series.** These are published in lines by individual publishing houses (such as Harlequin and Silhouette); each line has its own requirements as to word length, story content, and amount of sex.

**Single-title contemporary.** Longer contemporary romances that do not necessarily conform to the requirements of a specific romance line and therefore feature more complex plots and nontraditional characters.

**Erotica.** Deals mainly with the characters' sex lives and features graphic descriptions.

**Glitz.** So called because they feature (generally wealthy) characters with high-powered positions in careers that are considered to be glamorous—high finance, modeling/acting, publishing, fashion—and are set in exciting or exotic (often metropolitan) locales such as Monte Carlo, Hollywood, London, or New York. (Examples: Judith Krantz, Jackie Collins)

**Romantic comedy.** Has a fairly strong comic premise and/or a comic perspective in the author's voice or the voices of the characters (especially the heroine). (Example: Jennifer Crusie)

**Romantic suspense.** With a mystery or psychological thriller subplot in addition to the romance plot. (Examples: Barbara Michaels, Tami Hoag, Nora Roberts, Catherine Coulter)

**Paranormal.** Containing elements of the supernatural or science fiction/fantasy. There are numerous subcategories (many stories combine elements of more than one) including:

> **Time travel.** One or more of the characters travels to another time—usually the past—to find love. (Examples: Jude Deveraux, Diana Gabaldon)

> **Science fiction/futuristic.** Science-fiction elements are used for the story's setting: imaginary worlds, parallel universes, Earth in the near or distant future. (Examples: Jayne Ann Krentz, J.D. Robb)

> **Contemporary fantasy.** From modern ghost and vampire stories to New Age themes such as extraterrestrials and reincarnation. (Example: Linda Lael Miller)

**Multicultural.** Most currently feature African-American couples, but editors are looking for other ethnic stories as well. Multiculturals can be contemporary or historical, and fall into any subcategory.

**Christian.** Feature an inspirational, Christian message centering on the spiritual dynamic of the romantic relationship, and faith in God as the foundation for that relationship; sensuality is played down. (Examples: Janette Oke, Karen Kingsbury)

## WORD-COUNT GUIDELINES

Use the average word lengths below to help you decide what kind of manuscript you've written. Always check the specific guidelines of a publisher or agent before submitting. The word lengths below are not rigid guidelines—just the norms.

If you're writing fiction, then:

Up to 1,000 words: short-short, flash fiction, or vignette

1,000–6,000 words: short story

6,000–15,000 words: long story or novelette

15,000–45,000 words: novella

45,000–120,000 words: novel (80,000 words is common)

Anything more than 120,000 words may need to be broken up into a series of books or condensed.

If you're writing nonfiction, then:

Less than 1,000 words: filler, sidebar, or review

1,000–6,000 words: feature article

6,000–20,000 words: long feature

20,000–200,000 words: book length (though most commonly 50,000–100,000 words)

Nonfiction lengths can vary dramatically, depending on art and design elements (whether advertisements or sidebars) that run with the text.

## SAMPLE QUERY LETTERS

On the next few pages, you'll find model query letters that most editors or agents would find professional and successful. Each sample is prefaced by a general discussion of what needs to be in the query, as well as do's and don'ts.

**Sample magazine query.** The query is a time-honored traditional method for selling a magazine article. The sample query on page 353 is typical of how you query a magazine with an article idea. You can submit finished articles, but this is usually a recipe for disappointment. Most editors want queries before assigning articles.

**Sample nonfiction book query.** The sample query on page 355 can either be sent on its own to an agent or editor, or it can serve as a cover letter for a book proposal. Either way, it needs to be compelling and sum up why there's a need for the book, who will buy it, and who you are. Nonfiction book queries, because they have so much information to impart, may spill onto a second page, as illustrated in the sample.

**Sample novel query.** There are a few ways to submit your novel to an agent or editor, depending on the submission guidelines. Some want only a query letter, others request a query letter and the complete manuscript, others demand a query letter plus three sample chapters and a synopsis. No matter what the scenario, you need to write an incredibly succinct one-page query that conveys your story's hook. The sample on page 358 shows how this can be done.

# SAMPLE MAGAZINE QUERY

In a magazine or article query, you should:
- sell your idea using a catchy (but brief) hook
- tell the editor how you would handle or develop the article
- show that you're familiar with the publication and how your article would fit within it
- indicate why you're qualified to write the article

When applicable—and when possible within space constraints, the query should also:
- state the availability of art or illustration, especially if it is a key selling point
- provide a working title that succinctly and enticingly sums up your idea for the editor
- estimate an article length (but feel free to express flexibility; e.g., that you'd be happy to make it longer or shorter)
- outline possible sidebars or special features, and summarize the supporting material, such as anecdotes, interviews, statistics, etc

Formatting specifications:
- Use a standard font or typeface.
- Your name, address, phone, e-mail, and fax should appear in the top righthand corner (or on your letterhead).
- Use a one-inch margin on all sides.
- Address the query to a specific editor.
- Keep it to one page.
- Include a SASE for reply.
- Use block format—no indentations. Single-space the body of the letter and double-space between paragraphs.

Other do's and don'ts:
- Don't take up room listing credits of little interest to the editor.
- Don't tell the editor if the idea has been rejected elsewhere.
- Don't discuss payment terms. It's premature.

[your address, phone, e-mail here]

June 5, 2006

Edward Fictitious
Features Editor
*Inc.*
77 N. Washington St.
Boston, MA 02114

Dear Mr. Fictitious:

Custom Cleaner Inc.'s doom was sealed before the company's first home dry cleaning kit reached stores. Procter & Gamble already was preparing a competing product. And when P&G announced its plans, retailers wouldn't stock Custom Cleaner.

Clean Shower, another upstart cleaning product, seemed headed for a similar fate. After a promising initial reception in the market, the no-scrub daily shower cleanser inspired knockoffs from such well-heeled rivals as Clorox. But Automation Inc., maker of Clean Shower, fought back successfully, increasing sales by boosting advertising even as four competing brands hit the market.

In a 1,000-word article, I would like to use such case studies to explore how entrepreneurs respond, and sometimes even prevail, when established competitors invade their turf. I believe this would strongly appeal to *Inc.* readers who invest in new products—and usually harbor deep fears of sudden ruin at the hands of giant foes.

I am a freelance business writer who has published two books on start-up businesses, and for eight years I've covered the consumer products industry for *Advertising Age* and other national business publications. In this work, I've encountered numerous start-up companies that have launched novel products only to face potentially fatal competition.

Thanks for your time and consideration. You'll find my SASE and clippings enclosed. I look forward to hearing from you.

Sincerely,


[your name]

# SAMPLE NONFICTION BOOK QUERY

In a nonfiction book query, you should:
- make a convincing case for a compelling book concept
- show why you are the person to write the book
- outline the market potential for the book, including who the readers will be and what the competition is like

Sum up your concept in a single paragraph if possible. It may seem impossible, but if you're unable to do it now, your agent won't be able to do it later. This may be the same hook used by an editor to convince the committee that ultimately decides on your book. Later, it will be used by the publisher's sales rep to get your book into stores. Ultimately, it will be used on the jacket to convince readers to buy the book. So spend considerable time refining this paragraph.

Formatting specifications:
- Use a standard font or typeface.
- Use a one-inch margin.
- Single-space the body of the letter; double-space between paragraphs.
- Use letterhead or type your personal information in the top right-hand corner.
- Try to keep the query to a page, but two pages are OK.

Other do's and don'ts:
- Do address the editor or agent by name. Research what she handles, and include a paragraph that tells why you've chosen her for your query.
- Don't use caps, exclamation points, or other forms of exaggeration anywhere in the letter.
- Don't insert clip art, photos, or other illustrations into the letter. Keep it clean and simple.
- Don't come off as pompous, even if you do know everything about your topic.

[your address, phone, e-mail here]

June 5, 2006

Alison Lovesbooks
AMACOM Books
1601 Broadway
New York, NY 10019

Dear Ms. Lovesbooks:

When was the last time you tried selling an idea? Probably it was the last time you had a conversation.

In today's economy, regardless of your career, selling ideas is what you really do. And you do it in more directions than ever. Companies sell to customers, but they also sell ideas to suppliers. Employees pitch ideas to their bosses, and vice versa. In the modern team-filled corporation, you may be selling your ideas simultaneously to a wide array of peers, bosses, and subordinates. Until now, however, there was no definitive book on how to sell ideas to further your career.

That's about to change. I am preparing a book, *Selling Your Ideas: The Career Survival Strategy of the 21st Century*, to fill the void. Hundreds of highly successful books have addressed sales tactics for sales-people, and dozens of highly successful books address persuasion skills for everyone else. But, up to now, no one has addressed a book to cover the one sales job in which everyone in corporate America engages—selling ideas. Unlike other sales and presentation books, *Selling Your Ideas* addresses everyone in business on a department-by-department, function-by-function basis. Because virtually anyone at any level of corporate life will be reflected in this book, the appeal is considerably wider than that of any previous work of its kind.

Included will be dozens of real-life case studies drawn from my twenty years as a corporate executive, trainer, marketing consul-tant, and columnist for management publications. I am also an adjunct professor in the business department of the University of Denver and a past president of and consultant for the Business Executives Council.

I believe *Selling Your Ideas* would build on winning formulas of two successful AMACOM titles from recent years.

Like *The 2000 Percent Solution*, it will take an often humorous, case study–based approach to the challenging issues of making changes within organizations. But rather than approaching change from an organizational standpoint, *Selling Your Ideas* looks at the more approachable task of becoming a more effective individual agent for change.

Like *The Anatomy of Persuasion*, my book approaches persuasion as an important tool for everyone in business. But *Selling Your Ideas* goes beyond presentation tactics and communications issues to look at a broad range of strategies for selling ideas. I also will analyze strategies for persuading specific people in specific corporate functions, plus look extensively at strategies for selling ideas within corporate teams.

I would be interested in sharing my full proposal with you. Thank you for your time and consideration.

Sincerely,


[your name]

## SAMPLE NOVEL QUERY

In a novel book query, you should:
- deliver your novel's hook (usually in the first paragraph), which makes the editor or agent want to read your manuscript
- briefly describe who you are and your publishing credentials
- give a reason why this agent or editor and not another
- mention the novel's word count, title, and genre

Arguably the most important aspect of a novel query is the hook, which makes the reader want to see and read your book. The best hooks aren't more than a couple hundred words, and focus on the protagonist (main character), the protagonist's conflict or problem, and the setting or time period. Your hook should feel fresh and exciting, and pinpoint what sets your novel apart from all the others (without explicitly stating that yours is different or unique).

Formatting specifications:
- Follows the same standard as previous two query examples.

Other do's and don'ts:
- Do address the editor or agent by name. Research what she handles, and include a sentence or paragraph that tells why you've chosen her for your query.
- Don't belabor the fact you're unpublished, if that's the case.
- Don't spend time trying to sell yourself or hype your novel. Do describe the story in a compelling way—*without* using adjectives that tell rather than show, such as "in this page turner," "in this fast-paced adventure," "a heart-breaking story that will make you cry."
- Don't mention anything about yourself not pertinent to the novel. Do mention any expertise or background you have that might inform your novel (e.g., if a doctor writing a medical thriller).
- Don't say how much your mother or child or spouse loved it.
- Don't say how hard and long you've worked on the manuscript or mention how many times you've been rejected.

[address, phone, e-mail here]

October 29, 2005

Ann Rittenberg
Ann Rittenberg Literary Agency
30 Bond Street
New York, NY 10012

Dear Ms. Rittenberg,

My novel, *The Clearing*, is a supernatural love story told from the point of view of a young woman who has been dead 130 years. She's haunting a high school English teacher when one of the boys in his class sees her. No one has seen her since her death. When the two of them fall in love, the fact that he is in a body and she is not presents the first of their problems.

I read your recent interview with MediaBistro.com, where you mentioned that you enjoy books that toe the line between literary and commercial. I believe my book matches that description.

I have won several awards for fiction and poetry, and grew up in Pasadena, California, in a mildly haunted house.

*The Clearing* is 70,000 words and ready to send. I have enclosed an SASE. Thank you and I look forward to hearing from you.

Sincerely,


Laura Whitcomb

Editor's note: This letter is adapted from a query featured in *Your First Novel*, by agent Ann Rittenberg and author Laura Whitcomb. Chapter Fourteen, "Query Letter Babylon," is a must-read for any novelist attempting to write a sharp and impressive query.

# FORMATTING YOUR MANUSCRIPT

The next few pages illustrate what a typical manuscript looks like, whether it's an article or book. Manuscript formatting is fairly standard across all genres and should vary little from project to project.

The following visuals will show:

- what the cover page of a manuscript looks like
- how to format the first page of a manuscript
- how to format a typical manuscript page

Nearly all manuscripts should be double-spaced and have one-inch margins all around. A running head is typically used to indicate the author's name, the work's title, and page number. Limit yourself to standard fonts such as Times, Arial, or Courier.

These examples should serve as starting points that give you the confidence to go forward with your own projects. You will find, over time, that variations may work better for you and your editor. You will also find that different editors and applications require variations.

For more detail on how to properly format your work (especially for genres like poetry and scripts), consult *Formatting & Submitting Your Manuscript*, 2nd Edition.

# STANDARD MANUSCRIPT, COVER PAGE

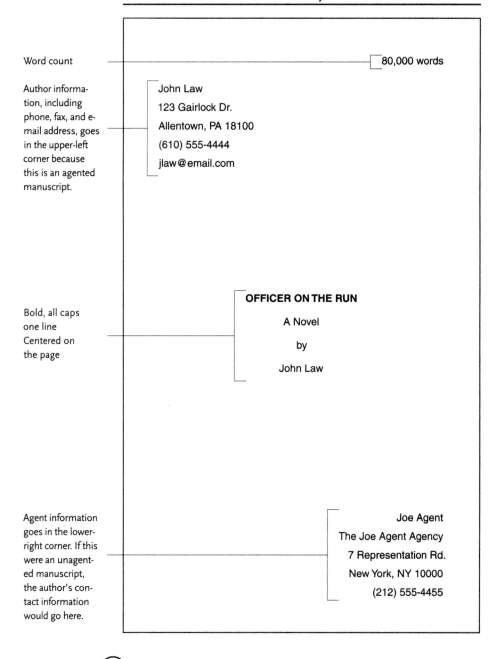

Word count — 80,000 words

Author informa-
tion, including
phone, fax, and e-
mail address, goes
in the upper-left
corner because
this is an agented
manuscript.

John Law
123 Gairlock Dr.
Allentown, PA 18100
(610) 555-4444
jlaw@email.com

Bold, all caps
one line
Centered on
the page

**OFFICER ON THE RUN**

A Novel

by

John Law

Agent information
goes in the lower-
right corner. If this
were an unagent-
ed manuscript,
the author's con-
tact information
would go here.

Joe Agent
The Joe Agent Agency
7 Representation Rd.
New York, NY 10000
(212) 555-4455

# STANDARD MANUSCRIPT, PAGE ONE

Law / OFFICER ON THE RUN                                    1

Slug line with novel's title in all caps. Page number (on the same line as the slug line).

**CHAPTER 1—THE BODY**

Chapter number and chapter title in all caps, separated by two hyphens, one-third of the way down the page.

    Marlene Preston walked like a freak but sang like a
bird. With aspirations to become a star, she sang in a
band on weekends but was a nightshift dispatcher during
the week. She was the Chief's latest affair, his Seventh
Deadly Sin. He would joke about her with the other officers and refer to her as Lucky No. 7. To her face he only
called her Lucky. She never figured out why. She just
wanted him to call her Marlene.

Justify left margin only.

Double-spaced text

Indent for each new paragraph.

One-inch margin

    Marlene grabbed the Chief's attention her second day
on the job, when she arrived at work after a rare midweek
gig. Because the band played until 11:30 and she had
to start her shift at midnight, Marlene didn't have time to
change into suitable work clothes. To everyone's surprise,
she showed up at the station in skin-hugging black leather
tights, six-inch silver pumps and a white halter top. Her
long, dark, untamed hair wrapped around her shoulders,

# STANDARD MANUSCRIPT PAGE

Slug line with novel's title in all caps. Page number (on the same line as the slug line).

Every officer on the force was checking out Marlene. That was for her one of the perks of the job—being the only woman in the company of men. She loved the attention, especially from the Chief. He was, after all, The Man—the guy all the other officers aspired to be. Marlene was flattered by his flirtations. She knew she was looking good, and it pleased her that the Chief noticed. And notice he did.

At 12:50, a call came in about a robbery. Two guys held up a 24-hour convenience store and shot a clerk in the shoulder. The Chief immediately directed all four officers on duty to hit the streets, two at the crime scene and two to find the getaway car. As soon as the station closed, the Chief was alone with Marlene. And he let her know he liked that.

"So, Marlene, this is your first major dispatch, isn't it?"

"Well, yeah."

"You handled that call really well, Marlene. Like a pro."

"Thanks."

Starts each change of dialogue on a new line, with a paragraph indent.

"But then again, you look like you could handle just about anything. You're so calm."

"Thanks."

"You gotta admit it's kind of exciting, isn't it?"

# PUBLISHERS AND THEIR IMPRINTS

The publishing world is in constant transition, and it's hard to keep publishers and their imprints straight. Here's a breakdown of major publishers (and their divisions)—who owns whom and which imprints are under each company umbrella. Keep in mind this information changes frequently.

## HARPERCOLLINS
www.harpercollins.com

### HarperCollins Australia/NZ
Angus & Robertson
Collins
Fourth Estate
Harper Perennial
HarperCollins
HarperSports
Voyager

### HarperCollins Canada
HarperCollinsPublishers
HarperPerennial Canada
HarperTrophyCanada
Phyllis Bruce Books

### HarperCollins Children's Books Group
Amistad
Avon
Eos
Greenwillow Books
HarperChildren's Audio
HarperFestival
HarperKidsEntertainment
HarperTempest
HarperTrophy
Joanna Cotler books
Julie Andrews Collection
Katherine Tegen Books
Laura Geringer Books
Rayo

### HarperCollins General Books Group
Amistad
Avon
Caedmon
Collins
Collins Design
Dark Alley
Ecco
Eos
Fourth Estate
Harper paperbacks
Harper Perennial
Harper Perennial
    Modern Classics
HarperAudio
HarperCollins
HarperEntertainment
HarperLargePrint

HarperSanFrancisco
HarperTorch
Morrow Cookbooks
PerfectBound
Rayo
ReganBooks
William Morrow

**HarperCollins UK**
Collins
General Books
   HarperFiction Voyager
   HarperEntertainment
     HarperCollins Audio

HarperSport
   Tolkien and Estates
HarperCollins Children's Books
HarperThorsons Harper Element
Press Books
   FourthEstate
   HarperPerennial
   HarperPress

**Zondervan**
Inspirio
Vida
Zonderkidz
Zondervan

---

## HOLTZBRINCK PUBLISHERS
www.holtzbrinck.com

**Farrar, Straus & Giroux**
Faber & Faber, Inc.
Farrar, Straus & Giroux Books
   for Young Readers
Hill & Wang (division)
North Point Press

**Henry Holt and Co. LLC**
Books for Young Readers
Metropolitan Books
Owl Books
Times Books

**The MacMillan Group**
MacMillan Education
Nature Publishing Group
Palgrave MacMillan
Pan MacMillan

Boxtree
Campbell Books
MacMillan
MacMillan Children's
Pan
Picador
Priddy Books
Sidgwick & Jackson

**St. Martin's Press**
Griffin Books
Let's Go
Minotaur
St. Martin's Paperbacks
St. Martin's Press
Thomas Dunne Books
Truman Tolley Books

**Tom Doherty Associates**
Forge
Tor Books

# PENGUIN GROUP (USA), INC.
www.penguingroup.com

## Penguin Adult Division
Ace Books
Alpha Books
Avery
Berkley Books
Chamberlain Bros.
Dutton
Gotham Books
HPBooks
Hudson Street Press
Jeremy P. Tarcher
Jove
New American Library
Penguin
Penguin Press
Perigree
Plume
Portfolio

Putnam
Riverhead Books
Sentinel
Viking

## Young Readers Division
Dial Books for Young Readers
Dutton Children's Books
Firebird
Frederick Warne
Grosset & Dunlap
Philomel
Price Stern Sloan
Puffin Books
Putnam
Razorbill
Speak
Viking Children's Books

# RANDOM HOUSE, INC.
www.randomhouse.com

## Ballantine Publishing Group
Ballantine Books
Ballantine Reader's Circle
Del Rey
Del Rey/Lucas Books
Fawcett

Ivy
One World
Wellspring

## Bantam Dell Publishing Group
Bantam Hardcover

Bantam Mass Market
Bantam Trade Paperback
Crimeline
Delacorte Press
Dell
Delta
Domain
DTP
Fanfare
Island
Spectra
The Dial Press

## Crown Publishing Group
Bell Tower
Clarkson Potter
Crown Business
Crown Publishers, Inc.
Harmony Books
Prima
Shaye Arehart Books
Three Rivers Press

## Doubleday Broadway
## Publishing Group
Black Ink/Harlem Moon
Broadway Books
Currency
Doubleday
Doubleday Image
Doubleday Religious Publishing
Main Street Books
Morgan Road Books
Nan A. Talese

## Knopf Publishing Group
Alfred A. Knopf

Anchor Books
Everyman's Library
Pantheon Books
Schocken Books
Vintage Anchor Publishing
Vintage Books

## Random House
## Adult Trade Group
Random House Trade Group
Random House Trade Paperbacks
Strivers Row Books
The Modern Library
Villard Books

## Random House Audio
## Publishing Group
Listening Library
Random House Audio
Random House Audio Assets
Random House Audio Dimensions
Random House Audio Price-less
Random House Audio Roads
Random House Audio Voices

## Random House Children's Books
BooksReportsNow.com
GoldenBooks.com
Junie B. Jones
Kids@Random
Knopf/Delacorte/Dell Young
Readers Group
   Alfred A. Knopf
   Bantam
   Crown
   David Fickling Books
   Delacorte Press

Dell Dragonfly
Dell Laurel-Leaf
Dell Yearling Books
Doubleday
Magic Tree House
Parents@Random
Wendy Lamb Books
Random House Young
Readers Group
   Akiko
   Arthur
   Barbie
   Beginner Books
   The Berenstain Bears
   Bob the Builder
   Disney
   Dragon Tales
   First Time Books
   Golden Books
   Landmark Books
   Little Golden Books
   Lucas Books
   Mercer Mayer
   Nickelodeon
   Nick, Jr.
   pat the bunny
   Picturebacks
   Precious Moments
   Richard Scarry
   Sesame Street Books
   Step Into Reading
   Stepping Stones
   Star Wars
   Thomas the Tank Engine
Seussville

Teachers@Random
Teens@Random

**Random House Direct, Inc.**
Bon Apetit
Gourmet Books
Pillsbury

**Random House
Information Group**
Fodor's Travel Publications
House of Collectibles
Living Language
Prima Games
The Princeton Review
Random House Espanol
Random House Puzzles & Games
Random House Reference
   Publishing

**Random House International**
Arete
McClelland & Stewart Ltd.
Plaza & Janes
Random House Australia
Random House of Canada Ltd.
Random House of Mondadori
Random House South Africa
Random House South America
Random House United Kingdom
Transworld UK
Verlagsgruppe Random House

**Random House Value Publishing**
Children's Classics
Crescent
Derrydale

Gramercy
Testament
Wings

**Waterbrook Press**
Fisherman Bible Study Guides
Shaw Books
Waterbrook Press

## SIMON & SCHUSTER
www.simonsays.com

**Simon & Schuster Adult Publishing**
Atria Books
Kaplan
Pocket Books
Scribner
Simon & Schuster
Strebor
The Free Press
The Touchstone & Fireside Group

**Simon & Schuster Children's Publishing**
Aladdin Paperbacks
Atheneum Books

Libros Para Ninos
Little Simon
Little Simon Inspirational
Margaret K. McElderry Books
Simon & Schuster Books for Young Readers
Simon Pulse
Simon Spotlight
Simon Spotlight Entertainment

**Simon & Schuster Audio**
Pimsleur
Simon & Schuster Audioworks
Simon & Schuster Sound Ideas

## HACHETTE BOOK GROUP USA
(formerly Time Warner Book Group)
www.twbookmark.com

**Warner Books**
Aspect
Back Bay Books
Mysterious Press
Springboard
Time Warner Book Group UK
Warner Business Books
Warner Faith

Warner Forever
Warner Vision

**Little, Brown & Company**
Bulfinch Press
Little, Brown Adult Trade
Little, Brown for Young Readers
Megan Tngley Books

### Advertising, Copywriting & Public Relations

| | PER HOUR | | | PER PROJECT | | | OTHER | | |
|---|---|---|---|---|---|---|---|---|---|
| | HIGH | LOW | AVG | HIGH | LOW | AVG | HIGH | LOW | AVG |
| Advertising copywriting | $150 | $35 | $92 | $9,000 | $150 | $2,278 | $3/word | 25¢/word | $1.63/word |
| Advertorials | $180 | $50 | $97 | n/a | n/a | n/a | $3/word / $1,875/page | 75¢/word / $300/page | $1.92/word / $550/page |
| Book jacket copywriting | $100 | $40 | $71 | $700 | $350 | $500 | $1/word | 50¢/word | 75¢/word |
| Campaign development or product launch | $150 | $50 | $89 | $8,750 | $1,500 | $4,250 | n/a | n/a | n/a |
| Catalog copywriting | $100 | $25 | $60 | n/a | n/a | n/a | $350/item | $25/item | $84/item |
| Copyediting for advertising | $100 | $20 | $58 | n/a | n/a | n/a | $1/word | 25¢/word | 65¢/word |
| Direct-mail copywriting | $150 | $50 | $87 | $50,000 | $600 | $8,248 | $4/word / $1,200/page | $1/word / $200/page | $1.50/word / $400/page |
| E-mail ad copywriting | $100 | $50 | $80 | $3,500 | $200 | $836 | n/a | n/a | $2/word |
| Event promotions/publicity | $85 | $50 | $63 | n/a | n/a | n/a | n/a | n/a | $500/day |
| Fundraising campaign brochure | $110 | $69 | $91 | $3,500 | $300 | $1,525 | n/a | n/a | $1/word |
| Political campaigns, public relations | $125 | $45 | $88 | n/a | n/a | $2,334 | n/a | n/a | n/a |
| Press kits | $180 | $30 | $96 | $5,000 | $1,000 | $479 | $2/word | 50¢/word | $1.30/word |
| Press/news release | $180 | $35 | $97 | $1,500 | $125 | n/a | $500/page | $150/page | $297/page |
| Public relations for businesses | $180 | $50 | $89 | n/a | n/a | n/a | $500/day | $200/day | $367/day |
| Public relations for government | $90 | $50 | $64 | n/a | n/a | n/a | n/a | n/a | n/a |
| Public relations for organizations or nonprofits | $80 | $20 | $53 | n/a | n/a | n/a | n/a | n/a | n/a |

1 Per project figures based on 30-minute speech.
2 Other figures based on length of speech (min=minute).
3 Run min=run minute.

| | PER HOUR | | | PER PROJECT | | | OTHER | | |
|---|---|---|---|---|---|---|---|---|---|
| | HIGH | LOW | AVG | HIGH | LOW | AVG | HIGH | LOW | AVG |
| Public relations for schools or libraries | $80 | $50 | $60 | n/a | n/a | n/a | | n/a | n/a |
| Speech writing/editing (general)[1] | $167 | $43 | $81 | $10,000 | $2,700 | $5,480 | n/a | n/a | n/a |
| Speech writing for government officials | $200 | $30 | $86 | n/a | n/a | n/a | n/a | n/a | $4,500/20 min |
| Speech writing for political candidates | $150 | $60 | $92 | | | | n/a | n/a | $650/15 min |
| **Audiovisuals & Electronic Communications** | | | | | | | | | |
| Book summaries (narrative synopsis) for film producers[2] | n/a | n/a | n/a | n/a | n/a | n/a | $1,269/15 min | $2,114/30 min | $4,006/60 min |
| Business film scripts[3] (training and info) | $150 | $85 | $100 | n/a | $600 | n/a | $34/page | $15/page | $20/page |
| Copyediting audiovisuals | $88 | $22 | $36 | n/a | n/a | n/a | $500/run min | $50/run min | $229/run min |
| Corporate product film | $150 | $85 | $129 | n/a | n/a | n/a | n/a | n/a | $50/page |
| Educational/training film scripts | $110 | $75 | $96 | n/a | n/a | n/a | $300/run min | $100/run min | $300/run min |
| Movie novelization | $100 | $35 | $68 | $15,000 | $3,000 | $6,750 | n/a | n/a | n/a |
| Radio commercials/PSAs | $85 | $30 | $56 | n/a | n/a | n/a | $300/run min | $100/run min | $300/run min |
| Radio editorials & essays (no production) | $70 | $50 | $60 | $1,500 | $150 | $400 | $850/run min | $120/run min | $504/run min |
| Radio interviews (3 minute interview) | n/a | n/a | n/a | n/a | n/a | n/a | n/a | n/a | n/a |
| Radio stories (over 2 minutes with sound production) | $1,500 | $100 | $400 | n/a | n/a | n/a | $200/run min | $45/run min | $109/run min |

| | PER HOUR | | | PER PROJECT | | | OTHER | | |
|---|---|---|---|---|---|---|---|---|---|
| | HIGH | LOW | AVG | HIGH | LOW | AVG | HIGH | LOW | AVG |
| Screenwriting (original screenplay) | n/a | n/a | n/a | $106,070 | $56,500 | $81,285 | n/a | n/a | n/a |
| Script synopsis for agent or film producer | n/a | n/a | n/a | $75 | $60 | $65 | n/a | n/a | n/a |
| Script synopsis for business | $70 | $45 | $58 | $100 | $60 | $75 | n/a | n/a | n/a |
| Scripts for nontheatrical films for education, business, industry | $125 | $55 | $80 | $5,000 | $3,000 | $4,083 | $500/run min | $100/run min | $300/run min |
| TV commercials/PSAs[1] | $85 | $60 | $73 | n/a | n/a | n/a | $2,500/ 30 sec spot | $150/ 30 sec spot | $963/ 30 sec spot |
| TV news story/feature[2] | $100 | $70 | $90 | n/a | n/a | n/a | n/a | n/a | n/a |
| TV scripts (nontheatrical) | $150 | $35 | $89 | $20,000 | $10,000 | $15,000 | $1,000/day | $550/day | $800/day |
| TV scripts (teleplay/MOW)[3] | n/a | n/a | n/a | n/a | n/a | n/a | $500/run min | $100/run min | $300/run min |
| **Book Publishing** | | | | | | | | | |
| Abstracting and abridging | $125 | $35 | $75 | n/a | n/a | n/a | $2/word | $1/word | $1.50/word |
| Anthology editing | $80 | $23 | $52 | $7,900 | $4,000 | $5,967 | n/a | n/a | n/a |
| Book proposal consultation | $100 | $40 | $57 | $1,500 | $250 | $792 | n/a | n/a | n/a |
| Book proposal writing | $100 | $40 | $65 | $10,000 | $500 | $4,512 | n/a | n/a | n/a |
| Book query critique | $100 | $50 | $60 | $300 | $200 | $250 | n/a | n/a | n/a |
| Book query writing | n/a | n/a | n/a | $500 | $120 | $200 | n/a | n/a | n/a |
| Children's book writing (advance against royalties) | n/a | n/a | n/a | n/a | n/a | n/a | $4,000 | $1,500 | $2,920 |
| Children's book writing (work for hire) | $75 | $50 | $63 | n/a | n/a | n/a | $5/word | $1/word | $3/word |

1 30 sec spot=30-second spot

2 $1,201 Writers Guild of America minimum/story.

3 TV scripts 30 minutes or less average $6,535/story, $19,603 with teleplay; TV scripts 60 minutes or less average $11,504/story, $28,833 with teleplay.

1 Per project figures do not include royalty arrangements, which vary from publisher to publisher.
2 Other figures in cents are per target word.

| | PER HOUR | | | PER PROJECT | | | OTHER | | |
|---|---|---|---|---|---|---|---|---|---|
| | HIGH | LOW | AVG | HIGH | LOW | AVG | HIGH | LOW | AVG |
| Content editing (scholarly) | $125 | $30 | $51 | $15,000 | $525 | $6,119 | $20/page | $4/page | $6/page |
| Content editing (textbook) | $100 | $23 | $52 | $4,500 | $500 | $1,859 | $9/page | $3/page | $4/page |
| Content editing (trade) | $125 | $19 | $49 | $20,000 | $1,000 | $7,988 | $40/page | $3.75/page | $7.50/page |
| Copyediting | $75 | $20 | $34 | $5,500 | $2,000 | $3,500 | $6/page | $1/page | $4.10/page |
| Fiction book writing (own) | n/a | n/a | n/a | n/a | n/a | n/a | $40,000 | $525 | $14,203 |
| Ghostwriting, as told to [1] | $100 | $50 | $73 | $80,000 | $5,500 | $22,800 | n/a | n/a | n/a |
| Ghostwriting, no credit | $115 | $30 | $70 | $100,000 | $5,000 | $36,229 | $3/word | 50¢/word | $1.65/word |
| Indexing | $40 | $22 | $30 | n/a | n/a | n/a | $5/page | $2/page | $3.69/page |
| Manuscript evaluation and critique | $100 | $36 | $72 | $2,000 | $150 | $835 | n/a | n/a | n/a |
| Nonfiction book writing (collaborative) | $100 | $70 | $85 | $75,000 | $1,300 | $25,297 | n/a | n/a | n/a |
| Nonfiction book writing (own) (advance against royalties) | n/a | n/a | n/a | n/a | n/a | n/a | $50,000 | $4,000 | $17,909 |
| Novel synopsis (general) | $60 | $30 | $45 | $400 | $150 | $275 | $30/page | $10/page | $20/page |
| Proofreading | $75 | $15 | $30 | n/a | n/a | n/a | $5/page | $2/page | $3.09/page |
| Research for writers or book publishers | $150 | $15 | $46 | n/a | n/a | n/a | $600/day | $450/day | $525/day |
| Rewriting | $120 | $25 | $63 | $50,000 | $4,000 | $14,500 | n/a | n/a | n/a |
| Translation (fiction) [2] | n/a | n/a | n/a | $10,000 | $7,000 | $8,500 | 12¢ | 6¢ | 9¢ |
| Translation (nonfiction) | n/a | n/a | n/a | n/a | n/a | n/a | 15¢ | 8¢ | 10¢ |
| Translation (poetry) | n/a | n/a | n/a | n/a | n/a | n/a | $15/page | $0/page | $7.50/page |

## Business

| | PER HOUR | | | PER PROJECT | | | OTHER | | |
|---|---|---|---|---|---|---|---|---|---|
| | HIGH | LOW | AVG | HIGH | LOW | AVG | HIGH | LOW | AVG |
| Annual reports | $180 | $45 | $87 | $15,000 | $500 | $6,147 | $600/day | $400/day | $494/day |
| Associations and organizations (writing for) | $125 | $20 | $68 | n/a | n/a | n/a | $400/day | $300/day | $350/day |
| Brochures, fliers, booklets for business | $150 | $30 | $86 | $15,000 | $300 | $2,777 | $2/word | 35¢/word | $1.28/word |
| | | | | | | | $800/page | $50/page | $387/page |
| Business & sales letters | $150 | $36 | $81 | $2,000 | $150 | $762 | $2/word | $1/word | $1.42/word |
| Business & government research | $100 | $35 | $69 | n/a | n/a | n/a | n/a | n/a | n/a |
| Business editing (general) | $150 | $25 | $72 | n/a | n/a | n/a | n/a | n/a | $1/word |
| Business plan | $150 | $50 | $88 | $15,000 | $1,000 | $6,000 | n/a | n/a | n/a |
| Business-writing seminars | $200 | $60 | $103 | $8,600 | $550 | $2,450 | $1,500/page | $200/page | $684/page |
| Catalogs for businesses | $90 | $35 | $65 | $10,000 | $2,000 | $5,000 | $1,200/day | $500/day | $740/day |
| Consultation on communications | $180 | $70 | $120 | n/a | n/a | n/a | $4/page | $2/page | $3/page |
| Copyediting for businesses | $125 | $25 | $61 | n/a | n/a | n/a | $2/word | $1/word | $1.50/word |
| Corporate histories | $180 | $35 | $87 | $35,000 | $1,000 | $12,500 | n/a | n/a | n/a |
| Corporate periodicals, editing | $125 | $40 | $70 | $7,500 | $1,000 | $4,000 | $3/word | $1/word | $1.75/word |
| Corporate periodicals, writing | $135 | $50 | $93 | n/a | n/a | n/a | $2/word | $1/word | $1.50/word |
| Corporate profile | $180 | $65 | $102 | n/a | n/a | $750 | $2/word | 50¢/word | $1/word |
| Ghostwriting for business (usually trade magazine articles for business columns) | $135 | $25 | $96 | n/a | n/a | n/a | n/a | n/a | $500/day |
| Government writing | $75 | $20 | $50 | n/a | n/a | n/a | $1/word | 25¢/word | 63¢/word |

[1] Per project figures based on four-page newsletters.

| | PER HOUR | | | PER PROJECT | | | OTHER | | |
|---|---|---|---|---|---|---|---|---|---|
| | HIGH | LOW | AVG | HIGH | LOW | AVG | HIGH | LOW | AVG |
| Grant proposal writing for nonprofits | $150 | $43 | $96 | $3,000 | $500 | $1,767 | n/a | n/a | n/a |
| Newsletters, desktop publishing/production | $135 | $35 | $76 | n/a | n/a | n/a | $750/page | $150/page | $391/page |
| Newsletters, editing | $100 | $30 | $63 | n/a | n/a | n/a | $230/page | $150/page | $185/page |
| Newsletters, writing[1] | $125 | $30 | $82 | $5,000 | $800 | $2,000 | $5/word | $1/word | $2/word |
| Translation (commercial for government agencies, technical) | n/a | n/a | n/a | | | | $1.40/ target line | $1/ target line | $1.20/ target line |

## Computer, Scientific & Technical

| | PER HOUR | | | PER PROJECT | | | OTHER | | |
|---|---|---|---|---|---|---|---|---|---|
| | HIGH | LOW | AVG | HIGH | LOW | AVG | HIGH | LOW | AVG |
| Computer-related manual writing | $165 | $60 | $105 | n/a | n/a | n/a | n/a | n/a | n/a |
| E-mail copywriting | $100 | $35 | $73 | n/a | n/a | n/a | $2/word | 30¢/word | $1.12/word |
| Medical and science editing | $125 | $30 | $66 | n/a | n/a | n/a | $4/page | $3/page | $3.50/page |
| Medical and science proofreading | $125 | $18 | $51 | n/a | n/a | n/a | n/a | n/a | n/a |
| Medical and science writing | $180 | $30 | $98 | $5,000 | $1,000 | $2,875 | $2/word | 25¢/word | 90¢/word |
| Online editing | $110 | $30 | $58 | n/a | n/a | n/a | $4/page | $3/page | $3.50/page |
| Technical editing | $100 | $33 | $72 | n/a | n/a | n/a | n/a | n/a | n/a |
| Technical writing | $125 | $30 | $84 | n/a | n/a | n/a | n/a | n/a | n/a |
| Web page design | $150 | $50 | $90 | $4,000 | $500 | $2,000 | n/a | n/a | n/a |
| Web page editing | $100 | $32 | $62 | n/a | n/a | n/a | n/a | n/a | n/a |
| Web page writing | $150 | $30 | $83 | $7,000 | $100 | $1,251 | $1.25/word | 35¢/word | 86¢/word |
| White Papers | $135 | $45 | $107 | n/a | n/a | n/a | n/a | n/a | n/a |

## Editorial/Design Packages[1]

| | PER HOUR | | | PER PROJECT | | | OTHER | | |
|---|---|---|---|---|---|---|---|---|---|
| | HIGH | LOW | AVG | HIGH | LOW | AVG | HIGH | LOW | AVG |
| Desktop publishing | $125 | $20 | $57 | $2,500 | $800 | $1,650 | $150/page | $35/page | $92/page |
| Greeting card ideas | n/a | n/a | n/a | n/a | n/a | n/a | $300/card | $50/card | $125/card |
| Photo brochures[2] | $75 | $65 | $70 | $15,000 | $400 | $4,913 | n/a | n/a | n/a |
| Photo research | $70 | $20 | $39 | n/a | n/a | n/a | n/a | n/a | n/a |
| Photography (corporate-commercial) | n/a | n/a | n/a | n/a | n/a | n/a | $2,500/day | $1,000/day | $2,000/day |
| Picture editing | $100 | $40 | $70 | n/a | n/a | n/a | $65/picture | $35/picture | $45/picture |
| Slides/Overhead | $100 | $50 | $55 | $2,500 | $500 | $1,000 | $90/slide | $50/slide | $63/slide |

## Educational & Literary Services

| | PER HOUR | | | PER PROJECT | | | OTHER | | |
|---|---|---|---|---|---|---|---|---|---|
| | HIGH | LOW | AVG | HIGH | LOW | AVG | HIGH | LOW | AVG |
| Educational consulting and designing business/adult education courses | $100 | $35 | $68 | n/a | n/a | n/a | $1,000/day | $600/day | $800/day |
| Educational grant and proposal writing | $100 | $35 | $56 | $15,000 | $500 | $8,084 | n/a | n/a | n/a |
| Manuscript evaluation for theses/ dissertations | $100 | $15 | $38 | $1,500 | $200 | $500 | n/a | n/a | n/a |
| Poetry manuscript critique | $90 | $30 | $85 | n/a | n/a | n/a | n/a | n/a | n/a |
| Presentations at national conventions (by well-known authors) | $500 | $125 | $294 | n/a | n/a | n/a | $30,000/ event | $1,000/ event | $5,000/ event |
| Presentations at regional writers' conferences | n/a | n/a | n/a | n/a | n/a | n/a | $1,000/ event | $50/ event | $336/ event |
| Presentations to local groups, librarians or teachers | n/a | n/a | n/a | n/a | n/a | n/a | $400/event | $50/event | $228/event |

1 For more information about photography rates, see 2007 Photographer's Market.
2 Per project figures based on 4 pages/8 photos

1 For specific pay rate information for feature articles, columns/departments, fillers, etc., see individual market listings.

| | PER HOUR | | | PER PROJECT | | | OTHER | | |
|---|---|---|---|---|---|---|---|---|---|
| | HIGH | LOW | AVG | HIGH | LOW | AVG | HIGH | LOW | AVG |
| Presentations to school classes (5-day visiting artists program) | n/a | n/a | n/a | n/a | n/a | n/a | $3,400 | $2,500 | $2,750 |
| Readings by poets, fiction writers (highest fees for celebrity writers) | n/a | n/a | n/a | n/a | n/a | n/a | $3,000/event | $50/event | $200/event |
| Short story manuscript critique | $115 | $35 | $72 | n/a | n/a | n/a | $175/story | $50/story | $115/story |
| Teaching college course/seminar (includes adult education) | $125 | $35 | $84 | $5,000 | $550 | $2,502 | $550/day | $150/day | $367/day |
| Writers' workshops | $220 | $30 | $75 | n/a | n/a | n/a | $4,400/event | $250/event | $1,663/event |
| Writing for scholarly journals | $60 | $40 | $50 | n/a | n/a | n/a | $450/article | $100/article | $252/article |

## Magazines & Trade Journals [1]

| | PER HOUR | | | PER PROJECT | | | OTHER | | |
|---|---|---|---|---|---|---|---|---|---|
| | HIGH | LOW | AVG | HIGH | LOW | AVG | HIGH | LOW | AVG |
| Article manuscript critique | $100 | $40 | $64 | n/a | n/a | n/a | n/a | n/a | n/a |
| Arts reviewing | n/a | n/a | n/a | $300 | $100 | $167 | $1/word | 10¢/word | 78¢/word |
| Book reviews | n/a | n/a | n/a | $500 | $50 | $190 | $1/word | 15¢/word | 48¢/word |
| City magazine, calendar of events column | n/a | n/a | n/a | n/a | n/a | n/a | $250/column | $50/column | $134/column |
| Consultation on magazine editorial | $150 | $50 | $90 | n/a | n/a | n/a | n/a | n/a | $450/day |
| Consumer magazine column | n/a | n/a | n/a | n/a | n/a | n/a | $1.50/word; $2,500/column | 37¢/word; $75/column | 75¢/word; $717/column |
| Consumer magazine feature articles | n/a | n/a | n/a | $11,700 | $100 | $2,993 | n/a | n/a | n/a |
| Content editing | $125 | $20 | $48 | n/a | n/a | n/a | $3/word | 14¢/word | $1.28/word |
| Copyediting magazines | $75 | $25 | $40 | n/a | n/a | n/a | $6,500/issue | $2,000/issue | $4,250/issue |
| Fact checking | $125 | $20 | $41 | n/a | n/a | n/a | $10/page | $2.90/page | $6.30/page |
| Ghostwriting articles (general) | $200 | $50 | $100 | $3,500 | $1,100 | $2,088 | $2/word | 60¢/word | $1.08/word |

| | PER HOUR | | | PER PROJECT | | | OTHER | | |
|---|---|---|---|---|---|---|---|---|---|
| | HIGH | LOW | AVG | HIGH | LOW | AVG | HIGH | LOW | AVG |
| Magazine research | $50 | $20 | $37 | n/a | n/a | n/a | $500/item | $100/item | $225/item |
| Proofreading | $75 | $20 | $34 | n/a | n/a | n/a | n/a | n/a | n/a |
| Reprint fees | n/a | n/a | n/a | $1,500 | $25 | $397 | $1.50/word | 10¢/word | 59¢/word |
| Rewriting | $125 | $20 | $60 | n/a | n/a | n/a | n/a | n/a | n/a |
| Trade journal column | $70 | $35 | $56 | n/a | n/a | n/a | $1/word<br>$600/column | 27¢/word<br>$250/column | 78¢/word<br>$342/column |
| Trade journal feature article | $100 | $44 | $75 | $2,000 | $150 | $962 | $3/word | 17¢/word | 95¢/word |
| **Miscellaneous** | | | | | | | | | |
| Cartoons (gag, plus illustration) | n/a | n/a | n/a | n/a | n/a | n/a | $575 | $15 | $100 |
| Comedy writing for nightclub entertainers | n/a | n/a | n/a | n/a | n/a | n/a | $150/joke<br>$500/group | $5/joke<br>$100/group | $50/joke<br>$250/group |
| Craft projects with instructions | n/a | n/a | n/a | $300 | $50 | $175 | $2,000/article | $50/article | $300/article |
| Encyclopedia articles | n/a | n/a | n/a | n/a | n/a | n/a | 35¢/word | 15¢/word | 25¢/word |
| Family histories | $80 | $30 | $65 | $30,000 | $7,000 | $17,400 | n/a | n/a | n/a |
| Gagwriting for cartoonists | n/a | n/a | n/a | n/a | n/a | n/a | n/a | n/a | $30/gag |
| Institutional history (church school) | n/a | n/a | $50 | n/a | n/a | n/a | $125/page | $75/page | $100/page |
| Manuscript typing | n/a | n/a | $20 | n/a | n/a | n/a | $3/page | $1/page | $1.27/page |
| Résumés | n/a | n/a | n/a | $500 | $200 | $300 | n/a | n/a | n/a |
| Writing contest judging[1] | n/a | n/a | $50 | $250 | $0 | $55 | $20/entry | $10/entry | $15/entry |

1 Some pay in gift certificates or books. Judging of finalists may be duty included in workshop speaker's fee.

## Newspapers

| | PER HOUR | | | PER PROJECT | | | OTHER | | |
|---|---|---|---|---|---|---|---|---|---|
| | HIGH | LOW | AVG | HIGH | LOW | AVG | HIGH | LOW | AVG |
| Arts reviewing | n/a | n/a | n/a | $200 | $15 | $93 | 60¢/word | 10¢/word | 37¢/word |
| Book reviews | n/a | n/a | n/a | $200 | $15 | $98 | 60¢/word | 25¢/word | 40¢/word |
| Column, local | n/a | n/a | n/a | n/a | n/a | n/a | $250/column | $50/column | $103/column |
| Copyediting | $35 | $25 | $30 | n/a | n/a | n/a | n/a | n/a | n/a |
| Editing/manuscript evaluation | $35 | $25 | $35 | n/a | n/a | n/a | n/a | n/a | n/a |
| Feature | n/a | n/a | n/a | $1,000 | $75 | $338 | $1.50/word | 10¢/word | 54¢/word |
| Obituary copy | n/a | n/a | n/a | n/a | n/a | n/a | $225/story | $35/story | $112/story |
| Proofreading | $25 | $18 | $20 | n/a | n/a | n/a | n/a | n/a | n/a |
| Reprints | n/a | n/a | n/a | $300 | $50 | $163 | n/a | n/a | n/a |
| Stringing | n/a | n/a | n/a | n/a | n/a | n/a | $2,400/story | $40/story | $378/story |
| Syndicated column, self-promoted (rate depends on circulation) | n/a | n/a | n/a | n/a | n/a | n/a | $35/insertion | $4/insertion | $8/insertion |

Lynn Wasnak (www.lynnwasnak.com) has freelanced full time for nearly three decades as a writer, editor, and small publisher.
Her international newsletter for childhood trauma survivors, Many Voices (www.manyvoicespress.com) is now in its seventeenth year.

# HELPFUL WEB SITES

The following sites (some of which are mentioned in the main section of the book) can provide invaluable information, connections, and advice, as well as keep you informed about the industry.

## SITES TO BOOKMARK TODAY

Publishers Lunch (www.publisherslunch.com) is a free weekday newsletter that highlights major book publishing news and deals. Industry professionals consider it a must-read.

Publishers Marketplace (www.publishersmarketplace.com) is the subscription version of Publishers Lunch. The most valuable feature is the searchable database of publishing deals, which can help you pinpoint the right agent, editor, or publisher for your book.

MediaBistro (www.mediabistro.com) serves up news and features primarily for magazine freelancers, but it's informative for all writers.

Arts Journal (www.artsjournal.com) tracks arts and culture stories in the media (including publishing) and offers compelling blogs.

BoSacks (www.bosacks.com) sends three notable media stories to your e-mail inbox each weekday.

## ALSO VALUABLE (OR FUN)

Everyone Who's Anyone (http://everyonewhosanyone.com) should be used responsibly.

Miss Snark (misssnark.blogspot.com), a blog by a literary agent, answers questions about querying, submissions, and the industry.

Mr. Magazine (www.mrmagazine.com) helps you keep tabs on new magazine launches and other trends.

Bookslut (www.bookslut.com) is a popular literary blog and a must-read for many book lovers.

Booksquare (www.booksquare.com) reliably rounds up notable book publishing news and trends.

Backspace (www.bksp.org) is a community of writers, editors, and agents. Some information here is free, but if you want the best services and information, you'll have to pay a modest membership fee.

Funds for Writers (www.fundsforwriters.com) helps you find grants, contests, and markets.

Preditors & Editors (www.anotherealm.com/prededitors) posts warnings about and recommendations for publications, editors, and agents.

Writer Beware (www.sfwa.org/beware), hosted by the Science Fiction & Fantasy Writers of America, keeps tabs on agencies, editors, and companies with questionable practices.

Absolute Write (www.absolutewrite.com) is well-known for its active and informative message boards.

Web del Sol (www.webdelsol.com) hosts more than two dozen literary arts publications and has great information for creative writers.

Buzz, Balls, and Hype (www.mjrose.com) is a blog hosted by M.J. Rose. Excellent information on self-promotion and book marketing.

## WRITER'S DIGEST SITES

Visit www.writersdigest.com for articles from *Writer's Digest* magazine, online message boards, Q&A, and other resources.

WritersMarket.com offers paid subscriptions to a searchable database of market listings from *Writer's Market* and *Guide to Literary Agents*. Includes hundreds of listings that don't fit in the print editions.

Also look for the sites of other Market Books, where you can sign up for e-newletters and find other useful information, including www. cwim.com (*Children's Writer's & Illustrator's Market*), www.noveland shortstory.com (*Novel & Short Story Writer's Market*), www.poetsmarket. com (*Poet's Market*), www.songwritersmarket.com (*Songwriter's Market*), and www.guidetoliteraryagents.com (*Guide to Literary Agents*).

# APPENDIX 2

## COMPLETE CATALOG OF QUESTIONS

## Chapter 8: How do book publishers work? ................. 92

## CHAPTER 21: SHOULD I COLLABORATE ON A PROJECT? .......256

## CHAPTER 26: HOW DO I MARKET MY SCRIPTS? .................. 309

# Index

to create derivative works,
221–222, 233, 235
electronic, 222, 295, 339
for fillers, 177
first North American serial,
40–41, 54, 154
first serial, 40–41, 156, 291
foreign copyright, 219
ghostwriting and, 258–259
magazine articles and, 156–161
movie, 99, 221
for nonfiction books, 132
one-time, 154, 156, 216
option, 314
paperback, 95
for poetry, 291, 295–297
for print-on-demand publishing,
336–337
reprint, 54, 95, 156–157, 228, 291
reversion of, 105–106, 161,
216, 217
second, 156–157
selling, through co-agents, 76–77
simultaneous serial, 219
for songs, 317
subsequent electronic, 222
subsidiary, 99–100
terminating, 217
translation, 99, 171, 219
romances, 108, 109
routine, writing, 13
royalties, 38, 94, 97, 98–100, 102,
268, 307
song, 317–318
royalty statements, 93, 98, 102
SASE, 34, 47, 48, 65, 66
scams, 313, 320
scenes, 116, 274, 276
scientific documents, copyright
and, 229, 233
screenplays. *See* scripts
scripts, 309–315
finding agents for, 81–82,
309, 310
searching the Internet, 183,
189, 190
seasonal queries, 49–50

secondary sources, 184
second-person point of view, 111
self-doubt, 4, 5, 6
self-education, 19, 20–21, 26–27
self-publishing, 97, 127, 134, 170,
296, 297, 331–340
series, 56, 120, 307, 311
service articles, 206
sex, 114
sexism, 245–246
shipping manuscripts, 65–67
short stories, 78, 110, 222, 233,
235, 270–282
short-short stories, 279
*show, don't tell,* 114, 117
sidebars, 63–64, 138, 187
simultaneous submissions,
36, 48, 52, 55–56, 73–74,
77, 288, 327
skills, writing, 13
slant, 12, 42, 44, 48, 87, 137, 140,
157, 158, 172, 187, 206, 326, 327
slice-of-life stories, 278
slush pile, 35, 43–44. *See also*
submissions, unsolicited
social security, 164
social security numbers, 62
SESAC, 231, 318, 321
software, 14, 15
song sharks, 294, 320
songs, quoting, 231
songwriters associations, 317
songwriting, 316–322
sources, 187, 202–207, 327
attributing, 186, 199, 205, 224–
227, 229, 230, 232, 233, 234
primary and secondary, 184
spec scripts, 311
spec, writing on, 48, 144, 152–153
specialization, 13
speed, writing, 6–7
stationery, 17
stilted writing, 213
story books, 301
story problems, 271
stringers, 323–324
style, 12, 211–215

## ABOUT WRITER'S DIGEST BOOKS

Writing is a lifelong pursuit, and dedicated writers know that the learning process never ends. Understanding this, Writer's Digest Books strives to offer the most practical and aesthetic books on craft and technique, ideas and inspiration, and publishing know-how, for all writing skill levels.

For more than eighty years, Writer's Digest Books has published the number one best-selling writing reference book, *Writer's Market*, and its catalog features the most comprehensive selection of writing how-to titles in the world. Writer's Digest authors and editors are leading experts, teachers, and publishing professionals who are commited and passionate about advising and mentoring writers.

We hope that you enjoy our books and that you discover something meaningful to your writing life in each one, and we especially hope they contribute to your persistence and confidence to write and publish.

## ABOUT THE EDITOR

Jane Friedman is editorial director of Writer's Digest Books and Writer's Market annuals. Her publishing experience includes turns at *Writer's Digest* magazine, *Novel Writer* and *Publishing Success* magazines, North Light Books, and *The Evansville Review*. Since 2001, she has spoken at dozens of writing conferences and book festivals nationwide, and she also organizes the annual Book Expo America/Writer's Digest Books Writers Conference.

In addition to her work at Writer's Digest, Jane serves as fiction editor for IdentityTheory.com and teaches composition at the University of Cincinnati. She holds a BFA in creative writing and a master's in English. Please e-mail your comments and suggestions for the next edition of this book to Jane.Friedman@fwpubs.com.

## NEED A SPEAKER?

Writer's Digest is staffed by industry insiders who can speak about the basics of publishing, as well as trends. If you're hosting a writing conference or an event that attracts writers, we'd love to present a workshop tailored to your needs. We're reliable, fun, and eager to please. E-mail Jane.Friedman@fwpubs.com to find out how we can serve your event.